COWLES FOUNDATION
for Research in Economics at Yale University

MONOGRAPH 19

COWLES FOUNDATION
For Research in Economics at Yale University

The Cowles Foundation for Research in Economics at Yale University, established as an activity of the Department of Economics in 1955, has as its purpose the conduct and encouragement of research in economics, finance, commerce, industry, and technology, including problems of the organization of these activities. The Cowles Foundation seeks to foster the development of logical, mathematical and statistical methods of analysis for application in economics and related social sciences. The professional research staff are, as a rule, faculty members with appointments and teaching responsibilities in the Department of Economics and other departments.

The Cowles Foundation continues the work of the Cowles Commission for Research in Economics founded in 1932 by Alfred Cowles at Colorado Springs, Colorado. The Commission moved to Chicago in 1939 and was affiliated with the University of Chicago until 1955. In 1955 the professional research staff of the Commission accepted appointments at Yale and, along with other members of the Yale Department of Economics, formed the research staff of the newly established Cowles Foundation.

MONOGRAPHS

1. Charles F. Roos, *Dynamic Economics* (out of print)
2. Charles F. Roos, *NRA Economic Planning* (out of print)
3. Alfred Cowles and Associates, *Common-Stock Indexes* (second edition)
4. Dickson H. Leavens, *Silver Money*
5. Gerhard Tintner, *The Variate Difference Method* (out of print)
6. Harold T. Davis, *The Analysis of Economic Time Series* (out of print)
7. Jacob L. Mosak, *General-Equilibrium Theory in International Trade* (out of print)
8. Oscar Lange, *Price Flexibility and Employment*
9. George Katona, *Price Control and Business*
10. Tjalling C. Koopmans, Editor, *Statistical Inference in Dynamic Economic Models*
11. Lawrence R. Klein, *Economic Fluctuations in the United States, 1921–1941*
12. Kenneth J. Arrow, *Social Choice and Individual Values* (second edition)
13. Tjalling C. Koopmans, Editor, *Activity Analysis of Production and Allocation*
14. William C. Hood and Tjalling C. Koopmans, Editors, *Studies in Econometric Method*
15. Clifford Hildreth and F. G. Jarrett, *A Statistical Study of Livestock Production and Marketing*
16. Harry M. Markowitz, *Portfolio Selection*
17. Gerard Debreu, *Theory of Value*
18. Alan S. Manne and Harry M. Markowitz, Editors, *Studies in Process Analysis*
19. Donald D. Hester and James Tobin, Editors, *Risk Aversion and Portfolio Choice*
20. Donald D. Hester and James Tobin, Editors, *Studies of Portfolio Behavior*
21. Donald D. Hester and James Tobin, Editors, *Financial Markets and Economic Activity*

Orders for Monographs **3, 4, 8,** and **9** should be sent to
PRINCIPIA PRESS OF TRINITY UNIVERSITY, *715 Stadium Drive, San Antonio, Texas*

Orders for Monographs **10 to 21** should be sent to
JOHN WILEY & SONS, INC., *605 Third Avenue, New York 2, N.Y.* 10016

Risk Aversion and Portfolio Choice

EDITED BY

Donald D. Hester and James Tobin

Contributors

GEORGE J. FEENEY

KOICHI HAMADA

DONALD D. HESTER

SUSAN LEPPER

EDMUND S. PHELPS

SHOICHI ROYAMA

RICHARD N. ROSETT

JAMES TOBIN

John Wiley & Sons, Inc.   NEW YORK · LONDON · SYDNEY

Foreword

This monograph is one of three (Monographs 19, 20, and 21) that bring together nineteen essays on theoretical and empirical monetary economics written by recent Yale graduate students and staff members of the Cowles Foundation. Seven of these are based on doctoral dissertations approved by the Yale Economics Department, supervised by Cowles Foundation staff members and other members of the Department.

The sixteen authors do not necessarily have common views about monetary theory and policy or about empirical methods and findings. Their contributions do not fit together in any prearranged master research plan; the idea that they would make a coherent collection is a product of afterthought, not forethought. But the essays do have a certain unity, the result of a common intellectual climate which suggested many of the questions to be asked and many of the theoretical and empirical approaches to finding the answers.

The conception of "monetary" economics underlying this collection of essays is a very broad one. Monetary phenomena are not confined to those involving the quantity of currency and demand deposits, and commercial banks are not the only financial intermediary considered to be of monetary interest. There is no sharp dividing line between assets which are "money" and those which are not or between institutions that emit "money" and those that do not. The emphasis is on differences of degree, not differences in kind. To justify this emphasis, it is only necessary to recall the great difficulty which economists who stress the sovereign importance of the "quantity of money" have in drawing the dividing line to define money.

Monetary theory broadly conceived is simply the theory of portfolio management by economic units: households, businesses, financial institutions, and governments. It takes as its subject matter stocks of assets and debts (including money proper) and their values and yields; its accounting framework is the balance sheet. It can be distinguished from branches of economic theory which take the income statement as their accounting framework and flows of income, saving, expenditure, and production as their subject matter.

Of course, separation of the theory of stocks from the theory of flows is artificial and tentative. Economists work toward the synthesis of the two, and many attempts at combining them have been made, with varying degrees of simplification and success. Nevertheless, the artificial distinction seems a useful one, especially for the development of monetary economics. The processes which determine why one balance sheet or portfolio is chosen in preference to another are just beginning to be studied and understood. In studying these processes it helps to keep the links between capital account and income account as simple as possible. At any rate, that is the approach of most of the essays in this collection.

Like other branches of economic theory, monetary theory has both a microeconomic and a macroeconomic side. Monetary microeconomics concerns the balance sheet or portfolio choices of individual units—households, businesses, or financial institutions. The choices are constrained by the wealth of the unit and by its opportunities to buy and sell assets and to incur or retire debt. Within these constraints, the choices are affected by the objectives, expectations, and uncertainties of the unit. Monetary macroeconomics concerns the general equilibrium of the capital accounts in the economy as a whole, the way in which asset prices and yields adjust to equate the demands to the supplies of the various assets and debts.

Monetary economics is as old as any branch of economics, but until fairly recently it lacked a solid microeconomic foundation. Elsewhere in economic theory this foundation is supplied by some assumption of optimizing behavior, for example, maximization of utility by consumers or of profits by firms. But the usual assumptions of pure economic theory—perfect certainty, perfect markets, no transactions costs or other frictions—provide no rationale for the holding of diversified portfolios and balance sheets (much less for the holding of money and other low-yield assets) or for the existence of financial institutions. Monetary theory was therefore based for the most part on *ad hoc* generalizations about capital account behavior, based on common sense or empirical observation rather than on any logically developed notion of optimal behavior.

During the last twenty years, economic theory, stimulated in part by the upsurge of interest in management science and operations research, has tackled directly the problem of defining optimal behavior in situations involving market imperfections, transactions costs and other "frictions," and uncertainties about future prospects. The tools developed have proved to have some fruitful applications to monetary behavior. For example, the theory of optimal inventory policy gave solid theoretical explanations of the transactions and precautionary demands for cash— phenomena that have long played a central role in traditional monetary economics.[1]

Another theoretical tool with important uses in monetary analysis originated in the general study of decision-making under uncertainty. It became possible to give a precise expression to the common-sense observation that distaste for risk leads investors to diversify portfolios and to hold assets with widely differing expected yields simultaneously. In an earlier Cowles Foundation Monograph, Harry Markowitz proposed a way in which the risk and expected yield of a portfolio could be defined and calculated from the subjective probabilities assigned by an investor to the various future prospects of the assets included in the portfolio.[2] He showed further how to compute *efficient* portfolios; an efficient portfolio is one whose expected return could not be raised by altering its composition without also increasing risk. Markowitz's interest was mainly normative; that is, his objective was to show investors how to be rational. However, if it is assumed that investors are in fact behaving rationally, the same approach can be fruitfully applied in positive monetary analysis. An early application of this kind to the famous question of the "speculative" demand for money was made in the article reprinted here as Chapter 1 of Monograph 19.

The seven essays in Monograph 19, *Risk Aversion and Portfolio Choice*, have both normative implications, as pieces of advice to investors, and positive implications, as descriptions of the economy. They are partly theoretical and partly empirical. They concern, on the one hand, the *attitudes* of investors toward risk and average return and, on the other, the *opportunities* which the market and the tax laws afford investors for purchasing less risk at the expense of expected return.

Monograph 20, *Studies of Portfolio Behavior*, is institutionally oriented. The six essays draw on the theoretical developments mentioned above and seek to apply them to the particular circumstances and objectives of various kinds of economic units: households, nonfinancial corporations,

---

[1] See William J. Baumol, "The Transactions Demand for Cash: An Inventory Theoretic Approach," *Quarterly Journal of Economics*, Vol. LXVI, No. 4 (November 1952), pp. 545–56; James Tobin, "The Interest-Elasticity of Transactions Demand for Cash," *The Review of Economics and Statistics*, Vol. XXXVIII, No. 3 (August 1956), pp. 241–8; and Don Patinkin, *Money, Interest and Prices* (Evanston, Ill.: Row, Peterson and Company, 1956), Chap. 7.

[2] Harry M. Markowitz, *Portfolio Selection: Efficient Diversification of Investments* (New York: John Wiley and Sons, 1959).

banks, and life insurance companies. It is our hope that the analytical tools contribute to the interpretation of the statistical data available on balance sheets and capital accounts.

The subjects of Monograph 21, *Financial Markets and Economic Activity*, are macroeconomic. They concern the conditions of equilibrium in economy-wide financial markets. The microeconomic principles discussed in the first two monographs are assumed to guide the behavior of individual economic units, including financial intermediaries, in demanding and supplying assets and debts in these markets. But the main focus is on the adjustment of interest rates and other yields to create equilibrium in various financial markets simultaneously. From this standpoint, the quantity of money as conventionally defined is not an autonomous variable controlled by governmental authority but an endogenous or "inside" quantity reflecting the economic behavior of banks and other private economic units. Commercial banks are seen to differ from other financial intermediaries less basically in the nature of their liabilities than in the controls over reserves and interest rates to which they are legally subject. Models of financial market equilibrium can be used to analyze a wide variety of questions about the behavior of financial markets. The theoretical studies in Monograph 21 apply this framework to investigate the consequences of various institutions and regulations for the effectiveness of monetary control. In addition some empirical findings on the structure of interest rates by maturity and by risk category are reported.

Some of the essays were, as indicated in footnotes, written under a grant from the National Science Foundation. We are grateful for their continuing support of research in this area at the Cowles Foundation. The staff of the Cowles Foundation—secretaries, librarians, and research assistants—has contributed efficiently and cheerfully to the original preparation of the papers and to their assembly into Monographs 19, 20, and 21. Particular gratitude is due Miss Althea Strauss, whose loyal and indefatigable service as administrative assistant provides important continuity at the Foundation, and to Mrs. Amanda Slowen, on whom fell the exacting task of retyping some of the material. Finally, the editors and all the authors are in greater debt than they may realize to Karen Hester, who painstakingly and skillfully edited the papers for inclusion in the monograph. She improved them both in English and in economics, but she is not responsible for the defects that remain.

New Haven, Connecticut
October, 1966

DONALD D. HESTER
JAMES TOBIN

Contents

1 Liquidity Preference as Behavior Towards Risk
    JAMES TOBIN   1

2 Substitution and Complementarity in the Choice of Risky Assets
    SHOICHI ROYAMA and KOICHI HAMADA   27

3 Efficient Portfolios with Short Sales and Margin Holdings
    DONALD D. HESTER   41

*4 Effects of Alternative Tax Structures on Individuals' Holdings of
    Financial Assets*
    SUSAN LEPPER   51

5 Stock Market Indices: A Principal Components' Analysis
    GEORGE J. FEENEY and DONALD D. HESTER   110

*6 The Accumulation of Risky Capital: A Sequential Utility
    Analysis*
    EDMUND S. PHELPS   139

7 Estimating the Utility of Wealth from Call Options Data
    RICHARD N. ROSETT   154

Index   171

1

Liquidity Preference as Behavior Towards Risk*

JAMES TOBIN

One of the basic functional relationships in the Keynesian model of the economy is the liquidity preference schedule, an inverse relationship between the demand for cash balances and the rate of interest. This aggregative function must be derived from some assumptions regarding the behavior of the decision-making units of the economy, and those assumptions are the concern of this chapter. Nearly two decades of drawing downward-sloping liquidity preference curves in textbooks and on classroom blackboards should not blind us to the basic implausibility of the behavior they describe. Why should anyone hold the non-interest bearing obligations of the government instead of its interest bearing obligations? The apparent irrationality of holding cash is the same, moreover, whether the interest rate is 6%, 3% or $\frac{1}{2}$ of 1%. What needs to be explained is not only the existence of a demand for cash when its yield is less than the yield on alternative assets but an inverse relationship between the aggregate demand for cash and the size of this differential in yields.[1]

SOURCE. Reprinted from *The Review of Economic Studies*, No. 67, February, 1958.

* I am grateful to Challis Hall, Arthur Okun, Walter Salant, and Leroy Wehrle for helpful comments on earlier drafts of this paper.
[1] "... in a world involving no transaction friction and no uncertainty, there would be no reason for a spread between the yield on any two assets, and hence there would be no difference in the yield on money and on securities.... in such a world securities themselves would circulate as money and be acceptable in transactions; demand bank deposits would bear interest, just as they often did in this country in the period of the

TRANSACTIONS BALANCES AND INVESTMENT BALANCES

Two kinds of reasons for holding cash are usually distinguished: transactions reasons and investment reasons.

Transactions Balances: Size and Composition

No economic unit—firm or household or government—enjoys perfect synchronization between the seasonal patterns of its flow of receipts and its flow of expenditures. The discrepancies give rise to balances which accumulate temporarily, and are used up later in the year when expenditures catch up. Or, to put the same phenomenon the other way, the discrepancies give rise to the need for balances to meet seasonal excesses of expenditures over receipts. These balances are *transactions balances*. The aggregate requirement of the economy for such balances depends on the institutional arrangements that determine the degree of synchronization between individual receipts and expenditures. Given these institutions, the need for transactions balances is roughly proportionate to the aggregate volume of transactions.

The obvious importance of these institutional determinants of the demand for transactions balances has led to the general opinion that other possible determinants, including interest rates, are negligible.[2] This may be true of the size of transactions balances, but the composition of transactions balances is another matter. Cash is by no means the only asset in which transactions balances may be held. Many transactors have large enough balances so that holding part of them in earning assets, rather than in cash, is a relevant possibility. Even though these holdings are always for short periods, the interest earnings may be worth the cost and inconvenience of the financial transactions involved. Elsewhere[3] I have shown that, for such transactors, the proportion of cash in transactions balances

---

[2] The traditional theory of the velocity of money has, however, probably exaggerated the invariance of the institutions determining the extent of lack of synchronization between individual receipts and expenditures. It is no doubt true that such institutions as the degree of vertical integration of production and the periodicity of wage, salary, dividend, and tax payments are slow to change. But other relevant arrangements can be adjusted in response to money rates. For example, there is a good deal of flexibility in the promptness and regularity with which bills are rendered and settled.

[3] "The Interest Elasticity of the Transactions Demand for Cash," *Review of Economics and Statistics*, Vol. 38 (August 1956), pp. 241–247.

---

twenties." Paul A. Samuelson, *Foundations of Economic Analysis* (Cambridge: Harvard University Press, 1947), p. 123. The section, pp. 122–124, from which the passage is quoted makes it clear that liquidity preference must be regarded as an explanation of the existence and level not of the interest rate but of the differential between the yield on money and the yields on other assets.

varies inversely with the rate of interest; consequently this source of interest-elasticity in the demand for cash will not be further discussed here.

Investment Balances and Portfolio Decisions

In contrast to transactions balances, the investment balances of an economic unit are those that will survive all the expected seasonal excesses of cumulative expenditures over cumulative receipts during the year ahead. They are balances which will not have to be turned into cash within the year. Consequently the cost of financial transactions—converting other assets into cash and vice versa—does not operate to encourage the holding of investment balances in cash.[4] If cash is to have any part in the composition of investment balances, it must be because of expectations or fears of loss on other assets. It is here, in what Keynes called the speculative motives of investors, that the explanation of liquidity preference and of the interest-elasticity of the demand for cash has been sought.

The alternatives to cash considered, both in this paper and in prior discussions of the subject, in examining the speculative motive for holding cash are assets that differ from cash only in having a variable market yield. They are obligations to pay stated cash amounts at future dates, with no risk of default. They are, like cash, subject to changes in real value due to fluctuations in the price level. In a broader perspective, all these assets, including cash, are merely minor variants of the same species, a species we may call monetary assets—marketable, fixed in money value, free of default risk. The differences of members of this species from each other are negligible compared to their differences from the vast variety of other assets in which wealth may be invested: corporate stocks, real estate, unincorporated business and professional practice, etc. The theory of liquidity preference does not concern the choices investors make between the whole species of monetary assets, on the one hand, and other broad classes of assets, on the other.[5] Those choices are the concern of other branches of economic theory, in particular theories of investment and of consumption. Liquidity preference theory takes as given the choices determining how much wealth is to be invested in monetary assets and

---

[4] Costs of financial transactions have the effect of deterring changes from the existing portfolio, whatever its composition; they may thus operate against the holding of cash as easily as for it. Because of these costs, the *status quo* may be optimal even when a different composition of assets would be preferred if the investor were starting over again.

[5] For an attempt by the author to apply to this wider choice some of the same theoretical tools that are here used to analyze choices among the narrow class of monetary assets, see "A Dynamic Aggregative Model," *Journal of Political Economy*, Vol. 63 (April 1955), pp. 103–115.

concerns itself with the allocation of these amounts among cash and alternative monetary assets.

Why should any investment balances be held in cash, in preference to other monetary assets? We shall distinguish two possible sources of liquidity preference, while recognizing that they are not mutually exclusive. The first is inelasticity of expectations of future interest rates. The second is uncertainty about the future of interest rates. These two sources of liquidity preference will be examined in turn.

INELASTICITY OF INTEREST RATE EXPECTATIONS

Some Simplifying Assumptions

To simplify the problem, assume that there is only one monetary asset other than cash, namely consols. The current yield of consols is r per "year". $1 invested in consols today will purchase an income of $$r$ per "year" in perpetuity. The yield of cash is assumed to be zero; however, this is not essential, as it is the current and expected differentials of consols over cash that matter. An investor with a given total balance must decide what proportion of this balance to hold in cash, A_1, and what proportion in consols, A_2. This decision is assumed to fix the portfolio for a full "year".[6]

Fixed Expectations of Future Rate

At the end of the year, the investor expects the rate on consols to be r_e. This expectation is assumed, for the present, to be held with certainty and to be independent of the current rate r. The investor may therefore expect with certainty that every dollar invested in consols today will earn over the year ahead not only the interest $$r$, but also a capital gain or loss g:

$$g = \frac{r}{r_e} - 1. \tag{1}$$

---

[6] As noted above, it is the costs of financial transactions that impart inertia to portfolio composition. Every reconsideration of the portfolio involves the investor in expenditure of time and effort as well as of money. The frequency with which it is worth while to review the portfolio will obviously vary with the investor and will depend on the size of his portfolio and on his situation with respect to costs of obtaining information and engaging in financial transactions. Thus the relevant "year" ahead for which portfolio decisions are made is not the same for all investors. Moreover, even if a decision is made with a view to fixing a portfolio for a given period of time, a portfolio is never so irrevocably frozen that there are no conceivable events during the period which would induce the investor to reconsider. The fact that this possibility is always open must influence the investor's decision. The fiction of a fixed investment period used here is, therefore, not a wholly satisfactory way of taking account of the inertia in portfolio composition due to the costs of transactions and of decision making.

For this investor, the division of his balance into proportions A_1 of cash and A_2 of consols is a simple all-or-nothing choice. If the current rate is such that $r + g$ is greater than zero, then he will put everything in consols. But if $r + g$ is less than zero, he will put everything in cash. These conditions can be expressed in terms of a critical level of the current rate r_c, where:

$$r_e = r_c(1+r_e)$$

$$r_c = \frac{r_e}{1 + r_e}. \qquad r_e = \frac{r_c}{1 - r_c} \qquad (2)$$

At current rates above r_c, everything goes into consols; but for r less than r_c, everything goes into cash.

Sticky and Certain Interest Rate Expectations

So far the investor's expected interest rate r_e has been assumed to be completely independent of the current rate r. This assumption can be

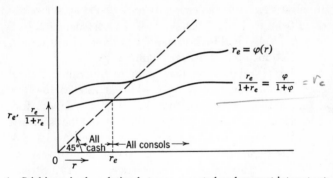

Figure 1 Stickiness in the relation between expected and current interest rate.

modified so long as some independence of the expected rate from the current rate is maintained. In Figure 1, for example, r_e is shown as a function of r, namely $\varphi(r)$. Correspondingly $r_e/(1 + r_e)$ is a function of r. As shown in the figure, this function $\varphi/(1 + \varphi)$ has only one intersection with the 45° line, and at this intersection its slope $\varphi'/(1 + \varphi)^2$ is less than one. If these conditions are met, the intersection determines a critical rate r_c such that if r exceeds r_c the investor holds no cash, while if r is less than r_c he holds no consols.

Differences of Opinion and the Aggregate Demand for Cash

According to this model, the relationship of the individual's investment demand for cash to the current rate of interest would be the discontinuous step function shown by the heavy vertical lines $LMNW$ in Figure 2. How then do we get the familiar Keynesian liquidity preference function, a

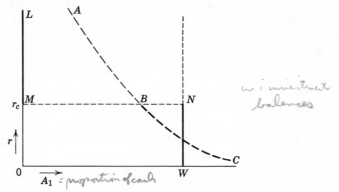

Figure 2 Individual demand for cash assuming certain but inelastic interest rate expectations.

smooth, continuous inverse relationship between the demand for cash and the rate of interest? For the economy as a whole, such a relationship can be derived from individual behavior of the sort depicted in Figure 2 by assuming that individual investors differ in their critical rates r_c. Such an aggregate relationship is shown in Figure 3.

At actual rates above the maximum of individual critical rates the aggregate demand for cash is zero, while at rates below the minimum critical rate it is equal to the total investment balances for the whole economy. Between these two extremes the demand for cash varies inversely with the rate of interest r. Such a relationship is shown as $LMN \sum W$ in Figure 3. The demand for cash at r is the total of investment balances controlled by investors whose critical rates r_c exceed r. Strictly speaking, the curve is a step function; but, if the number of investors is large, it can be approximated by a smooth curve. Its shape depends on the distribution of dollars of investment balances by the critical rate of the investor

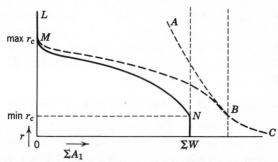

Figure 3 Aggregate demand for cash assuming differences among individuals in interest rate expectations.

controlling them; the shape of the curve in Figure 3 follows from a unimodal distribution.

Capital Gains or Losses and Open Market Operations

In the foregoing analysis the size of investment balances has been taken as independent of the current rate on consols r. This is not the case if there are already consols outstanding. Their value will depend inversely on the current rate of interest. Depending on the relation of the current rate to the previously fixed coupon on consols, owners of consols will receive capital gains or losses. Thus the investment balances of an individual owner of consols would not be constant at W but would depend on r in a manner illustrated by the curve ABC in Figure 2.[7] Similarly, the investment balances for the whole economy would follow a curve like ABC in Figure 3, instead of being constant at $\sum W$. The demand for cash would then be described by $LMBC$ in both figures. Correspondingly the demand for consols at any interest rate would be described by the horizontal distance between $LMBC$ and ABC. The value of consols goes to infinity as the rate of interest approaches zero; for this reason, the curve BC may never reach the horizontal axis. The size of investment balances would be bounded if the monetary assets other than cash consisted of bonds with definite maturities rather than consols.

According to this theory, a curve like $LMBC$ depicts the terms on which a central bank can engage in open market operations, given the claims for future payments outstanding in the form of bonds or consols. The curve tells what the quantity of cash must be in order for the central bank to establish a particular interest rate. However, the curve will be shifted by open market operations themselves, since they will change the volume of outstanding bonds or consols. For example, to establish the rate at or below $min\ r_c$, the central bank would have to buy all outstanding bonds or consols. The size of the community's investment balances would then be independent of the rate of interest; it would be represented by a vertical line through, or to the right of, B, rather than the curve ABC. Thus the new relation between cash and interest would be a curve lying above LMB, of the same general contour as $LMN\sum W$.

Keynesian Theory and Its Critics

I believe the theory of liquidity preference I have just presented is essentially the original Keynesian explanation. The *General Theory* suggests a number of possible theoretical explanations, supported and

---

[7] The size of their investment balances, held in cash and consols, may not vary by the full amount of these changes in wealth; some part of the changes may be reflected in holdings of assets other than monetary assets. But presumably the size of investment balances will reflect at least in part these capital gains and losses.

enriched by the experience and insight of the author. But the explanation to which Keynes gave the greatest emphasis is the notion of a "normal" long-term rate, to which investors expect the rate of interest to return. When he refers to uncertainty in the market, he appears to mean disagreement among investors concerning the future of the rate rather than subjective doubt in the mind of an individual investor.[8] Thus Kaldor's correction of Keynes is more verbal than substantive when he says, "It is . . . not so much the *uncertainty* concerning future interest rates as the *inelasticity* of interest expectations which is responsible for Mr Keynes' 'liquidity preference function' . . . ."[9]

Keynes' use of this explanation of liquidity preference as a part of his theory of underemployment equilibrium was the target of important criticism by Leontief and Fellner. Leontief argued that liquidity preference must necessarily be zero *in equilibrium*, regardless of the rate of interest. Divergence between the current and expected interest rate is bound to vanish as investors learn from experience; no matter how low an interest rate may be, it can be accepted as "normal" if it persists long enough. This criticism was a part of Leontief's general methodological criticism of Keynes, that unemployment was not a feature of equilibrium, subject to analysis by tools of static theory, but a phenomenon of disequilibrium requiring analysis by dynamic theory.[10] Fellner makes a similar criticism of the logical appropriateness of Keynes' explanation of liquidity preference for the purposes of his theory of underemployment equilibrium. Why, he asks, are interest rates the only variables to which inelastic expectations attach? Why don't wealth owners and others regard pre-depression price levels as "normal" levels to which prices will return? If they did, consumption and investment demand would respond to reductions in money wages and prices, no matter how strong and how elastic the liquidity preference of investors.[11]

---

[8] J. M. Keynes, *The General Theory of Employment, Interest, and Money* (New York: Harcourt Brace, 1936), Chapters 13 and 15, especially pp. 168–172 and 201–203. One quotation from p. 172 will illustrate the point: "It is interesting that the stability of the system and its sensitiveness to changes in the quantity of money should be so dependent on the existence of a *variety* of opinion about what is uncertain. Best of all that we should know the future. But if not, then, if we are to control the activity of the economic system by changing the quantity of money, it is important that opinions should differ."
[9] N. Kaldor, "Speculation and Economic Stability," *Review of Economic Studies*, Vol. 7 (1939), p. 15.
[10] W. Leontief, "Postulates: Keynes' General Theory and the Classicists," Chapter XIX in S. Harris, editor, *The New Economics* (New York: Knopf, 1947), pp. 232–242. Section 6, pp. 238–239, contains the specific criticism of Keynes' liquidity preference theory.
[11] W. Fellner, *Monetary Policies and Full Employment* (Berkeley: University of California Press, 1946), p. 149.

These criticisms raise the question whether it is possible to dispense with the assumption of stickiness in interest rate expectations without losing the implication that Keynesian theory drew from it. Can the inverse relationship of demand for cash to the rate of interest be based on a different set of assumptions about the behavior of individual investors? This question is the subject of the next section.

UNCERTAINTY, RISK AVERSION, AND LIQUIDITY PREFERENCE

The Locus of Opportunity for Risk and Expected Return

Suppose that an investor is not certain of the future rate of interest on consols; investment in consols then involves a risk of capital gain or loss. The higher the proportion of his investment balance that he holds in consols, the more risk the investor assumes. At the same time, increasing the proportion in consols also increases his expected return. In the upper half of Figure 4, the vertical axis represents expected return and the horizontal axis risk. A line such as OC_1 pictures the fact that the investor can expect more return if he assumes more risk. In the lower half of Figure 4, the left-hand vertical axis measures the proportion invested in consols. A line like OB shows risk as proportional to the share of the total balance held in consols.

The concepts of expected return and risk must be given more precision.

The individual investor of the previous section was assumed to have, for any current rate of interest, a definite expectation of the capital gain or loss g (defined in equation 1 above) he would obtain by investing one dollar in consols. Now he will be assumed instead to be uncertain about g but to base his actions on his estimate of its probability distribution. This probability distribution, it will be assumed, has an expected value of zero and is independent of the level of r, the current rate on consols. Thus the investor considers a doubling of the rate just as likely when the rate is 5% as when it is 2%, and a halving of the rate just as likely when it is 1% as when it is 6%.

A portfolio consists of a proportion A_1 of cash and A_2 of consols, where A_1 and A_2 add up to 1. We shall assume that A_1 and A_2 do not depend on the absolute size of the initial investment balance in dollars. Negative values of A_1 and A_2 are excluded by definition; only the government and the banking system can issue cash and government consols. The return on a portfolio R is:

$$R = A_2(r + g), \qquad 0 \leq A_2 \leq 1. \tag{3}$$

Since g is a random variable with expected value zero, the expected return on the portfolio is:

$$E(R) = \mu_R = A_2 r. \tag{4}$$

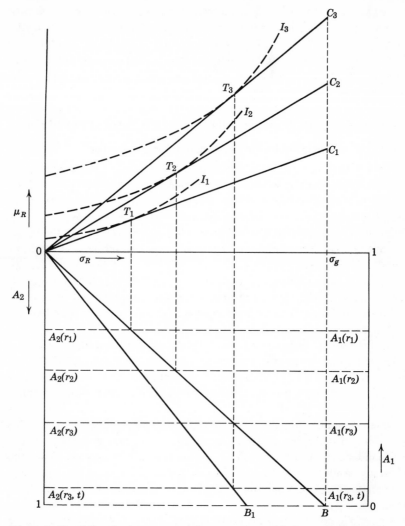

Figure 4 Portfolio selection at various interest rates and before and after taxation.

The risk attached to a portfolio is to be measured by the standard deviation of R, σ_R. The standard deviation is a measure of the dispersion of possible returns around the mean value μ_R. A high standard deviation means, speaking roughly, high probability of large deviations from μ_R, both positive and negative. A low standard deviation means low probability of large deviations from μ_R; in the extreme case, a zero standard deviation would indicate certainty of receiving the return μ_R. Thus a high σ_R portfolio offers the investor the chance of large capital gains at the price of equivalent chances of large capital losses. A low σ_R portfolio protects the investor from capital loss, and likewise gives him little prospect of unusual gains. Although it is intuitively clear that the risk of a portfolio is to be identified with the dispersion of possible returns, the standard deviation is neither the sole measure of dispersion nor the obviously most relevant measure. The case for the standard deviation will be further discussed in a following section.

The standard deviation of R depends on the standard deviation of g, σ_g, and on the amount invested in consols:

$$\sigma_R = A_2\sigma_g \qquad 0 \leq A_2 \leq 1. \tag{5}$$

Thus the proportion the investor holds in consols A_2 determines both his expected return μ_R and his risk σ_R. The terms on which the investor can obtain greater expected return at the expense of assuming more risk can be derived from equations 4 and 5:

$$\mu_R = \frac{r}{\sigma_g}\,\sigma_R \qquad 0 \leq \sigma_R \leq \sigma_g. \tag{6}$$

Such an *opportunity locus* is shown as line OC_1 (for $r = r_1$) in Figure 4. The slope of the line is r_1/σ_g. For a higher interest rate r_2, the opportunity locus would be OC_2; and for r_3, a still higher rate, it would be OC_3. The relationship (in equation 5) between risk and investment in consols is shown as line OB in the lower half of Figure 4. Cash holding $A_1 (= 1 - A_2)$ can also be read off the diagram on the right-hand vertical axis.

Loci of Indifference between Combinations of Risk and Expected Return

The investor is assumed to have preferences between expected return μ_R and risk σ_R that can be represented by a field of indifference curves. The investor is indifferent between all pairs (μ_R, σ_R) that lie on a curve such as I_1 in Figure 4. Points on I_2 are preferred to those on I_1; for given risk, an investor always prefers a greater to a smaller expectation of return. Conceivably, for some investors, *risk-lovers*, these indifference curves have negative slopes. Such individuals are willing to accept lower expected return in order to have the chance of unusually high capital gains afforded by high values of σ_R. *Risk-averters*, on the other hand, will not be satisfied to accept more risk unless they can also expect greater expected return. Their indifference curves will be positively sloped. Two kinds of risk-averters need to be distinguished. The first type, who may be called *diversifiers* for reasons that will become clear below, have indifference curves that are concave upward, like those in Figure 4. The second type, who may be called *plungers*, have indifference curves that are upward sloping, but either linear or convex upward.

Indifference Curves as Loci of Constant Expected Utility of Wealth

The reader who is willing to accept the indifference fields that have just been introduced into the analysis may skip to "Effects of Changes in the Rate of Interest" without losing the main thread of the argument. But these indifference curves need some explanation and defense. Indifference curves between μ_R and σ_R do not necessarily exist. It is a simplification to assume that the investor chooses among the alternative probability distributions of R available to him on the basis of only two parameters of those distributions. Even if this simplification is accepted, the mean and standard deviation may not be the pair of parameters that concern the investor.

One justification for the use of indifference curves between μ_R and σ_R would be that the investor evaluates the future of consols only in terms of some two-parameter family of probability distributions of g. For example, the investor might think in terms of a range of equally likely gains or losses, centered on zero. Or he might think in terms that can be approximated by a normal distribution. Whatever two-parameter family is assumed— uniform, normal, or some other—the whole probability distribution is determined as soon as the mean and standard deviation are specified. Hence the investor's choice among probability distributions can be analyzed by μ_R-σ_R indifference curves; any other pair of independent parameters could serve equally well.

If the investor's probability distributions are assumed to belong to some two-parameter family, the shape of his indifference curves can be inferred from the general characteristics of his utility-of-return function. This function will be assumed to relate utility to R, the percentage growth in the investment balance by the end of the period. This way of formulating the utility function makes the investor's indifference map, and therefore his choices of proportions of cash and consols, independent of the absolute amount of his initial balance.

On certain postulates, it can be shown that an individual's choice among probability distributions can be described as the maximization of the expected value of a utility function.[12] The ranking of probability

---

[12] See von Neumann, J. and Morgenstern, O., *Theory of Games and Economic Behavior*, 3rd Edition (Princeton: Princeton University Press, 1953), pp. 15–30, pp. 617–632; Herstein, I. N. and Milnor, J., "An Axiomatic Approach to Measurable Utility," *Econometrica*, Vol. 23 (April 1953), pp. 291–297; Marschak, J., "Rational Behavior, Uncertain Prospects, and Measurable Utility", *Econometrica*, Vol. 18 (April 1950), pp. 111–141; Friedman, M. and Savage, L. J., "The Utility Analysis of Choices Involving Risk," *Journal of Political Economy*, Vol. 56 (August 1948), pp. 279–304, and "The Expected Utility Hypothesis and the Measurability of Utility," *Journal of Political Economy*, Vol. 60 (December 1952), pp. 463–474. For a treatment which also provides an axiomatic basis for the subjective probability estimates here assumed, see Savage, L. J., *The Foundations of Statistics* (New York: Wiley, 1954).

distributions with respect to the expected value of utility will not be changed if the scale on which utility is measured is altered either by the addition of a constant or by multiplication by a positive constant. Consequently we are free to choose arbitrarily the zero and unit of measurement of the utility function $U(R)$ as follows: $U(0) = 0$; $U(-1) = -1$.

Suppose that the probability distribution of R can be described by a two-parameter density function $f(R; \mu_R, \sigma_R)$. Then the expected value of utility is:

$$E[U(R)] = \int_{-\infty}^{\infty} U(R)f(R; \mu_R, \sigma_R) \, dR. \tag{7}$$

Let

$$z = \frac{R - \mu_R}{\sigma_R}.$$

$$E[U(R)] = E(\mu_R, \sigma_R) = \int_{-\infty}^{\infty} U(\mu_R + \sigma_R z)f(z; 0, 1) \, dz. \tag{8}$$

An indifference curve is a locus of points (μ_R, σ_R) along which expected utility is constant. We may find the slope of such a locus by differentiating equation 8 with respect to σ_R.

$$0 = \int_{-\infty}^{\infty} U'(\mu_R + \sigma_R z)\left[\frac{d\mu_R}{d\sigma_R} + z\right]f(z; 0, 1) \, dz.$$

$$\frac{d\mu_R}{d\sigma_R} = -\frac{\int_{-\infty}^{\infty} zU'(R)f(z; 0, 1) \, dz}{\int_{-\infty}^{\infty} U'(R)f(z; 0, 1) \, dz}. \tag{9}$$

$U'(R)$, the marginal utility of return, is assumed to be everywhere nonnegative. If it is also a decreasing function of R, then the slope of the indifference locus must be positive; an investor with such a utility function is a risk-averter. If it is an increasing function of R, the slope will be negative; this kind of utility function characterizes a risk-lover.

Similarly, the curvature of the indifference loci is related to the shape of the utility function. Suppose that (μ_R, σ_R) and (μ'_R, σ'_R) are on the same indifference locus, so that $E(\mu_R, \sigma_R) = E(\mu'_R, \sigma'_R)$. Is

$$\left(\frac{\mu_R + \mu'_R}{2}, \frac{\sigma_R + \sigma'_R}{2}\right),$$

on the same locus, or on a higher or a lower one? In the case of declining marginal utility we know that for every z:

$$\tfrac{1}{2}U(\mu_R + \sigma_R z) + \tfrac{1}{2}U(\mu'_R + \sigma'_R z) < U\left(\frac{\mu_R + \mu'_R}{2} + \frac{\sigma_R + \sigma'_R}{2} z\right).$$

Consequently

$$E\left(\frac{\mu_R + \mu_R'}{2}, \frac{\sigma_R + \sigma_R'}{2}\right)$$

is greater than $E(\mu_R, \sigma_R)$ or $E(\mu_R', \sigma_R')$, and

$$\left(\frac{\mu_R + \mu_R'}{2}, \frac{\sigma_R + \sigma_R'}{2}\right),$$

which lies on a line between (μ_R, σ_R) and (μ_R', σ_R'), is on a higher locus than those points. Thus it is shown that a risk-averter's indifference curve is necessarily concave upwards, provided it is derived in this manner from a two-parameter family of probability distributions and declining marginal utility of return. All risk-averters are diversifiers; plungers do not exist. The same kind of argument shows that a risk-lover's indifference curve is concave downwards.

In the absence of restrictions on the subjective probability distributions of the investor, the parameters of the distribution relevant to his choice can be sought in parametric restrictions on his utility-of-return function. Two parameters of the utility function are determined by the choice of the utility scale. If specification of the utility function requires no additional parameters, one parameter of the probability distribution summarizes all the information relevant for the investor's choice. For example, if the utility function is linear $[U(R) = R]$, then the expected value of utility is simply the expected value of R, and maximizing expected utility leads to the same behavior as maximizing return in a world of certainty. If, however, one additional parameter is needed to specify the utility function, then two parameters of the probability distribution will be relevant to the choice; and so on. Which parameters of the distribution are relevant depends on the form of the utility function.

Focus on the mean and standard deviation of return can be justified on the assumption that the utility function is quadratic. Following our conventions as to utility scale, the quadratic function would be:

$$U(R) = (1 + b)R + bR^2 \qquad (10)$$

Here $0 < b < 1$ for a risk-lover, and $-1 < b < 0$ for a risk-averter. However equation 10 cannot describe the utility function for the whole range of R, because marginal utility cannot be negative. The function given in equation 10 can apply only for:

$$(1 + b) + 2bR \geq 0;$$

that is, for:
$$R \geq -\left(\frac{1+b}{2b}\right) \ (b > 0) \quad \text{(Risk-lover)} \tag{11}$$

$$R \leq -\left(\frac{1+b}{2b}\right) \ (b < 0) \quad \text{(Risk-averter).}$$

In order to use equation 10 therefore, we must exclude from the range of possibility values of R outside the limits of equation 11. At the maximum investment in consols ($A_2 = 1$), $R = r + g$. A risk-averter must be assumed therefore, to restrict the range of capital gains g to which he attaches non-zero probability so that, for the highest rate of interest r to be considered:
$$r + g \leq -\left(\frac{1+b}{2b}\right). \tag{12}$$

The corresponding limitation for a risk-lover is that, for the lowest interest rate r to be considered:
$$r + g \geq -\left(\frac{1+b}{2b}\right). \tag{13}$$

Given the utility function of equation 10, we can investigate the slope and curvature of the indifference curves it implies. The probability density function for $R, f(R)$, is restricted by the limit of equation 12 or equation 13; but otherwise no restriction on its shape is assumed.

$$E[U(R)] = \int_{-\infty}^{\infty} U(R)f(R) \ dR = (1 + b)\mu_R + b(\sigma_R^2 + \mu_R^2). \tag{14}$$

Holding $E[U(R)]$ constant and differentiating with respect to σ_R to obtain the slope of an indifference curve, we have:
$$\frac{d\mu_R}{d\sigma_R} = \frac{\sigma_R}{-\dfrac{1+b}{2b} - \mu_R} \tag{15}$$

For a risk-averter, $-[(1 + b)/2b]$ is positive and is the upper limit for R, according to equation 11; $-[(1 + b)/2b]$ is necessarily larger than μ_R. Therefore the slope of an indifference locus is positive. For a risk-lover, on the other hand, the corresponding argument shows that the slope is negative.

Differentiating equation 15 leads to the same conclusions regarding curvature as the previous alternative approach, namely that a risk-averter is necessarily a diversifier.

$$\frac{d^2\mu_R}{d\sigma_R^2} = \frac{1 + \left(\dfrac{d\mu_R}{d\sigma_R}\right)^2}{-\dfrac{1+b}{2b} - \mu_R} \tag{16}$$

For a risk-averter, the second derivative is positive and the indifference locus is concave upwards; for a risk-lover, it is concave downwards.

Effects of Changes in the Rate of Interest

On pages 12 to 15 two alternative rationalizations of the indifference curves introduced on page 11 have been presented. Both rationalizations assume that the investor (1) estimates subjective probability distributions of capital gain or loss in holding consols, (2) evaluates his prospective increase in wealth in terms of a cardinal utility function, (3) ranks alternative prospects according to the expected value of utility. The first rationalization derives the indifference curves by restricting the subjective probability distributions to a two-parameter family. The second rationalization derives the indifference curves by assuming the utility function to be quadratic within the relevant range. On either rationalization, a risk-averter's indifference curves must be concave upwards, characteristic of the *diversifiers*, and those of a risk-lover concave downwards. If the category defined as *plungers* exists at all, their indifference curves must be determined by some process other than those described on pages 12 to 15.

The opportunity locus for the investor is described on pages 9 to 11 and summarized in equation 6. The investor decides the amount to invest in consols so as to reach the highest indifference curve permitted by his opportunity-locus. This maximization may be one of three kinds:

1. Tangency between an indifference curve and the opportunity locus, as illustrated by points T_1, T_2, and T_3 in Figure 4. A regular maximum of this kind can occur only for a risk-averter, and will lead to diversification. Both A_1, cash holding, and A_2, consol holding, will be positive. They too are shown in Figure 4, in the bottom half of the diagram, where, for example, $A_1(r_1)$ and $A_2(r_1)$ depict the cash and consol holdings corresponding to point T_1.

2. A corner maximum at the point $\mu_R = r$, $\sigma_R = \sigma_g$, as illustrated in Figure 5.

In Figure 5 the opportunity locus is the ray OC, and point C represents the highest expected return and risk obtainable by the investor, i.e., the expected return and risk from holding his entire balance in consols. A utility maximum at C can occur either for a risk-averter or for a risk-lover. I_1 and I_2 represent indifference curves of a diversifier; I_2 passes through C and has a lower slope, both at C and everywhere to the left of C, than the opportunity locus. I_1' and I_2' represent the indifference curves of a risk-lover, for whom it is clear that C is always the optimum position. Similarly, a plunger may, if his indifference curves stand with respect to his opportunity locus as in Figure 6 (OC_2), plunge his entire balance in consols.

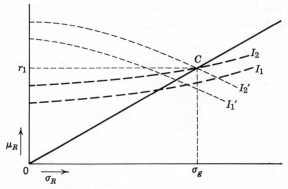

Figure 5 "Risk-lovers" and "diversifiers": optimum portfolio at maximum risk and expected return.

3. A corner maximum at the origin, where the entire balance is held in cash. For a plunger, this case is illustrated in Figure 6 (OC_1). Conceivably it could also occur for a diversifier, if the slope of his indifference curve at the origin exceeded the slope of the opportunity locus. However, case 3 is entirely excluded for investors whose indifference curves represent the constant-expected-utility loci of page 13. Such investors, we have already noted, cannot be plungers. Furthermore, the slope of all constant-expected-utility loci at $\sigma_R = 0$ must be zero, as can be seen from equations 9 and 15.

We can now examine the consequences of a change in the interest rate r, holding constant the investor's estimate of the risk of capital gain or loss. An increase in the interest rate will rotate the opportunity locus OC to the

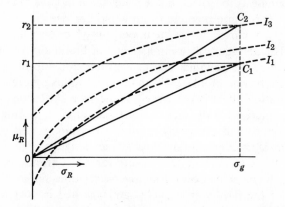

Figure 6 "Plungers": optimum portfolio at minimum or maximum risk and expected return.

left. How will this affect the investor's holdings of cash and consols? We must consider separately the three cases.

Case 1. In Figure 7, OC_1, OC_2, and OC_3 represent opportunity loci for successively higher rates of interest. The indifference curves I_1, I_2, and I_3 are drawn so that the points of tangency T_1, T_2, and T_3, correspond to successively higher holdings of consols A_2. In this diagram, the investor's demand for cash depends inversely on the interest rate.

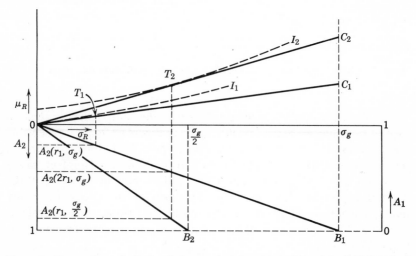

Figure 7 Comparison of effects of changes in interest rate (r) and in "risk" (σ_g) on holding of consols.

This relationship is, of course, in the direction liquidity preference theory has taught us to expect, but it is not the only possible direction of relationship. It is quite possible to draw indifference curves so that the point of tangency moves left as the opportunity locus is rotated counterclockwise. The ambiguity is a familiar one in the theory of choice, and reflects the ubiquitous conflict between income and substitution effects. An increase in the rate of interest is an incentive to take more risk; so far as the substitution effect is concerned, it means a shift from security to yield. But an increase in the rate of interest also has an income effect, for it gives the opportunity to enjoy more security along with more yield. The ambiguity is analogous to the doubt concerning the effect of a change in the interest rate on saving; the substitution effect argues for a positive relationship, the income effect for an inverse relationship.

However, if the indifference curves are regarded as loci of constant expected utility, part of this ambiguity can be resolved. We have already observed that these loci all have zero slopes at $\sigma_R = 0$. As the interest rate r rises from zero, so also will consol holding A_2. At higher interest rates, however, the inverse relationship may occur.

This reversal of direction can, however, be virtually excluded in the case of the quadratic utility function. The condition for a maximum is that the slope of an indifference locus as given by equation 15 equals the slope of the opportunity locus of equation 6.

$$\frac{r}{\sigma_g} = \frac{A_2\sigma_g}{-\dfrac{1+b}{2b} - A_2 r}; \qquad A_2 = \frac{r}{r^2 + \sigma_g^2}\left(-\frac{1+b}{2b}\right). \tag{17}$$

Equation 17 expresses A_2 as a function of r, and differentiating gives:

$$\frac{dA_2}{dr} = \frac{\sigma_g^2 - r^2}{(\sigma_g^2 + r^2)^2}\left(-\frac{1+b}{2b}\right); \qquad \frac{r}{A_2}\frac{dA_2}{dr} = \frac{\sigma_g^2 - r^2}{\sigma_g^2 + r^2}. \tag{18}$$

Thus the share of consols in the portfolio increases with the interest rate for r less than σ_g. Moreover, if r exceeds σ_g, a tangency maximum cannot occur unless r also exceeds g_{max}, the largest capital gain the investor conceives possible (see equation 12).[13] The demand for consols is less elastic at high interest rates than at low, but the elasticity is not likely to become negative.

Cases 2 and 3. A change in the interest rate cannot cause a risk-lover to alter his position, which is already the point of maximum risk and expected yield. Conceivably a "diversifier" might move from a corner maximum to a regular interior maximum in response either to a rise in the interest rate or to a fall. A "plunger" might find his position altered by an increase in the interest rate, as from r_1 to r_2 in Figure 6; this would lead him to shift his entire balance from cash to consols.

Effects of Changes in Risk

Investors' estimates, σ_g, of the risk of holding monetary assets other than cash, "consols," are subjective. But they are undoubtedly affected by

---

[13] For this statement and its proof, I am greatly indebted to my colleague Arthur Okun. The proof is as follows: If $r^2 \geq \sigma_g^2$, then by equations 12 and 17:

$$1 \geq A_2 \geq \frac{r}{2r^2}\left(-\frac{1+b}{2b}\right) \geq \frac{1}{2r}(r + g_{max}).$$

From the two extremes of this series of inequalities it follows that $2r \geq r + g_{max}$ or $r \geq g_{max}$. Professor Okun also points out that this condition is incompatible with a tangency maximum if the distribution of g is symmetrical. For then $r \geq g_{max}$ would imply $r + g_{min} \geq 0$. There would be no possibility of net loss on consols and thus no reason to hold any cash.

market experience, and they are also subject to influence by measures of monetary and fiscal policy. By actions and words, the central bank can influence investors' estimates of the variability of interest rates; its influence on these estimates of risk may be as important in accomplishing or preventing changes in the rate as open-market operations and other direct interventions in the market. Tax rates, and differences in tax treatment of capital gains, losses, and interest earnings, affect in calculable ways the investor's risks and expected returns. For these reasons it is worthwhile to examine the effects of a change in an investor's estimate of risk on his allocation between cash and consols.

In Figure 7, T_1 and $A_2(r_1, \sigma_g)$ represent the initial position of an investor, at interest rate r_1 and risk σ_g. OC_1 is the opportunity locus (equation 6), and OB_1 is the risk-consols relationship (equation 5). If the investor now cuts his estimate of risk in half, to $\sigma_g/2$, the opportunity locus will double in slope, from OC_1 to OC_2, and the investor will shift to point T_2. The risk-consols relationship will have also doubled in slope, from OB_1 to OB_2. Consequently point T_2 corresponds to an investment in consols of $A_2(r_1, \sigma_g/2)$. This same point T_2 would have been reached if the interest rate had doubled while the investor's risk estimate σ_g remained unchanged. But in that case, since the risk-consols relationship would remain at OB_1, the corresponding investment in consols would have been only half as large, i.e., $A_2(2r_1, \sigma_g)$. In general, the following relationship exists between the elasticity of the demand for consols with respect to risk and its elasticity with respect to the interest rate:

$$\frac{\sigma_g}{A_2} \frac{dA_2}{d\sigma_g} = -\frac{r}{A_2} \frac{dA_2}{dr} - 1. \tag{19}$$

The implications of this relationship for analysis of effects of taxation may be noted in passing, with the help of Figure 7. Suppose that the initial position of the investor is T_2 and $A_2(2r_1, \sigma_g)$. A tax of 50% is now levied on interest income and capital gains alike, with complete loss offset provisions. The result of the tax is to reduce the expected net return per dollar of consols from $2r_1$ to r_1 and to reduce the risk to the investor per dollar of consols from σ_g to $\sigma_g/2$. The opportunity locus will remain at OC_2, and the investor will still wish to obtain the combination of risk and expected return depicted by T_2. To obtain this combination, however, he must now double his holding of consols, to $A_2(r_1, \sigma_g/2)$; the tax shifts the risk-consols line from OB_1 to OB_2. A tax of this kind, therefore, would reduce the demand for cash at any market rate of interest, shifting the investor's liquidity preference schedule in the manner shown in Figure 8. A tax on interest income only, with no tax on capital gains and no offset

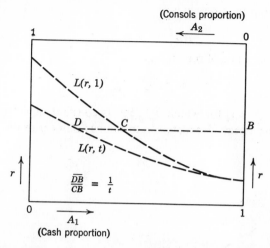

Figure 8 Effect of tax (at rate 1-*t*) on liquidity preference function.

privileges for capital losses, would have quite different effects. If the Treasury began to split the interest income of the investor in Figure 7 but not to share the risk, the investor would move from his initial position, T_2 and $A_2(2r_1, \sigma_g)$, to T_1 and $A_2(r_1, \sigma_g)$. His demand for cash at a given market rate of interest would be increased and his liquidity preference curve shifted to the right.

Multiple Alternatives to Cash

So far it has been assumed that there is only one alternative to cash, and A_2 has represented the share of the investor's balance held in that asset, "consols." The argument is not essentially changed, however, if A_2 is taken to be the aggregate share invested in a variety of non-cash assets, e.g., bonds and other debt instruments differing in maturity, debtor, and other features. The return R and the risk σ_g on "consols" will then represent the average return and risk on a composite of these assets.

Suppose that there are m assets other than cash, and let x_i ($i = 1, 2, \ldots, m$) be the amount invested in the ith of these assets. All x_i are non-negative, and

$$\sum_{i=1}^{m} x_i = A_2 \leq 1.$$

Let r_i be the expected yield, and let g_i be the capital gain or loss, per dollar invested in the ith asset. We assume $E(g_i) = 0$ for all i. Let v_{ij} be the variance or covariance of g_i and g_j as estimated by the investor.

$$v_{ij} = E(g_i g_j) \qquad (i, j = 1, 2, \ldots, m) \tag{20}$$

The over-all expected return is:

$$\mu_R = A_2 r = \sum_{i=1}^{m} x_i r_i. \tag{21}$$

The over-all variance of return is:

$$\sigma_R{}^2 = A_2{}^2 \sigma_g{}^2 = \sum_{i=1}^{m} \sum_{j=1}^{m} x_i x_j v_{ij}. \tag{22}$$

A set of points x_i for which $\sum_{i=1}^{m} x_i r_i$ is constant may be defined as a *constant-return locus*. A constant-return locus is linear in the x_i. For two

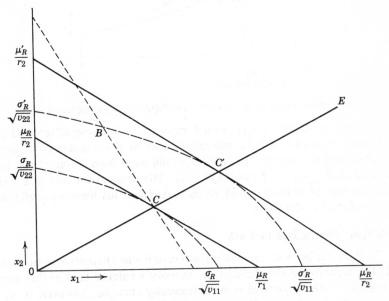

Figure 9 Dominant combinations of two assets.

assets x_1 and x_2, two loci are illustrated in Figure 9. One locus of combinations of x_1 and x_2 that gives the same expected return μ_R is the line from μ_R/r_2 to μ_R/r_1, through C; another locus, for a higher constant, μ'_R, is the parallel line from μ'_R/r_2 to μ'_R/r_1, through C'.

A set of points x_i for which $\sigma_R{}^2$ is constant may be defined as a *constant-risk locus*. These loci are ellipsoidal. For two assets x_1 and x_2, such a locus is illustrated by the quarter-ellipse from $\sigma_R/\sqrt{v_{22}}$ to $\sigma_R/\sqrt{v_{11}}$, through point C. The equation of such an ellipse is:

$$x_1{}^2 v_{11} + 2x_1 x_2 v_{12} + x_2{}^2 v_{22} = \sigma_R{}^2 = \text{constant}.$$

Another such locus, for a higher risk level, σ'_R, is the quarter-ellipse from $\sigma'_R/\sqrt{v_{22}}$ to $\sigma'_R/\sqrt{v_{11}}$ through point C'.

From Figure 9, it is clear that C and C' exemplify *dominant* combinations of x_1 and x_2. If the investor is incurring a risk of σ, somewhere on the ellipse through C, he will want to have the highest possible expectation of return available to him at that level of risk. The highest available expected return is represented by the constant-expected-return line tangent to the ellipse at C. Similarly C' is a dominant point: it would not be possible to obtain a higher expected return than at C' without incurring additional risk, or to diminish risk without sacrificing expected return.

In general, a dominant combination of assets is defined as a set x_i which minimizes $\sigma_R{}^2$ for μ_R constant:

$$\sum_i \left(\sum_j v_{ij}x_j\right) x_i - \lambda\left(\sum_i r_i x_i - \mu_R\right) = \min \qquad (23)$$

where λ is a Lagrange multiplier. The conditions for the minimum are that the x_i satisfy the constraint (equation 21) and the following set of m simultaneous linear equations, written in matrix notation:

$$[v_{ij}][x_i] = [\lambda r_i]. \qquad (24)$$

All dominant sets lie on a ray from the origin. That is, if $[x_i^{(0)}]$ and $[x_i^{(1)}]$ are dominant sets, then there is some non-negative scalar κ such that $[x_i^{(1)}] = [\kappa x_i^{(0)}]$. By definition of a dominant set, there is some $\lambda^{(0)}$ such that:

$$[v_{ij}][x_i^{(0)}] = [\lambda^{(0)}r_i],$$

and some $\lambda^{(1)}$ such that:

$$[v_{ij}][x_i^{(1)}] = [\lambda^{(1)}r_i].$$

Take $\kappa = \lambda^{(1)}/\lambda^{(0)}$. Then:

$$[v_{ij}][\kappa x_i^{(0)}] = [\kappa\lambda^{(0)}r_i] = [\lambda^{(1)}r_i] = [v_{ij}][x_i^{(1)}].$$

At the same time,

$$\sum_i r_i x_i^{(0)} = \mu_R^{(0)}$$

and

$$\sum_i r_i x_i^{(1)} = \mu_R^{(1)}.$$

Hence, $\mu_R^{(1)} = \kappa\mu_R^{(0)}$. Conversely, every set on this ray is a dominant set. If $[x_i^{(0)}]$ is a dominant set, then so is $[\kappa x_i^{(0)}]$ for any non-negative constant κ. This is easily proved. If $[x_i^{(0)}]$ satisfies equations 21 and 24 for $\mu_R^{(0)}$ and $\lambda^{(0)}$, then $[\kappa x_i^{(0)}]$ satisfies equations 21 and 24 for $\lambda^{(k)} = \kappa\lambda^{(0)}$ and $\mu_R^{(k)} = \kappa\mu_R^{(0)}$. In the two dimensional case pictured in Figure 9, the dominant pairs lie along the ray $OCC'E$.

There will be some point on the ray (say E in Figure 9) at which the investor's holdings of non-cash assets will exhaust his investment balance $(\sum_i x_i = 1)$ and leave nothing for cash holding. Short of that point the balance will be divided among cash and non-cash assets in proportion to the distances along the ray; in Figure 9 at point C, for example, OC/OE of the balance would be non-cash and CE/OE cash. But the convenient fact that has just been proved is that the proportionate composition of the non-cash assets is independent of their aggregate share of the investment balance. This fact makes it possible to describe the investor's decisions as if there were a single non-cash asset, a composite formed by combining the multitude of actual non-cash assets in fixed proportions.

Corresponding to every point on the ray of dominant sets is an expected return μ_R and risk σ_R; these pairs (μ_R, σ_R) are the opportunity locus of pages 11 and 16. By means of equation 24 the opportunity locus can be expressed in terms of the expected return and variances and covariances of the non-cash assets. Let:

$$[V_{ij}] = [V_{ij}]^{-1}.$$

Then:

$$\mu_R = \lambda \sum_i \sum_j r_i r_j V_{ij} \tag{25}$$

$$\sigma_R{}^2 = \lambda^2 \sum_i \sum_j r_i r_j V_{ij}. \tag{26}$$

Thus the opportunity locus is the line:

$$\mu_R = \sigma_R \sqrt{\sum_i \sum_j r_i r_j V_{ij}} = \sigma_R \frac{r}{\sigma_g}. \tag{27}$$

This analysis is applicable only so long as cash is assumed to be a riskless asset. In the absence of a residual riskless asset, the investor has no reason to confine his choices to the ray of dominant sets. This may be easily verified in the two-asset case. Using Figure 9 for a different purpose now, suppose that the entire investment balance must be divided between x_1 and x_2. The point (x_1, x_2) must fall on the line $x_1 + x_2 = 1$, represented by the line through BC in the diagram. The investor will not necessarily choose point C. At point B, for example, he would obtain a higher expected yield as well as a higher risk; he may prefer B to C. His opportunity locus represents the pairs (μ_R, σ_R) along the line through BC $(x_1 + x_2 = 1)$ rather than along the ray OC, and is a hyperbola rather than a line. It is still possible to analyze portfolio choices by the apparatus of (μ_R, σ_R) indifference and opportunity loci, but such analysis is beyond the scope of the present chapter.[14]

---

[14] Harry Markowitz, in *Portfolio Selection*, New York: John Wiley & Sons, 1959, treats the general problem of finding dominant sets and computing the corresponding opportunity locus, for sets of securities all of which involve risk. Markowitz's main interest is prescription of rules of rational behavior for investors; the main concern of this paper is the implications for economic theory, mainly comparative statics, that can be derived from assuming that investors do in fact follow such rules. For the general nature of Markowitz's approach, see his article, "Portfolio Selection," *Journal of Finance*, Vol. VII, No. 1 (March 1952), pp. 77–91.

It is for this reason that the present analysis has been deliberately limited to choices among monetary assets. Among these assets cash is relatively riskless, even though in the wider context of portfolio selection, the risk of changes in purchasing power, which all monetary assets share, may be relevant to many investors. Breaking down the portfolio selection problem into stages at different levels of aggregation—allocation first among, and then within, asset categories—seems to be a permissible and perhaps even indispensable simplification both for the theorist and for the investor himself.

IMPLICATIONS OF THE ANALYSIS FOR LIQUIDITY PREFERENCE THEORY

The theory of risk-avoiding behavior has been shown to provide a basis for liquidity preference and for an inverse relationship between the demand for cash and the rate of interest. This theory does not depend on inelasticity of expectations of future interest rates, but can proceed from the assumption that the expected value of capital gain or loss from holding interest-bearing assets is always zero. In this respect, it is a logically more satisfactory foundation for liquidity preference than the Keynesian theory previously described. Moreover, it has the empirical advantage of explaining diversification—the same individual holds both cash and "consols"—while the Keynesian theory implies that each investor will hold only one asset.

The risk aversion theory of liquidity preference mitigates the major logical objection to which, according to the argument on page 8, the Keynesian theory is vulnerable. But it cannot completely meet Leontief's position that in a strict stationary equilibrium liquidity preference must be zero unless cash and consols bear equal rates. By their very nature consols and, to a lesser degree, all time obligations contain a potential for capital gain or loss that cash and other demand obligations lack. Presumably, however, there is some length of experience of constancy in the interest rate that would teach the most stubbornly timid investor to ignore that potential. In a pure stationary state, it could be argued, the interest rate on consols would have been the same for so long that investors would unanimously estimate σ_g to be zero. So stationary a state is of very little interest. Fortunately the usefulness of comparative statics does not appear to be confined to comparisons of states each of which would take a generation or more to achieve. As compared to the Keynesian theory of liquidity preference, the risk aversion theory widens the applicability of comparative statics in aggregative analysis; this is all that need be claimed for it.

The theory, however, is somewhat ambiguous concerning the direction of relationship between the rate of interest and the demand for cash. For low interest rates, the theory implies a negative elasticity of demand for cash with respect to the interest rate, an elasticity that becomes larger and larger in absolute value as the rate approaches zero. This implication, of course, is in accord with the usual assumptions about liquidity preference. But for high interest rates, and especially for individuals whose estimates, σ_g, of the risk of capital gain or loss on "consols" are low, the demand for cash may be an increasing, rather than a decreasing, function of the interest rate. However, the force of this reversal of direction is diluted by recognition that the size of investment balances is not independent of the current rate of interest r. We have considered the proportionate allocation between cash and "consols" on the assumption that it is independent of the size of the balance. An increase in the rate of interest may lead an investor to desire to shift towards cash. But to the extent that the increase in interest also reduces the value of the investor's consol holdings, it automatically gratifies this desire, at least in part.

The assumption that investors expect on balance no change in the rate of interest has been adopted for the theoretical reasons explained rather than for reasons of realism. Clearly investors do form expectations of changes in interest rates and differ from each other in their expectations. For the purposes of dynamic theory and of analysis of specific market situations, the two theories discussed here are complementary rather than competitive. The formal apparatus considered previously will serve just as well for a non-zero expected capital gain or loss as for a zero expected value of g. Stickiness of interest rate expectations would mean that the expected value of g is a function of the rate of interest r, going down when r goes down and rising when r goes up. In addition to the rotation of the opportunity locus due to a change in r itself, there would be a further rotation in the same direction due to the accompanying change in the expected capital gain or loss. At low interest rates expectation of capital loss may push the opportunity locus into the negative quadrant, so that the optimal position is clearly no consols, all cash. At the other extreme, expectation of capital gain at high interest rates would increase sharply the slope of the opportunity locus and the frequency of no cash, all consols positions, like that of Figure 6. The stickier the investor's expectations, the more sensitive his demand for cash will be to changes in the rate of interest.

2

Substitution and Complementarity in the Choice of Risky Assets*

SHOICHI ROYAMA and KOICHI HAMADA

INTRODUCTION

The response of the demand for assets to a change in the expected return on an asset is of crucial importance in asset-choice theory. The effectiveness of monetary control or debt management depends heavily on the direction and the magnitude of the response of the demand for assets to changes in their expected returns and risks.

This chapter is designed to develop a theory of the choice of risky assets analogous to consumer demand theory. The effect of the change in expected returns on the demand for assets can be decomposed into two terms: the substitution effect and the income (or wealth) effect. The sign of the substitution effect determines whether assets are substitutes or complements. Several properties of the substitutes-complements relationship will be derived. In particular, it will be shown that the substitutes-complements relationship is closely related to the sign of the correlation coefficients of assets. The response of the demand for assets to changes in risk is also related to the above classification of assets.

* We are greatly indebted to Professor Ryuichiro Tachi who suggested this topic to us. We are also grateful to Professors Ryutaro Komiya, N. Liviatan, Takashi Negishi and Hirofumi Uzawa for many helpful comments; but responsibility for any errors or imperfections remains strictly with us. After this chapter was completed, an unpublished paper by Gordon Pye came to our attention. It deals with a problem similar to that on pages 31 to 33 but his formulation differs somewhat from ours.

Throughout the chapter, it is assumed that an investor has a quadratic utility function with decreasing marginal utility of wealth. Most of the results can be generalized to the case of a two-parameter (expected return and risk) utility function.

Brownlee and Scott [1] and Lintner [3] treated money (or savings deposits) as a riskless asset. However, in the actual world where the price level can vary, even money is subject to risk of appreciation or depreciation in real value. Therefore, we shall assume in this paper that all assets have some risk. For a meaningful discussion of debt management or inflation, for example, one cannot neglect this aspect of money.

MAXIMIZATION OF EXPECTED UTILITY

Suppose an investor has a utility function of the von Neumann-Morgenstern type.

$$U(W) = W - \tfrac{1}{2}aW^2 \qquad a > 0$$

where U is an index of the utility of wealth invariant up to a linear transformation, and W is the amount of real wealth.[1] The positive sign of a implies decreasing marginal utility of wealth. In order to keep the marginal utility of wealth non-negative, we restrict our attention to the range of W such that $1 - aW > 0$, or

$$W < \frac{1}{a}. \tag{1}$$

Suppose there are n types of assets. The ith asset has a rate of return q_i which is a stochastic variable. q_i's are distributed with the following expected returns and variance-covariance matrix.

$$E(q_i) = r_i \qquad i = 1, 2, \ldots, n$$

$$\text{Cov.}(q_i, q_j) = E[(q_i - r_i)(q_j - r_j)] = \sigma_{ij} \qquad i, j = 1, 2, \ldots, n$$

We shall allow the case where some r_i's are negative. The matrix $V = \|\sigma_{ij}\|$ is symmetric and positive semi-definite. Let us assume here that $\|\sigma_{ij}\|$ is positive definite. That is, all q_i's are not linearly dependent in the mathematical sense. In particular, $\sigma_{ii} > 0$ for all i. This means that there exist no riskless assets.

In this chapter, we concentrate our attention on a single-period asset choice. That is, we are interested in the combination of assets that maximizes the expected utility of wealth held at the end of the period.[2]

---

[1] The real value of an asset is measured in terms of non-durable goods. In order to exclude the existence of an asset without any risk, we assume that there is no forward-trading market for the composite of these consumer goods.

[2] This model was first introduced by Markowitz [4].

Let x_i be the real value of the ith asset held at the beginning of the period, and W_0 be the real value of an investor's wealth then. Since money is also included in the list of assets,

$$\sum_{i=1}^{n} x_i = W_0. \tag{2}$$

At the end of the period the value of his wealth will be

$$W = \sum_{i=1}^{n} (1 + q_i)x_i,$$

which is also a stochastic variable. An investor will choose x_i's to maximize $E[U(W)]$, if he follows the rule of expected utility maximization.

$$E[U(W)] = E\left[\sum_{i=1}^{n} (1 + q_i)x_i \right] - \frac{1}{2} aE\left[\left(\sum_{i=1}^{n} (1 + q_i)x_i \right)^2 \right] \tag{3}$$

If we define $1 + r_i = \mu_i$, then

$$E(1 + q_i) = \mu_i$$

$$\text{Cov. } [(1 + q_i), (1 + q_j)] = \text{Cov. } (q_i, q_j) = \sigma_{ij}.$$

Then, from equation 3

$$E(U) = \sum_{i=1}^{n} \mu_i x_i - \frac{1}{2}a \sum_{i=1}^{n} \sum_{j=1}^{n} (\sigma_{ij} + \mu_i \mu_j)x_i x_j. \tag{4}$$

Thus our maximization problem reduces to a quadratic programming problem. Maximize:

$$E(U) = \sum_{i=1}^{n} \mu_i x_i - \frac{1}{2}a \sum_{i=1}^{n} \sum_{j=1}^{n} (\sigma_{ij} + \mu_i \mu_j)x_i x_j$$

subject to

$$\sum_{i=1}^{n} x_i = W_0. \tag{5}$$

Since $\|\sigma_{ij} + \mu_i \mu_j\|$ is positive definite by assumption, $E(U)$ is a concave function of the x_i's. Therefore this maximization problem has an optimum solution.

Define a Lagrangean

$$L = E(U) - \lambda\left(\sum_{i=1}^{n} x_i - W_0 \right).$$

The necessary condition for a maximum is

$$\frac{\partial L}{\partial x_i} = \mu_i - a\sum_{j=1}^{n} (\sigma_{ij} + \mu_i \mu_j)x_j - \lambda = 0 \qquad \text{for } x_i > 0 \tag{6}$$

and

$$\frac{\partial L}{\partial x_{i'}} = \mu_{i'} - a\sum_{j=1}^{n} (\sigma_{i'j} + \mu_{i'} \mu_j)x_j - \lambda \leq 0 \qquad \text{for } x_{i'} = 0.$$

In order to concentrate our attention on relationships between assets, let us assume that every asset x_i is held in an optimum portfolio.[3] Then, for all i equation 6 is valid. Therefore if we put $m_{ij} \equiv -a(\sigma_{ij} + \mu_i\mu_j)$, we get the following equations from equation 6.

$$\sum_{j=1}^{n} m_{ij}x_j - \lambda = -\mu_i \qquad i = 1, 2, \ldots, n$$

(7)

$$-\sum_{j=1}^{n} x_j = -W_0$$

Define

$$H = \begin{bmatrix} m_{11} & \cdots & m_{1n} & -1 \\ \cdot & & \cdot & \cdot \\ \cdot & & \cdot & \cdot \\ \cdot & & \cdot & \cdot \\ m_{n1} & \cdots & m_{nn} & -1 \\ -1 & \cdots & -1 & 0 \end{bmatrix}.$$

(8)

Then x_i and λ can be written in matrix form:

$$\begin{bmatrix} x_1 \\ \cdot \\ \cdot \\ \cdot \\ x_n \\ \lambda \end{bmatrix} = H^{-1} \begin{bmatrix} -\mu_1 \\ \cdot \\ \cdot \\ \cdot \\ -\mu_n \\ W_0 \end{bmatrix}.$$

In order that this solution be maximal the bordered principal minor in the following form has the sign equal to that of $(-1)^l$.

$$\begin{bmatrix} m_{11} & \cdots & m_{1l} & -1 \\ \cdot & & \cdot & \cdot \\ \cdot & & \cdot & \cdot \\ \cdot & & \cdot & \cdot \\ m_{l1} & \cdots & m_{ll} & -1 \\ -1 & \cdots & -1 & 0 \end{bmatrix} \qquad l = 2, 3, \ldots, n$$

[3] If we allow the "short-sale" of assets, x_i can be negative and equation (6) holds for any assets whether they are held or issued by the investor. (See Lintner [3] p. 19ff.)

Accordingly

$$\frac{D_{ii}}{D} < 0 \qquad (9)$$

where D is the determinant of H and D_{ij} is the cofactor of the (i,j)th element of D (cf. Samuelson [5] p. 378).

THE RESPONSE OF DEMAND TO CHANGES IN EXPECTED RETURNS

We are interested in the effects of a change in expected returns on the demand for assets.

Since $\mu_i = 1 + r_i$,

$$\frac{\partial x_j}{\partial r_i} = \frac{\partial x_j}{\partial \mu_i} \qquad \text{(for any } i, j\text{)}.$$

Accordingly we shall develop our discussion in terms of $\partial x_j / \partial \mu_i$.
Totally differentiating equation 7, keeping σ_{ij} constant,

$$-a \sum_{j=1}^{n} (\sigma_{ij} + \mu_i \mu_j)\, dx_j - d\lambda = -d\mu_i + a \sum_{j=1}^{n} (\mu_j\, d\mu_i + \mu_i\, d\mu_j) x_j$$

$$-\sum_{j=1}^{n} dx_j = -dW_0 \qquad (10)$$

By matrix notation

$$
\begin{bmatrix}
m_{11} & \cdots & m_{1n} & -1 \\
\cdot & & \cdot & \cdot \\
\cdot & & \cdot & \cdot \\
\cdot & & \cdot & \cdot \\
m_{n1} & \cdots & m_{nn} & -1 \\
-1 & \cdots & -1 & 0
\end{bmatrix}
\begin{bmatrix}
dx_1 \\
\cdot \\
\cdot \\
\cdot \\
dx_n \\
d\lambda
\end{bmatrix}
=
\begin{bmatrix}
-d\mu_1 + a \sum_{j=1}^{n} (\mu_j\, d\mu_1 + \mu_1\, d\mu_j) x_j \\
\cdot \\
\cdot \\
\cdot \\
-d\mu_n + a \sum_{j=1}^{n} (\mu_j\, d\mu_n + \mu_n\, d\mu_j) x_j \\
-dW_0
\end{bmatrix}
$$

Therefore

$$
\begin{bmatrix}
dx_1 \\
\cdot \\
\cdot \\
\cdot \\
dx_n \\
d\lambda
\end{bmatrix}
= H^{-1}
\begin{bmatrix}
-d\mu_1 + a \sum_{j=1}^{n} (\mu_j\, d\mu_1 + \mu_1\, d\mu_j) x_j \\
\cdot \\
\cdot \\
\cdot \\
-d\mu_n + a \sum_{j=1}^{n} (\mu_j\, d\mu_n + \mu_n\, d\mu_j) x_j \\
-dW_0
\end{bmatrix}
$$

Then, we get

$$\left(\frac{\partial x_j}{\partial W_0}\right)_{\mu_i \text{ const.}} = -\frac{D_{n+1,j}}{D},\tag{11}$$

and

$$\left(\frac{\partial x_j}{\partial \mu_i}\right)_{W_0 \text{ const.}} = -\left(1 - a\sum_{k=1}^{n} \mu_k x_k\right)\frac{D_{ij}}{D} + ax_i\sum_{k=1}^{n} \mu_k \frac{D_{kj}}{D}\tag{12}$$

If we define

$$S_{ij} \equiv -\left(1 - a\sum_{k=1}^{n} \mu_k x_k\right)\frac{D_{ij}}{D},$$

equation 12 can be written as follows:

$$S_{ij} = \left(\frac{\partial x_j}{\partial \mu_i}\right)_{W_0 \text{ const.}} - ax_i\sum_{k=1}^{n} \mu_k \frac{D_{kj}}{D}.\tag{13}$$

Before interpreting the second term of equation 13, let us consider the effect of an increase in the total expected return to the investor without any change in risk. For example, we may imagine a case where the government imposes a lump-sum tax or subsidizes the investor at the end of the planning period.

Then the expected value of the total wealth will be

$$E(W) = \sum_{i=1}^{n} \mu_i x_i - \tau\tag{14}$$

$$\text{Var. }(W) = \sum_{i=1}^{n}\sum_{j=1}^{n} \sigma_{ij} x_i x_j.$$

where τ is the amount of tax (subsidy if negative) paid by the investor. In matrix form, the equilibrium condition will be:

$$H \begin{bmatrix} x_1 \\ \cdot \\ \cdot \\ \cdot \\ x_n \\ \lambda \end{bmatrix} = \begin{bmatrix} -(1 + a\tau)\mu_1 \\ \cdot \\ \cdot \\ \cdot \\ -(1 + a\tau)\mu_n \\ -W_0 \end{bmatrix}$$

By differentiating both sides by τ, one can easily get

$$-\left(\frac{\partial x_j}{\partial E(W)}\right)_{\mu_i \text{ const.}} = \left(\frac{\partial x_j}{\partial \tau}\right)_{\mu_i \text{ const.}} = -\frac{a\sum_{k=1}^{n} \mu_k D_{kj}}{D},\tag{15}$$

where $E(W)$ should be understood in the sense of equation 14.

From equation 15, the second term of equation 13 can be interpreted as follows. Suppose all x_k's remain unchanged in spite of a small increase in the expected return on the ith asset, $d\mu_i$. Then the investor automatically enjoys an increase in the value of his future expected wealth by $x_i\,d\mu_i$ without increasing risk. Also suppose this amount is taken away from the investor to keep him at the same combination of risk and return. Then the effect of a deduction from expected wealth will change the demand for x_j by $-x_i a \sum_{k=1}^{n} \mu_k(D_{kj}/D)\,d\mu_i$. This is exactly equal to the second term of the right hand side of equation 13. In other words, S_{ij} is the effect of the change in μ_i on x_j provided that *the investor is compensated for the change in μ_i so as to enable him to enjoy the same expected wealth with the same risk*. This is essentially the same as the interpretation of the substitution term by Hicks in the Mathematical Appendix of *Value and Capital* [2]. We may call the second term the (expected) wealth effect or the future wealth effect.

Schematically,

$$S_{ij} = \left(\frac{\partial x_j}{\partial \mu_i}\right)_{W_0\text{ const.}} - x_i\left[\frac{\partial x_j}{\partial E(W)}\right]_{\mu_k\text{ const.}} \tag{16}$$

This is the Slutsky equation of asset-choice theory. By analogy to consumer demand theory, let us call an asset x_j a *normal asset* if $\partial x_j/\partial E(W) > 0$, *an inferior asset* if $\partial x_j/\partial E(W) < 0$.[4] Naturally, all assets cannot be inferior nor normal.

SUBSTITUTES AND COMPLEMENTS RELATIONSHIP

In this section we shall investigate the properties of the substitution term S_{ij}.

Let us define assets x_i and x_j ($i \neq j$) as *substitutes* if $S_{ij} < 0$, and *complements* if $S_{ij} > 0$.

Two assets are substitutes if the rise in the return on one asset decreases the demand for the other; complements if the rise in the return on one asset increases the demand for the other, provided that the wealth effect is neglected. Since

$$\left(1 - a\sum_{k=1}^{n} \mu_k x_k\right) = 1 - aE(W) > 0$$

by assumption of equation 1,

$$S_{ij} = -\left(1 - a\sum_{k=1}^{n} \mu_k x_k\right) \cdot \frac{D_{ij}}{D} \tag{17}$$

---

[4] In our model, it is easily proved that a rise in the value of total wealth W_0, *ceteris paribus*, increases (decreases) the ratio of demand for the normal (inferior) asset to total wealth, x_i/W_0.

has the opposite sign to that of D_{ij}/D. We can state the following proposition by using properties of matrix H.

(i) $$S_{ij} = S_{ji}; \quad \text{for } H \text{ is symmetric.}$$

The substitution effect is reciprocal

(ii) $S_{ii} > 0$ by the second order condition for an optimum portfolio given by equation 9. If we neglect the wealth effect, *the rise in the expected return on an asset will increase its own demand.*

By expanding the matrix by the last row

(iii) $$\sum_{j=1}^{n} S_{ij} = 0$$

Since $S_{ii} > 0$, $\sum_{j \neq i} S_{ij} < 0$. This shows that *substitution dominates complementary* just as in the case of usual demand theory. The remarks by Hicks on this topic are valid in this case without any modification (Hicks [2] Mathematical Appendix pp. 311–312). All assets cannot be complementary with one another. If $n = 2$, the two assets are necessarily substitutes.

Because matrix H is negative definite subject to a linear constraint, we have

$$\sum_{i=1}^{m} \sum_{j=1}^{m} \frac{D_{ij}}{D} y_i y_j < 0 \quad (\text{for } 1 \leq m \leq n),$$

where the y_i's are not all zero and, when $m = n$, not all proportional to the coefficient of our linear restriction.

Then,

(iv) $$\sum_{i=1}^{m} \sum_{j=1}^{m} S_{ij} y_i y_j > 0, \quad (1 \leq m \leq n).$$

The property (ii) above is one particular case of (iv). From (iv), we get

$$\sum_{i=1}^{m} \sum_{j=1}^{m} S_{ij} > 0, \quad (1 \leq m < n).$$

Taking account of (iii), we obtain the following property of S_{ij}'s.

$$\sum_{i=1}^{m} \sum_{j=m+1}^{n} S_{ij} < 0, \quad (1 \leq m < n).$$

Suppose the n assets are divided into two groups in any possible manner. If the substitution effects within each group are negligible, then these two bundles of assets can be treated as substitutes for each other.

Furthermore, multiplying equation 15 by μ_{ij} and summing over $j = 1$, 2, ..., n, we obtain

(v)
$$\sum_{j=1}^{n} \mu_j \left(\frac{\partial x_j}{\partial \tau} \right)_{\mu_i \text{ const.}} = -a \sum_{j=1}^{n} \sum_{k=1}^{n} \frac{D_{kj}}{D} \mu_k \mu_j > 0.$$

That is, if we raise the parameter τ, e.g., by imposing a lump sum tax, the investor will react to this by increasing the expected value of his wealth. The *rationale* for this is that the imposition of such a tax upon an investor with a quadratic utility function, at any combination of $E(W)$ and Var. (W), increases the marginal utility of the former.

THE RESPONSE OF DEMAND TO CHANGE IN RISK

Let us turn to the effect of the change in risk on the demand for assets. This problem has considerable practical significance if we want to analyze the effect of taxation or that of price expectations. Taxation with loss-offset changes the variance of the return on a particular asset and price expectations may increase the covariance of the returns on some assets, say, bonds and money.

Suppose only σ_{ij} is variable and r_i, and accordingly μ_i, and other variances and covariances are kept constant. Then differentiating equation 7 with respect to x_i and σ_{ij},

$$\sum_{j=1}^{n} m_{ij} \, dx_j - d\lambda = a \sum_{j=1}^{n} x_j \, d\sigma_{ij}$$

$$-\sum_{j=1}^{n} dx_j = -dW_0.$$

Therefore, defining $T_{ij}{}^k \equiv \partial x_k / \partial \sigma_{ij}$,

$$T_{ij}{}^k = a \frac{x_i D_{jk} + x_j D_{ik}}{D} \quad (i \neq j),$$

$$T_{ii}{}^k = a \frac{x_i D_{ik}}{D}.$$

(18)

Since D_{ik}/D is positive if x_i and x_k are substitutes and negative if they are complements, we can see the following properties:

(i) $\qquad T_{ii}{}^i < 0$

The demand for an asset is reduced when it becomes more risky.

(ii) For $i \neq k$,

$$T_{ii}{}^k > 0, \quad \text{if } x_i \text{ and } x_k \text{ are substitutes,}$$

$$T_{ii}{}^k < 0, \quad \text{if } x_i \text{ and } x_k \text{ are complements.}$$

The increase in risk of a particular asset increases the demand for all assets that are substitutes for it and reduces the demand for all assets that are complements with it.[5]

(iii) For $i \neq j$,

$$T_{ij}{}^{i} = a\, \frac{x_i D_{ji} + x_j D_{ii}}{D} < 0,$$

if $D_{ij}/D < 0$.

If x_i, x_j are complements, the increase in σ_{ij} will reduce the demand for both x_i and x_j. An increase in the covariance of two assets works as if the variance of a composite asset consisting of the two increased. The direct effect of this increase is the reduction of the demand for the two as a whole. But if they are substitutes, the decrease in demand for one asset tends to increase the demand for the other. Thus the total effect of the increase in σ_{ij} on x_i or x_j may be negative or positive, if the two assets are substitutes.

(iv) For i, j and k all different,

$$T_{ij}{}^{k} = a\, \frac{x_i D_{jk} + x_j D_{ik}}{D} > 0,$$

if

$$D_{jk}/D > 0 \qquad \text{and} \qquad D_{ik}/D > 0;$$

i.e., x_j, x_k and x_i, x_k are substitutes.

$$T_{ij}{}^{k} < 0,$$

if

$$D_{jk}/D < 0 \qquad \text{and} \qquad D_{ik}/D < 0;$$

i.e., x_j, x_k and x_i, x_k are complements.

If σ_{ij} increases, the risk of a composite asset consisting of x_i and x_j increases. Therefore x_k increases if x_k is a substitute for x_i and x_j; x_k decreases if x_k is complementary with x_i and x_j.

---

[5] Multiplying $T_{ii}{}^{k}$ by x_k and summing over both k and i, we obtain the following property from the negative definiteness of matrix H under the constraint,

$$\sum_{k=1}^{m} \sum_{i=1}^{m} x_k T_{ii}{}^{k} = \sum_{k=1}^{m} \sum_{i=1}^{m} x_k \frac{\partial x_k}{\partial \sigma_{ii}}$$

$$= a \sum_{k=1}^{m} \sum_{i=1}^{m} \frac{D_{ik}}{D} x_i x_k \leq 0$$

or $1 \leq m \leq n$. Equality holds when all x_k's are identical.

Consider a subset of assets: $x_1, x_2, \ldots, x_m$. If all the assets in this subset increase their own risks, the weighted sum defined above of the changes in the demand for these assets will be nonpositive.

SUBSTITUTABILITY AND CORRELATION BETWEEN THE RETURNS ON ASSETS

It is often maintained that, if the returns on two assets are positively correlated, these assets are likely to be good substitutes. If the returns on two assets are negatively correlated, on the other hand, the holding of both assets at the same time will tend to reduce the total risk. Accordingly they are likely to be complements (e.g., Tobin [6] pp. 162 ff.).[6]

We are interested in how S_{ij} is related to σ_{ij}, which indicates the degree of correlation between the returns on x_i and x_j. Let us evaluate the following expression:

$$\left(\frac{\partial S_{ij}}{\partial \sigma_{ij}}\right)_{\mu_k \text{ const.}} \qquad i \neq j$$

In other words, other things being equal, what happens if the correlation of the two returns changes?

If we write

$$\frac{\partial Y}{\partial t} \equiv \left\| \frac{\partial y_{ij}}{\partial t} \right\|$$

where $Y = \|y_{ij}\|$ is a square and nonsingular matrix, and t is a scalar.

$$\frac{\partial Y^{-1}}{\partial t} = -Y^{-1} \frac{\partial Y}{\partial t} Y^{-1}.$$

Therefore

$$\frac{\partial H^{-1}}{\partial \sigma_{ij}} = -H^{-1} \frac{\partial H}{\partial \sigma_{ij}} H^{-1}$$

where $\partial H/\partial \sigma_{ij}$ is a matrix whose (i,j)th and (j,i)th element are $(-a)$ and all other elements are zero. Therefore

$$\frac{\partial h^{ij}}{\partial \sigma_{ij}} = a[(h^{ij})^2 + h^{ii}h^{jj}] \qquad \begin{array}{l} i \neq j; \\ i, j = 1, 2, \ldots, n, \end{array}$$

where

$$\|h^{ij}\| = H^{-1}.$$

---

[6] Differentiating the expected utility with respect to x_i and x_j, we obtain,

$$\frac{\partial}{\partial x_i}\left\{ \frac{\partial E[U(W)]}{\partial x_j} \right\} = -a(\sigma_{ij} + \mu_i\mu_j).$$

Therefore, if one adopts the definition of related goods by Pareto, one will see that x_i and x_j are substitutes if $\sigma_{ij} + \mu_i\mu_j > 0$, complements if $\sigma_{ij} + \mu_i\mu_j < 0$. However, this definition hardly gives us any operational relationship with regard to the nature of demand in actual capital markets (cf., Hicks [2] pp. 42–43).

Since by equation 9,

$$h^{ii} = \frac{D_{ii}}{D} < 0, \qquad \text{(for } i = 1, 2, \ldots, n\text{)}$$

$$\frac{\partial h^{ij}}{\partial \sigma_{ij}} > 0.$$

Accordingly,

$$\left(\frac{\partial S_{ij}}{\partial \sigma_{ij}}\right)_{\mu_k \text{ const.}} = \frac{\partial}{\partial \sigma_{ij}}\left[-\left(1 - a\sum_{k=1}^{n} \mu_k x_k\right)h^{ij}\right]$$

$$= -\left(1 - a\sum_{k=1}^{n} \mu_k x_k\right)\frac{\partial h^{ij}}{\partial \sigma_{ij}} + ah^{ij}\sum_{k=1}^{n} \mu_k \frac{\partial x_k}{\partial \sigma_{ij}}$$

by equation 18,

$$= -\left(1 - a\sum_{k=1}^{n} \mu_k x_k\right)\frac{\partial h^{ij}}{\partial \sigma_{ij}} + a^2 h^{ij}\sum_{k=1}^{n} \mu_k \frac{x_i D_{jk} + x_j D_{ik}}{D}$$

$$= -\left(1 - a\sum_{k=1}^{n} \mu_k x_k\right)\frac{\partial h^{ij}}{\partial \sigma_{ij}} + a^2 h^{ij}\left(x_i \sum \mu_k \frac{D_{jk}}{D} + x_j \sum \mu_k \frac{D_{ik}}{D}\right)$$

by equation 15,

$$= -\left(1 - a\sum_{k=1}^{n} \mu_k x_k\right)\frac{\partial h^{ij}}{\partial \sigma_{ij}} + ah^{ij}\left[x_i \frac{\partial x_j}{\partial E(W)} + x_j \frac{\partial x_i}{\partial E(W)}\right].$$

Suppose that the wealth effects, $\partial x_j/\partial E(W)$ and $\partial x_i/\partial E(W)$, can be neglected. Then

$$\left(\frac{\partial S_{ij}}{\partial \sigma_{ij}}\right)_{\mu_k \text{ const.}} < 0.$$

If the wealth effect may be neglected, the higher the correlation in the algebraic sense, the stronger is the substitution (or the weaker the complementarity) between the two assets.[7] An increase in the correlation of the returns on two assets will probably strengthen the substitution effect between them. This can be interpreted as a rigorous representation of the statement by Tobin in his various works (e.g., [6, 7]).

CONCLUDING REMARKS

So far it has been assumed for analytical simplicity that the utility function is quadratic with decreasing marginal utility. The use of the

---

[7] The reader will easily see, if both x_i and x_j are normal assets and are complementary with each other, then the statement above will be correct even if we take account of wealth effects.

quadratic utility function may raise some uneasiness ([3] p. 18 note). However, most of the results in this paper can be generalized to any representation of expected utility by two parameters, that is, expected return and risk.[8] The discussion on pages 31 to 35 holds true without any modification. So does that on pages 35 and 36 so long as we define $T_{ij}{}^k$ as $\partial x_k/\partial \sigma_{ij}$ compensated for a change in total risk to enable the investor to have the same risk with the same expected wealth.

Also the assumption that all x_i's are positive can be relaxed. By allowing the investor to borrow or to sell short, one can eliminate the restriction that all x_i's should be non-negative. So long as the optimum solution is bounded, the above discussion will be valid with proper changes in signs.

The following example will illustrate how the above result can be applied to actual policy problems. Consider an economy with three kinds of assets: money, bonds and physical capital. Consider the effect of a change in price expectations on the demand for assets. The return on money depends on the change in the price level; that of bonds on the rate of interest, its change, and the change in the price level, and the return on capital on the changes in relative prices of capital and consumer goods and its future profitability. Thus, bonds and money share risk to some extent. If we define money, bonds and capital as x_1, x_2, and x_3 respectively, then σ_{12} is positive.

For simplicity we shall neglect the wealth effect, and assume that the whole economy behaves just as an individual risk-averting investor, and that all three assets are substitutes for each other.

Suppose prices are expected to rise. Then both μ_1 and μ_2 will decrease and demand for x_3, capital, will increase because of substitution effects, S_{13} and S_{23}. Furthermore the covariance σ_{12} is likely to increase and this effect reinforces the increase in the demand for capital.

Consider here the case where price-pegged bonds[9] are issued by the government in exchange for the existing bonds. Then σ_{12} will be reduced substantially. Not only will inflationary expectations not affect μ_2, but also they will not increase σ_{12}. Thus the inflationary pressure developed by expectations of a rising price level would be curtailed to a considerable degree.

---

[8] Even if the utility function is not quadratic, expected utility maximization can be represented as the maximization of a function with two parameters, expected return and standard deviation, provided that the future returns are distributed by the multivariate normal distribution.

[9] The price-pegged bond, or bond with purchasing power escalation, is a marketable bond with price and return expressed in terms of purchasing power ([6] pp. 202ff).

REFERENCES

1. Brownlee, O. H., and Scott, I. O., "Utility, Liquidity and Debt Management," *Econometrica*, XXXII (July 1963), pp. 349–362.
2. Hicks, J. R., *Value and Capital*, second edition, London: Oxford University Press, 1946.
3. Lintner, J. H., "The Valuation of Risk Assets and the Selection of Risky Investments in Stock Portfolios and Capital Budgets," *The Review of Economics and Statistics*, XXVII (February 1965), pp. 13–37.
4. Markowitz, Harry, *Portfolio Selection*, New York: John Wiley, 1959.
5. Samuelson, P. A. *Foundations of Economic Analysis*, Cambridge: Harvard University Press, 1947.
6. Tobin, James, "An Essay on the Principles of Debt Management," in *Fiscal and Debt Management Policies*, prepared for the Commission on Money and Credit, Englewood Cliffs, N.J.: Prentice-Hall, 1963.
7. Tobin, James, "The Theory of Portfolio Selection," in *The Theory of Interest Rates*, ed. by F. H. Hahn and F. P. R. Brechling, New York: Macmillan, 1965.

3

Efficient Portfolios with Short Sales and Margin Holdings

DONALD D. HESTER

This chapter demonstrates that relaxing constraints imposed in most discussions of portfolio selection with quadratic utility functions can admit more efficient portfolios. A portfolio is said to be efficient if, for its rate of return, no portfolio exists with a lower variance of rate of return. The discussion is not merely academic; short sales, margin loans, and investors' selecting liabilities are evident in contemporary capital markets. It is believed that there is little difficulty in generalizing the argument to an arbitrary set of common stocks, although computation of efficient solutions in the n asset case has not been thoroughly studied yet.

A portfolio is defined as $p = \sum \alpha_i Z_i$ where Z_i = a dollar invested in the ith security; α_i is a set of weights. In earlier discussions Markowitz and Tobin generally required that $\alpha_i \geq 0$, $\sum \alpha_i = 1$.[1] This chapter studies portfolios where those restrictions are relaxed. The new restrictions are $2 \geq \alpha_i \geq -1$, $1 \geq \sum \alpha_i \geq 0$.

A short sale is a transaction in which an investor sells a security which he does not own. In effect, when a broker is notified that a short sale is desired, the investor's account is credited with the current market value of the sale and is debited with a corresponding number of shares. The credit is merely a bookkeeping transaction which cannot be withdrawn. The investor is obliged to pay all dividends which the stock pays. If the

---

[1] H. M. Markowitz, *Portfolio Selection*, New York: John Wiley and Sons, Inc., 1959 and J. Tobin, "Liquidity Preference as Behavior Towards Risk," this volume, Chapter 1.

stock's price falls (rises) the investor has an unrealized capital gain (loss).

An investor may not obtain an unlimited short position; the total value of his short sales and margin loans are restricted by Federal Reserve margin requirements when transactions occur and by the willingness of brokers to tolerate low margins once positions are taken. For example, if margin requirements are 50%, an investor may acquire up to $1000 worth of stock with $500. Alternatively, the investor may buy $500 worth of some security and acquire a short position of $500 in another. Once a transaction is made, margin requirements no longer apply. I am informed that few brokers will allow margins to decrease below 30%. The minimum margin brokers allow is a function of the value of an individual's net worth; larger accounts have lower minimum margin requirements.

A margin loan is like most secured bank loans. Loan recipients are required to pay a rate of between $5\frac{1}{2}$ and $6\frac{1}{2}$%, the actual rate charged being a decreasing function of the investor's net worth.

I

The argument is best seen by studying orthogonal representations of covariance matrices. One simple orthogonal representation can be obtained by extracting characteristic roots from these matrices. The coefficients of vectors are normalized so that $\sum \alpha_i^2 = 1$.

A discussion of how relaxing constraints on the α's affects the set of efficient portfolios in a three asset world is presented in Section II. A brief empirical look at the relevance of those results to trading on the New York Stock Exchange follows in Section III. Finally some remarks on the state of portfolio analysis conclude the chapter.

II

Three simplifying assumptions are made here: (1) transactions costs (brokerage charges) are nil, (2) cash has a zero rate of return with probability one, and (3) investors believe that they will incur a margin call with probability zero.[2]

I find the last of these assumptions least palatable. Admitting a small risk will not destroy the conclusions but will substantially complicate all subsequent calculations. An alternative assumption is that the investor retains other assets which he may use to offset margin calls.

---

[2] A margin call is a notification from a broker to the effect that an investor's margin has deteriorated to an intolerable level. The investor must supply more cash or unencumbered securities if he wishes to prevent the broker from disposing of his portfolio in the market.

In addition, the existence of two assets, X_1 and X_2, besides cash is assumed; each has a positive expected rate of return and nonzero variance. Three special cases are studied: (a) $r_{X_1 X_2} = 1$, (b) $r_{X_1 X_2} = 0$, and (c) $r_{X_1 X_2} = -1$.

Suppose:

$$(1) \quad \sigma_{ij} = \begin{Vmatrix} \sigma_{11} & \sigma_{12} \\ \sigma_{12} & \sigma_{22} \end{Vmatrix}$$

The characteristic equation of this matrix is:

$$(2) \quad (\sigma_{11} - \lambda)(\sigma_{22} - \lambda) - (\sigma_{12})^2 = 0.$$

$$(3) \quad \lambda = \frac{\sigma_{11} + \sigma_{22} \pm \sqrt{\sigma_{11}^2 + \sigma_{22}^2 - 2\sigma_{11}\sigma_{22} + 4\sigma_{12}^2}}{2}.$$

Case a (Perfect Positive Correlation)

$$(4) \quad \sigma_{12} = +\sqrt{\sigma_{11}\sigma_{22}}; \qquad \lambda = \sigma_{11} + \sigma_{22}, 0.$$

The vector associated with λ_1 is

$$\left(\frac{\sigma_1}{\sqrt{\sigma_{11} + \sigma_{22}}} X_1 + \frac{\sigma_2}{\sqrt{\sigma_{11} + \sigma_{22}}} X_2 = V_1 \right)$$

and with λ_2 is

$$\left(\frac{\sigma_2}{\sqrt{\sigma_{11} + \sigma_{22}}} X_1 - \frac{\sigma_1}{\sqrt{\sigma_{11} + \sigma_{22}}} X_2 = V_2 \right).$$

Therefore a portfolio with zero variance has the ratio of holdings of $X_1/X_2 = -\sigma_2/\sigma_1$.

To illustrate the solution, assume that investors believe

$$(5) \quad \sigma_{ij} = \begin{Vmatrix} 0.0004 & 0.0006 \\ 0.0006 & 0.0009 \end{Vmatrix},$$

$$E(R_{X_1}) = 0.05,$$

and

$$E(R_{X_2}) = 0.10.$$

A zero variance portfolio with positive rate of return will be realized by an investor who invests two thirds of his net worth in X_2, holds one third as cash, and acquires a short position in X_1 equivalent to his net worth. Hereafter such a portfolio is called $(\frac{1}{3}, -1, \frac{2}{3})$. The expected return is 0.0167. The next points on the efficiency frontier are described by reducing cash to zero and purchasing X_2. This continues until the portfolio $(0, -1, 1)$, which has an expected return of 0.05 and standard deviation of 0.01. The next section of the frontier implies the investor

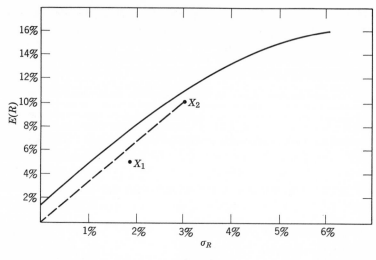

Figure 1

moves either to $(0, 0, 1)$ if the rate of interest on margin loans exceeds 0.05 or, if not, directly to $(-1, 0, 2)$. If this rate of interest exceeds 0.05 but is less than 0.10, the frontier passes from $(0, 0, 1)$ to $(-1, 0, 2)$ and is linear between these two points. If the rate of interest on margin loans is greater than or equal to 0.10 the efficient locus terminates at $(0, 0, 1)$. Figure 1 shows the argument when the rate on margin loans is 0.04 and the margin requirement is 50%. The dashed efficient set applies when neither short sales nor margin loans exist; the solid lines apply under the assumptions of this chapter.

It is instructive to examine the case when $E(R_{X_2}) = 0.06$. In this instance the previous riskless portfolio has a negative expected rate of

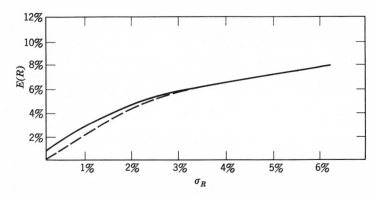

Figure 2

return, is dominated by cash, and is hence inefficient. However another riskless portfolio exists and is efficient; it is $(0, 1, -0.67)$. It also involves a short sale. Its expected rate of return is 1.0%. The next set of efficient points lie on a curve between $(0, 1, -0.67)$ and $(0, 1, 0)$. The reason that the portfolio shifts to this portfolio rather than $(0, 0, 1)$ is simply that the ratio of the expected rate of return to standard deviation is larger for X_1 than X_2; the opposite was true in the preceding example. The next set of points involve shifting from $(0, 1, 0)$ to $(0, 0, 1)$ along a straight line. Finally the efficient set is again linear between $(0, 0, 1)$ and $(-1, 0, 2)$.

Figure 2 illustrates this case. While in Figure 1 every point on the dotted efficiency locus is dominated, this is not the case in Figure 2. The importance of restrictions on α's depends on the structure of the first two moments of asset rates of return and is a function of the rate of interest on margin loans.

Case b (Zero Correlation)

$$(6) \quad \sigma_{12} = 0; \quad \lambda = \sigma_{11}, \sigma_{22}.$$

The vector associated with λ_1 is $(X_1 = V_1)$ and with λ_2 is $(X_2 = V_2)$. No portfolio with zero variance and positive rates of return is possible. The minimum variance portfolio, with cash excluded (and with the requirement that no one asset is held in both a long and short position), requires holding X_1 and X_2 in inverse proportion to their respective variances. This result is also obtained when short sales and margin loans are banned. Consequently, when assets are uncorrelated, investors should not make short sales unless an asset's expected rate of return is negative. To be sure, negative rates of return on assets would reinforce the incentives in Case *a* for short sales.

As in Figures 1 and 2, margin loans extend the efficiency locus so that an investor may control more than 100% of his net worth, provided, of course, that the expected rate of return on the high yield asset exceeds the interest rate on margin loans. However, investors should purchase securities on margin even before they reach the portfolio $(0, 0, 1)$, if the rate of interest on margin loans is less than the expected rate of return on the minimum risk no cash portfolio. The reason is that the rate of increase in risk can be reduced by retarding the rate at which X_2 is exchanged for X_1. Figure 3 illustrates this in the trivial (but easy to draw) case when margin loan interest rates are zero. For this example, $E(R_{X_1}) = 10\%$, $\sigma_{X_1} = 5\%$; $E(R_{X_2}) = 12\%$, $\sigma_{X_2} = 8\%$. A minimum risk, no cash portfolio is $(0, \frac{64}{89}, \frac{25}{89})$; its rate of return is 10.6% and its standard deviation is 4.33%. The no margin loan efficiency locus is sketched in dashed lines. When margin loan interest rates exist, but are less than

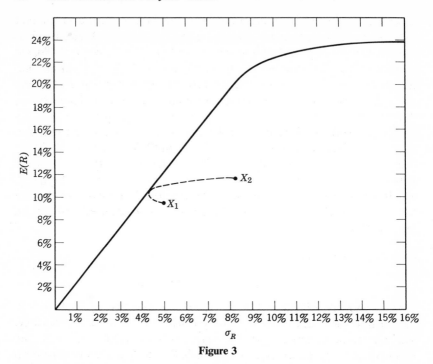

Figure 3

10.6%, the solid efficiency locus will be closer to the dashed line, but everywhere above it to the right of a tangency point defined by a line from the origin to the dashed locus.

To see this, by continuity we know that when $R_{X_2} > R_M > R_{X_1}$ and $1 > \alpha > 0$, there exists a range of values of β_1 and β_2 ($\beta_1 + \beta_2 \geq 1$) such that $\alpha R_{X_1} + (1 - \alpha)R_{X_2} = \beta_1 R_{X_1} + \beta_2 R_{X_2} - (\beta_1 + \beta_2 - 1)R_M$.[3]

First note that if $R_M > \hat\alpha R_{X_1} + (1 - \hat\alpha)R_{X_2}$, the minimum risk portfolio, portfolios with positive margin loans must be inefficient. This is because, if margin loans exist, X_2 must be held in larger quantities absolutely and relatively to X_1 than in nonmargin loan portfolios for a given rate of return. Holding larger quantities of X_2 will cause the variance of such portfolios to exceed that of equal return $(0, \alpha, 1 - \alpha)$ portfolios on the efficiency locus.

On the other hand, if $R_M < \hat\alpha R_{X_1} + (1 - \hat\alpha)R_{X_2}$, a portfolio with positive margin loans will be efficient. The proportion $X_2/(X_1 + X_2)$ in portfolios allowing margin loans is lower than in $(0, \alpha, 1 - \alpha)$ portfolios with equivalent rates of return. By specifying a small enough margin

---

[3] R_M is the interest rate on margin loans. To simplify notation expected value operators are dropped.

loan it is always possible to construct a portfolio with equal expected return and lower variance than for $(0, \alpha, 1 - \alpha)$ in the area to the right of the minimum variance portfolio $(0, \hat{\alpha}, 1 - \hat{\alpha})$.

Finally if $R_M = \hat{\alpha}R_{X_1} + (1 - \hat{\alpha})R_{X_2}$, the investor will always prefer not to acquire a margin loan. His rate of return is unchanged while the risk of his portfolio is increased.

Case c (Perfect Negative Correlation)

$$(7) \quad \sigma_{12} = -\sqrt{\sigma_{11} \cdot \sigma_{22}}, \qquad \lambda = \sigma_{11} + \sigma_{22}, 0.$$

The vector associated with λ_1 is

$$\frac{\sigma_1}{\sqrt{\sigma_{11} + \sigma_{22}}} X_1 - \frac{\sigma_2}{\sqrt{\sigma_{11} + \sigma_{22}}} X_2 = V_1$$

and with λ_2

$$\frac{\sigma_2}{\sqrt{\sigma_{11} + \sigma_{22}}} X_1 + \frac{\sigma_1}{\sqrt{\sigma_{11} + \sigma_{22}}} X_2 = V_2.$$

A portfolio with zero variance is described by the coefficients of the second characteristic vector; the required ratio of $X_1/X_2 = \sigma_2/\sigma_1$. In this case, the efficiency frontier when no margin loans exist is completely dominated by one which tolerates margin loans if the rate of return on the minimum risk no cash portfolio exceeds the interest rate on margin loans. This case is exhibited in Figure 4 which is constructed from the same data as Figure 1, except for the sign of the covariance which is reversed. The argument is exactly the same as the last in Case *b*.

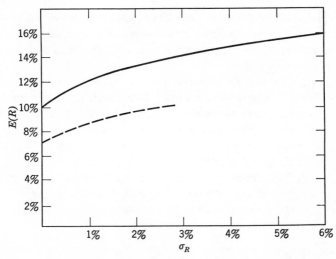

Figure 4

Short sales will not be made for purposes of diversification; they will of course exist if an investor's expected rate of return on an asset is (sufficiently) negative.

A common feature of the three cases is that minimum risk portfolios are weighted averages of pseudo portfolios, the characteristic vectors. The weights are the reciprocals of λ's. If a λ is zero then the minimum risk portfolio is its associated characteristic vector. The following observations apply in a world with no zero risk assets.

1. If a covariance matrix is singular a portfolio exists which has zero risk and a non-negative rate of return.

2. If more than one root is zero the efficient locus has a point consisting only of that zero variance vector with the highest rate of return.

3. If the covariance matrix is not singular and no margin requirements exist, a minimum risk portfolio is one in which characteristic vectors, normalized so $\sum \alpha_i^2 = 1$, $\sum \alpha_i > 0$, are held in inverse proportion to their associated roots.

Finally, few pairs of assets are described by any of the three cases here. Asset pairs lie between a and b or b and c. By an appeal to continuity it is likely that these intermediate cases exhibit the properties observed in both neighboring special cases. The argument is only that partial domination of the no short sale, no margin loan efficiency locus is likely in pairwise analysis of assets.

III

Data published by the New York Stock Exchange permits a crude but interesting experiment. We may draw some conclusions about the extent to which stock market investors are risk averse by analyzing their aggregate margin and short position.

First, what is known about the covariance matrix of rates of return on the New York Exchange? Very little! Markowitz reports a covariance matrix of annual rates of return on nine securities (1937–1954).[4] His matrix has only positive elements; the average correlation is 0.48. Preliminary results obtained by George Feeney and myself suggest that Markowitz's estimate also applies to a larger group of stocks.[5]

The average rate of return on stocks, at least over a large number of recent years has exceeded the margin loan rate of interest by a wide margin. No doubt, most linear (positive α's) combinations of stocks had rates of return which exceeded the margin loan rate.

[4] H. Markowitz, *op cit.*, p. 113.
[5] Feeney, George J. and Donald D. Hester this volume, Chapter 5.

Table 1[6]

	1963	1962
Value of stock listed on NYSE (billion dollars)	383.0	299.0
Volume of outstanding short sales (million shares)	5.654	5.168
Debit balance with member firms (billion dollars)	4.898	3.605
Credit balance with member firms (billion dollars)	1.152	1.374

[6] *Barrons*, August 19, 1963, p. 44.

To bring these observations into focus, assume that in June 1963 an individual believed that a covariance matrix and an expected rate of return estimated over the preceding ten years were reliable estimates from which to invest. The discussion in the preceding section suggests that if he placed great weight on expected return and was only a little concerned with risk, he would have margin loans. If he were concerned with risk he might have a moderate margin position and a smaller short position. Table 1 reports aggregate data for the New York Stock Exchange in June, 1963, and June, 1962.

The data are not ideal for the purpose at hand; an important share of shares outstanding is held by financial institutions and others who are prohibited from making margin and short sale transactions. Furthermore, investors may borrow against equities from banks rather than brokers; such margin positions are not observed. If all investors were permitted to buy on margin, theoretically debit balances with brokers (margin purchases) could reach something like $190 billion. Even allowing that only 50% of the market is free to buy on margin, it is abundantly clear that investors collectively do not invest only for rate of return; they appear strongly to desire low variance.

Second, for purposes of comparison, the volume of short shares must be multiplied by some average stock price. The August 19, 1963, *Barrons* reports the average price of actively traded stocks was in the neighborhood of $45. Thus the short position in the New York Stock Exchange is much smaller than the margin position; it is only about $200 million. Apparently there were few investors who believed that stocks had a negative expected return and few found it prudent to hedge against risk by selling short. Other safer assets, outside the stock market, exist to satisfy the investment desires of individuals who are extremely averse to risk. Examples may include mutual savings banks, savings and loan associations, annuities, bonds, etc.

This last argument is somewhat belied by the fact that investors keep cash balances with brokers of a little more than one billion dollars.

Perhaps the assumption that investors really believe in the past covariance matrix is in error; this could also account for their failure to exploit the structure with margin loans and/or short sales. It is more likely that transactions costs are the explanation for these balances; costs of odd lot transactions are high and the number of shareholders exceeds fifteen million.

Finally, it is likely that risk lovers, individuals preferring both high expected return and variance of return, are a negligible force in the market. By extending arguments by Tobin, it is clear that risk lovers will prefer short positions and/or margin loans when available.[7] The previous discussion argues that risk averters should have some short sale and margin positions. Only the remainder can be risk lovers.

IV

This analysis has been presented in terms of a modern stock market. This is a convenient expository vehicle because we may draw on an explicit set of margin and short sale restraints and because the market is more or less competitive. However, the behavior described appears in other "capital" transactions. A store manager who negotiates a bank loan and makes an improvement to his store with the proceeds has acquired a margin position. The problem is not easily analyzed because the expected rate of return is doubtless not constant when differently valued improvements are compared. Further, the budget constraint is not explicit, but determined subjectively by a banker. No doubt the covariance matrix of returns is only vaguely understood.

An example of a short sale would be renting a car to an individual while you make a two year sojourn in the Orient. The condition of the loan is that the borrower provide an equivalent car when you return two years later. The analytical difficulties associated with this case are: (1) the discrete nature of the transaction, (2) the lack of an organized market, and (3) the virtual nonexistence of an expected rate of return or covariance matrix from which to act.

In conclusion, a budget or net worth constraint is analytically misleading; consumer debt, margin loans, mortgages, and short positions exist in the world. Granting a quadratic utility function, there are a number of instances when part or all of the Markowitz efficient portfolio locus is dominated by a locus which allows short sales and margin positions. No doubt an analogous statement applies to models of consumer behavior. The nature of credit restraints on economic units needs further investigation.

---

[7] Tobin, this volume, Chapter 1.

4

Effects of Alternative Tax Structures on Individuals' Holdings of Financial Assets

SUSAN J. LEPPER

INTRODUCTION

The Problem—In Terms of Policy and Theory

No subject in economics is more vigorously debated in the political arena than taxation. In part, these controversies derive from differences in value judgments, exacerbated by vested financial interests. In part, they result from the equivocal conclusions of economic theory on the consequences of various taxes. One area of taxation in which opinions vary over a wide range is taxation of investment returns. On the one hand, there are those who are primarily concerned with effects of such taxation on the availability of risk capital. They emphasize that the availability of such capital at costs which are not prohibitive is essential to a free enterprise economy in order to permit easy entry of new firms into an industry and to encourage product and process innovation. The relatively recent concern with economic growth heightens the significance of these considerations. On the other hand, there is a view which focuses on the importance of progressive taxation of investment returns to the over-all progressivity of the tax system. The high concentration of property ownership makes returns from property a favorite target of those who wish to use the tax system to reduce the inequality of income. It must be the task of economic theory to determine the compatibility of these two goals.

Until fairly recently, the tools of economic theory have not been adequate to cope with this problem because they have not incorporated risk into a theoretical structure in such a way as to explain important

51

aspects of observed behavior. Recent developments have gone far in correcting this situation. Examination of the problem using newly available theoretical tools reveals that it is an over-simplification to claim that taxation, in particular progressive taxation of investment returns, reduces the incentive to hold risky assets merely by reducing the return available from such assets. Any form of tax does, of course, reduce the return from a risky asset. But two additional considerations must be kept in mind. First, the same tax also affects the returns from alternative forms of investment and, second, the tax may affect the amount of risk associated with a particular asset as well as its return. Weighing all of these considerations involves the use of a theory of portfolio diversification which incorporates a concept of subjectively measurable risk and a theory of choice under uncertainty.

Theoretical Tools

It is just these two characteristics of the theoretical model to be used in this study which were missing from neoclassical models of the demand for assets of various types. Most such theories of demand for real assets on both the micro- and the macro-levels have assumed the marginal equality of "the" rate of return on capital to "the" rate of interest. According to Keynesian theory, "the" rate of interest adjusts so as to reduce to zero any excess supply (demand) for cash balances—at given levels of income and prices—which also reduces to zero excess demand (supply) for bonds. It is assumed either that the relevant rates of return are the current rates, which are known, or that investors' expectations are single-valued. Even if risk is allowed for by assuming the existence of market-determined risk premia, rules of rational behavior dictate that an individual hold only that asset, either real or financial, on which the market offers the highest margin of return above his own risk premium. Thus, ownership of a variety of assets by the private sector as a whole can be explained only by difference among individuals' expectations of return and/or demands for risk premia. Diversification of individuals' portfolios and hence individuals' demands for assets—in particular, for cash which offers no yield except in periods of expected price deflation—cannot be explained by these assumptions about rational behavior in a world of certainty or by reducing risky alternatives to "certainty equivalents."[1]

---

[1] Both J. R. Hicks [*Value and Capital* (London: Oxford University Press, 1939), Chapter XIII, and "A Suggestion for Simplifying the Theory of Money," *Economica*, Vol. 2, No. 5 (1935), pp. 1–19] and F. A. Lutz ["The Structure of Interest Rates," *Quarterly Journal of Economics*, Vol. 55 (1940–41), pp. 36–63] recognized that the combined uncertainties of future returns and future expenditures affected the demand for assets of various kinds, primarily for bonds of various maturities, relative to the demand for cash.

An important step in the development of tools for analyzing the demand for assets with uncertain returns came with the introduction of the concept of a probability distribution as a description of the range and likelihood of various outcomes of an investment. It seems intuitively obvious that, assuming that a probability distribution describes the nature of an uncertain situation, risk is in some way associated with the dispersion of possible outcomes. Thus, Makower and Marschak[2] in 1938 suggested that the variance of returns (a measure of the deviation of possible returns from the mean return) should be considered as an investment criterion, as well as the mean, or expected return. Lange[3] suggests that individuals are concerned with the most probable—statistically, the mode—outcome of an action (in the context of his discussion, outcomes were deviations of the future from the present price of a good being bought or sold) and the range of probable outcomes. Roy's analysis of real investment[4] associates risk with the probability of returns falling below some "disaster" level and Telser[5] uses a very similar method in his discussion of hedging in commodity markets. The primary significance, for our purposes, of using probability distributions to describe uncertain situations is that this approach permits subjective measurement of risk.

A second important development in the analysis of behavior in risky situations was the formulation of a concept of preference functions to describe rational choice among actions with uncertain outcomes. One of the best-known works in this area is that of von Neumann and Morgenstern.[6] If an individual's preferences follow N-M, or similar axioms, they can be described by an index or utility function. This index or function assigns cardinal values or "utilities" to all the probable outcomes of any action—for our purpose, choices of investments. Using this function, it is possible to calculate the expected value, in the statistical sense, of any action. This "expected utility" equals the sum of the utilities of each of the outcomes multiplied by their probabilities and constitutes a scale for measuring the desirability of an action. Rational behavior is, naturally, equivalent to choosing that action which maximizes "expected utility."

---

[2] H. Makower and J. Marschak, "Assets, Prices and Monetary Theory," *Economica*, N.S. Vol. V (1938), pp. 261–288.

[3] O. Lange, *Price Flexibility and Full Employment* (Bloomington, Indiana: Principia Press, Inc., 1944), Chapter VI.

[4] A. D. Roy, "Safety First and the Holding of Assets," *Econometrica*, Vol. 20, No. 3 (July 1952), pp. 431–449.

[5] T. G. Telser, "Safety First and Hedging," *Review of Economic Studies*, Vol. XXIII (1), No. 60 (1955), pp. 1–16.

[6] J. von Neumann and O. Morgenstern, *Theory of Games and Economic Behavior* (3rd ed.; Princeton: Princeton University Press, 1953).

Consider, for example, an individual choosing between investment A, having equal chances of yielding $10 or $20, and investment B, having a 60 per cent chance of yielding $5 and a 40 per cent chance of yielding $25. Such an individual would prefer B if his "utility function" assigned utilities of, for example, 100 and 400 to the possible returns on A and 25 and 625 to the returns on B (i.e., his utility function is $U = r^2$) since the expected utility of A is $(0.5)(100) + (0.5)(400)$ or 250 and the expected utility of B is $(0.6)(25) + (0.4)(625)$ or 265. In the same way, this concept can be applied to the problem of portfolio diversification by assigning probabilities to the returns from complete portfolios of various compositions. Each particular portfolio has associated with it a different probability distribution of returns. Calculation of the expected utility of each portfolio permits the investor to select the optimum pattern of asset holdings. This model has been developed in some detail by Tobin,[7] who applied it to an analysis of liquidity preference, and by Markowitz,[8] who developed from it a prescriptive theory of portfolio diversification among large numbers of specific assets, intended to be used by investment advisers. The specific details of the model as it is used in this study are discussed in the following two sections.

A model quite similar to this was applied by Domar and Musgrave to an analysis of taxation and risk-taking in a path-breaking article published in 1944.[9] In their analysis, they assume that the return and risk associated with any portfolio are measured by characteristics of the probability distribution of returns (respectively, the average return and average loss). The effects on these statistics of proportional income taxes with and without loss offsets are derived. It is further assumed that, among portfolios with the same risk, investors would certainly prefer the portfolio with the largest return. This assumption makes it possible to construct what they term an "optimum-asset curve" (or "opportunity locus" in Tobin-Markowitz terminology) containing the risk-return points corresponding to all such

[7] J. Tobin, "Liquidity Preference as Behavior Towards Risk," in this volume, Chapter 1.

[8] H. Markowitz, *Portfolio Selection—Efficient Diversification of Investments* (Cowles Foundation for Research in Economics at Yale; New York: John Wiley and Sons, 1959).

[9] E. Domar and R. Musgrave "Proportional Taxation and Risk-taking," *Quarterly Journal of Economics*, Vol. XVIII (1944), pp. 388–422. This article and subsequent works by E. C. Brown ["Business-income Taxation and Investment Incentives" in *Income, Employment and Public Policy* (Essays in Honor of Alvin H. Hansen; New York: W. W. Norton and Company, 1948)] and Paul Streeten ["The Effect of Taxation on Risk-taking," *Oxford Economic Papers*, Vol. 5 (October 1953), pp. 271–287] are synthesized in Musgrave's *The Theory of Public Finance* (New York: McGraw-Hill Book Company, 1959), Chapter XIV.

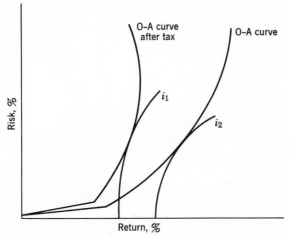

Figure 1 Equilibrium solutions before and after imposition of a proportional income tax without loss offset.

portfolios. If an investor's preferences among risk-return combinations are described by indifference curves (analogous to those used in the theory of consumer choice), his preferred portfolio is determined by the tangency of the optimum asset curve to his highest indifference curve (see Figures 1 and 2) and this tangency point is shifted as taxes shift the optimum asset curve.

The analysis of various taxes in this study is similar to Domar and Musgrave's in basic outline. It goes beyond theirs in two respects. First, use is made of a mathematical relationship, on the one hand, between the form of an investor's utility of returns function and the shape of his indifference curves and, on the other hand, between the utility of returns

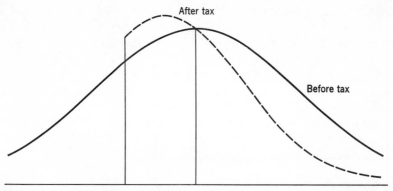

Figure 2 Probability distribution of returns showing effect of a proportional income tax without loss offset.

function and the appropriate measures of risk and return. This latter relationship has been developed by Tobin[10] and is used in an article by Richter[11] to derive more precise and mathematically general conclusions than Domar and Musgrave were able to do. Many of the properties of this model are found to be useful not only to determine the effects of taxes on total risk-taking, as Richter does, but also to determine the effects on the demand for risky assets. Unfortunately, however, even the qualitative effects of detailed tax provisions also depend on the form and parameters of the probability distribution of returns. Therefore, the functional form of the probability distribution of returns is postulated and estimates are made from empirical data of the parameters of the probability distribution which might have been assumed by a typical investor in 1961. From these assumptions, conclusions are deduced about shifts in demand which might occur in response to changes in tax structure.

A Preview of Conclusions

As we have already suggested, our analysis of the effects of taxes on the demand for assets depends upon two concepts: measurement of risk by some characteristic of a probability distribution of anticipated returns, and selection of the optimum portfolio in such a way as to maximize the expected value of the utility of returns.

The analysis focuses attention on the crucial role of investors' concepts of risk in determining the impact of various taxes. If investors are concerned about the entire dispersion of the distribution around its mean, a proportional tax—even one with incomplete loss offsets—tends to increase the demand for risky assets by all investors except those whose demands would be relatively small in any case. This occurs because the tax reduces the means and the dispersions of the distributions of returns in such a way as to make risky assets *relatively* more attractive than they would be without tax, thus leading some investors to try to compensate for part of the tax-induced loss of income. Addition of progressivity to the tax structure creates loss of incentive to hold risky assets, relative to a proportional tax, because it reduces the mean return from risky portfolios by a larger amount relative to the reduction in risk; it also expands slightly the range of portfolios for which there is a disincentive effect. On the other hand, if investors associate risk with actual losses (or, possibly, with negative skewness of the distribution of returns), risk is affected very little by taxes unless there are significant loss-offset provisions. There is, therefore, a disincentive to the holding of risky assets which is larger the greater

---

[10] Tobin, *op. cit.*
[11] M. K. Richter, "Cardinal Utility, Portfolio Selection and Taxation," *Review of Economic Studies*, Vol. XXVIII (3) (June 1960), pp. 152–166.

the tax-induced reduction in the mean return. Thus, progressive taxes without significant loss-offset provisions may or may not create a disincentive to holding risky assets, depending on the nature of investors' preferences.

Empirical observations of a fairly casual sort, and the study by Butters, Thompson, and Bollinger[12] seem to suggest that investors are primarily concerned with the negative, rather than with the entire, dispersion of a distribution. If this is the case, the possibility of tax-induced limitations of demand for risky assets is unequivocal. It is also easier to remedy, however, by loss-offset provisions. Thus it would appear from analysis of the mechanics of tax effects that there is reason for concern over the impact of taxes on the availability of risk capital. But it would also seem that the goals of those holding the different opinions mentioned above may not be incompatible. A tax code could be written which would include a progressive structure of rates at a level dictated by average revenue needs over a period of years *if* the Government were willing to absorb a sufficiently large proportion of investors' losses and the correspondingly increased variability in tax revenues. A variety of loss-offset schemes might be considered, including expanded current loss offsets, loss carry-forward and carry-back provisions and various income-averaging schemes (which also have advantages from the point of view of equity among taxpayers). The advantages of such provisions might prove well worth the cost of administration.

A Caveat

Any theoretical conclusions must be carefully interpreted with a view to recognizing the economic sector or segment of behavior to which they can be applied. This study is concerned with individuals' allocation of wealth among various kinds of financial assets. Attention is focused on the composition of portfolios because it is this which affects the availability of funds to their ultimate users by determining, *ceteris paribus*, the positions of the demand curves for assets. This study does not consider the magnitude of the flow of funds into investment channels which is essentially a question of the uses of income. Neither does it consider the ultimate market adjustments which might result from changes in the tax laws.[13]

---

[12] J. Butters, L. Thompson, and L. Bollinger, *Effects of Taxation on Investments by Individuals* (Cambridge: Harvard University, Graduate School of Business Administration, 1953).

[13] It is on this point that this study parts company from Hall's global analysis of aggregate relationships in a three sector-consumer, business, government-economy. [See Challis A. Hall, *Fiscal Policy for Stable Growth* (New York: Holt, Rinehart and Winston, 1960).]

It does not do so because the incentives for and constraints on asset holding differ significantly among the various major classes of individual and institutional investors.[14]

THE MODEL

The model which underlies our analysis of the disincentive to risk-taking which may result from various taxes on investment returns describes the behavior of an individual investor. This investor is faced with the problem of distributing a given amount of wealth among various financial assets. Once he has selected a portfolio, his assets will remain distributed in this pattern for one investment period, at the end of which a new portfolio can be selected. At the beginning of each investment period, the investor knows the length of the investment period, the size of his investment balance, and what assets are available. He does not know with certainty the return which each of these assets will yield. The investor is thus confronted with the necessity of making a decision under uncertainty.

The decision-making model to be developed assumes that two sets of parameters are relevant to investors' actions: parameters which describe their expectations, and parameters which determine their preferences. Taxes change the parameters which describe investors' expectations; preferences determine investors' responses to these tax-induced changes. The sections below describe, first, the assumptions which are made about the nature of investors' expectations and, hence, the parameters necessary to describe them and, second, the assumptions which are made about investors' preferences. The first set of assumptions makes it possible to specify in more detail the mechanical effects of various taxes on expectations. The second set of assumptions is necessary in order to define what decision parameters are relevant. It is also necessary to specify, below, certain simplifying assumptions which are required by institutional factors or by an absence of knowledge of the absolute magnitudes of some parameters.

Risk and Expectations

An action, such as choice of a portfolio, which must be undertaken without knowledge of its consequence may be said to involve risk. In such a situation, it is reasonable to assume that the individual acts on the basis of his expectations. It seems likely, furthermore, that these expectations are not single-valued, but rather that the individual conceives of several possible consequences of his action, some of which may be more likely

---

[14] See, for example, an unpublished dissertation by Ernest Bloch, *Corporate Liquidity Preference* (New School for Social Research, June, 1961).

than others. One formalization of this set of assumptions is the concept of "subjective probability." The subjective probability which an individual assigns to the outcome of an action is a measure of the degree of confidence he has in its occurrence. These probabilities are called "subjective" because they may not be verifiable through repeated observations. Implicit in this concept, however, is the assumption that they can be treated according to the normal rules of probability theory.[15]

It is assumed in this model of investment behavior that investors assign subjective probabilities to the possible returns (measured in per cent) from the various assets which they can buy. In order to manipulate these distributions analytically it is assumed that they can all be described by normal or Gaussian functions, truncated at −100 per cent. Investors' expectations are, therefore, defined by the parameters of the joint normal probability distribution of returns from the available assets. These constitute the first set of subjective parameters which are relevant to investors' decisions. The values assigned to the parameters by each investor depend on his views concerning the markets for each asset, the inter-relation of returns on the various assets, and likely developments in the economy at large. It is beyond the scope of this chapter to develop a theory of how these expectations are formed. It seems likely that institutional factors impose certain limits on the values of these parameters and that the historical frequencies of returns also influence expectations. These factors are explored on pp. 75–79.

Expectations of returns from an investor's total portfolio are obviously a function of the distribution of returns on the various component assets. The particular probability distribution which describes expected returns from the total portfolio depends on the proportion of total wealth held in each component asset. If the truncation of the distribution of returns at −100 per cent is ignored, the distribution of total returns would also be normal. It seems reasonable to assume that the probability of return from

---

[15] The concept of subjective probability is taken as the relevant one since it has been developed explicitly to deal with the problem of action under uncertainty without the constraint that the action must be repetitive. A classic work on subjective, or, as he calls it, "personal" probability, is Leonard J. Savage's *The Foundations of Statistics* (New York: John Wiley & Sons, 1954), in which he identifies the "personalistic view" as holding that "probability measures the confidence that a particular person has in the truth of a particular proposition" (p. 3). Savage develops a system of postulates which relates these "degrees of confidence," interpreted in a behavioral sense, to mathematical probabilities. Alternative views are mentioned as being the "objectivistic view," which holds that the concept of probability applies only to those repetitive events whose behavior is in agreement with mathematical probability theory, and the "necessary" view which holds that probability measures the extent to which one set of propositions confirms the truth of another.

any asset being equal to -100 per cent is very small. Therefore, little error is introduced by assuming that the distribution of total returns is normal[16] and truncated at -100 per cent.

Rational Decisions in Risky Situations

The decision which our investor must make consists, therefore, in making a choice among subjective (normal) probability distributions whose parameters are determined by his expectations of returns from various available assets and the proportion of the total portfolio held in each asset. It is further assumed that the investor makes a "rational" choice which consists in maximizing the expected value (in the statistical sense) of a function which assigns utilities to the possible outcomes of the investment. Such behavior is implied if rationality in the face of uncertainty is defined according to the Savage, von Neumann-Morgenstern, or similar axiom system.[17] The conclusions derived below follow specifically from this implication of the axiomatic theories of utility. It is intuitively reasonable, however, that the general conclusions might apply to some behavior which does not specifically fit any one of these axiom systems.

The voluminous literature dealing with axiomatic theories of utility has raised many questions, and suggested some answers, concerning the behavioral content of such axiom systems. A few of these questions are: can subjective beliefs about probabilities and subjective preferences be meaningfully distinguished; does behavior conform to the requirement that preferences among probabilities be "linear"; is there any behavioral analogue to the concept of indifference which plays a central role in these systems; and are preferences consistent. Two authors at least, Davidson

---

[16] If

r_i = return (in per cent) on the ith asset,

x_i = proportion of the total portfolio invested in the ith asset,

m_i = the mean of the probability distribution of returns on the ith asset,

v_i = the variance of expected returns on the ith asset,

$v_{i,j}$ = the covariance between returns on the ith and jth assets,

$R \equiv$ expected return from the total portfolio (in per cent),

M_R = the mean of the probability distribution of R,

V_R = The variance of the probability distribution of R,

then

$R = \Sigma\, x_i r_i,$

$M_R = \Sigma\, x_i m_i,$

$V_R = \Sigma \Sigma\, x_i x_j v_{i,j}.$

(It should be noted that, barring purchases on margin, $\Sigma\, x_i = 1$ and, barring short sales, $x_i \geq 0$ for all x_i.)

[17] I. N. Herstein and J. Milnor, "An Axiomatic Approach to Measurable Utility," *Econometrica*, Vol. 23, No. 2 (April, 1953), pp. 291–97, and their references contain discussions of such axiom systems.

and Suppes,[18] have given affirmative answers to these questions. They constructed an axiom system which provides for an interval-scale utility function, and developed a behavioristic analogue which permitted separate experimental measures of utility and subjective probability. Their experimental results suggest the following conclusions: (1) Subjects may bias the probabilities they assign to certain events so that their subjective probabilities do not equal objective probabilities. Once the subjective probabilities have been found, however, there are identifiable probability events such that, if the subject is asked in effect to assign utilities to two opportunities of winning the same stake, he will assign twice the utility to the opportunity which has twice the probability of winning. That is, subjects display linear preferences with respect to probabilities. (2) Subjects apparently try to find repetitive patterns when faced with some sequences of probability events, but there exist some events which are subjectively independent. This condition has been identified by Luce[19] as necessary if rational choice is to imply maximization of expected utility in a probabilistic sense. (3) When confronted with probability events which are subjectively independent and for which subjects' preferences are linear, subjects show consistent preferences. Thus it has been shown that some people, in some situations, behave in a manner consistent with the axioms underlying our model. On the other hand, Markowitz[20] has cited observations by himself and other authors on this subject which appear to indicate inconsistent preferences and hence to contradict the axioms. Experiments testing the applicability of the model to many people in situations involving large sums of money are, as yet, too limited in scope and sample size to yield statistically significant results.

Distinctly different approaches to the problem of decisions under uncertainty are those classified in a review article by Arrow[21] as "adaptive" rather than maximizing. It might be assumed, for example, that the subject, in each play, acts on the basis of a hypothesis derived from observing the sequence of outcomes of all previous plays without being concerned with the probable error of the hypothesis. Such a model might be better suited for analyzing the process by which the investor's expectations are formulated, than for analyzing his behavior in the face of the remaining uncertainty. One reason for this conclusion is that investors appear to the casual

[18] D. Davidson and P. Suppes (in collaboration with Seigel), *Decision Making: An Experimental Approach* (Stanford, California: Stanford University Press, 1957).
[19] R. Luce, "A Probabilistic Theory of Utility," *Econometrica*, Vol. 26, No. 2 (April, 1958), pp. 193–224.
[20] Markowitz, *op. cit.*
[21] K. Arrow, "Utility, Attitudes and Choices," *Econometrica*, Vol. 26, No. 1 (January, 1958), pp. 1–23.

observer to be more clearly concerned with risk than, e.g., the subject of an experimental game.

Another type of nonmaximizing approach, which appears likely to prove very fruitful as it is developed further, is that of heuristic, simulation models (models postulating a set of "rules of thumb" or binary tests). Such a model of the process of selection of common stocks by investment trust officers has been developed by G. P. E. Clarkson.[22] Although it has shown very interesting results, it by-passes certain stages of the process which are critical for our problem. One such stage is the association of investment in certain industries with certain investment goals which would seem to be differentiated partly on the basis of acceptable risk. Further development of such models may make them relevant to our problem but, in the meantime, it is useful to explore the conclusions of a somewhat less cumbersome system.

Granting the use of maximization of expected utility as the investment goal, it remains to define the time period considered in the maximizing process. The length of an investment period is likely to be determined primarily by the cost, either psychic or financial, of changing portfolios. It does seem reasonable, however, that an investor's utility horizon and his expectations horizon may both comprise several investment periods. The shorter of the investor's utility or expectations horizons determines the number of periods over which an investor might plan his investment strategy. One fairly simple model using a multi-period approach[23] assumes that the investor's utility horizon contains many investment periods but that only final utility is considered, that the investor reinvests all his returns, and that the same expectations of returns apply to each investment period. These assumptions appear highly restrictive. In addition, it is assumed that the investor decides on a strategy at the beginning of the utility period which is to be followed throughout. Markowitz points out[24] that true optimization in any period requires the investor to assume that, in each successive period, the optimum portfolio selection will be made. If utility of returns in any one period depends on which period is being considered, or on returns in the preceding period (e.g., because the investor has positive time preference, or because he reinvests part of his returns and has a nonlinear utility of wealth function), true maximization requires that the expected utility of optimum future portfolio selections be computed for

---

[22] G. P. E. Clarkson, *The Meno Anew: A Simulation of Trust Investment* (dittoed Behavioral Theory of the Firm Project, working paper #32; Pittsburgh: Carnegie Institute of Technology, 1961).

[23] H. Latané, "Criteria for Choice Among Risky Ventures," *Journal of Political Economy*, Vol. LXVII, No. 2 (April, 1959), pp. 144–155.

[24] Markowitz, *op. cit.*, Chapter XI.

each possible outcome of the current investment period. This analysis requires a large number of arbitrary assumptions. Thus it is desirable to introduce some simplification. Of the various ways in which this could be done, it seems preferable to assume single-period planning rather than to make other simplifying assumptions, such as assuming linear utility functions (which reduces the decision process to the selection of the portfolio with the highest mean regardless of risk).

The Shape of the Utility of Returns Function

The shape of investors' utility of returns functions determines which characteristics of portfolios are relevant to their decisions—that is, which parameters determine their preferences. If $U(R)$ is the utility function of R and $f(R)$ is the probability distribution of R, then the expected value of utility, $E[U(R)]$, is

$$\int U(R)f(R)\, dR.$$

If $U(R)$ equals some polynomial expression containing R in each term (except for a constant), $E[U(R)]$ is some sum of integrals where each term in the sum contains one of the powers of R appearing in $U(R)$. Since, by definition, the kth moment of $f(R)$ is

$$\int R^k f(R)\, dR$$

$E[U(R)]$ contains one moment of $f(R)$ (or expression containing a moment) for each power of R appearing in $U(R)$. Therefore, the number of properties of the probability distribution of returns which are relevant to an investor's choice depends on the degree of the polynomial defining his utility function; the specific properties depend on the terms [containing moments of $f(R)$] in the expression for $E[U(R)]$.

The assumption that investors' utility functions are generally of one shape or another is a highly arbitrary one which the theorist is forced to make largely on the basis of intuition—modified by the criterion of mechanical tractability. There is relatively little empirical evidence which can be applied reliably to this problem.

It seems intuitively likely that utility of returns functions should be related to utility of wealth functions, since returns can be thought of as increments to wealth. Indeed, a utility of returns function can be derived from a utility of wealth function. Thus if $U(W)$ describes the utility of wealth, utility of returns, R, can be derived from the function

$U[(1 + R)W_1]$, where W_1 is the initial value of wealth.[25] The utility of R and the values of all its derivatives depend on the coefficients of the utility of wealth function and the initial value of wealth.

Since returns constitute income as well, discussions of the utility of income should be helpful. The most common assumption about utility of income is that marginal utility diminishes as income increases. The apparent inconsistency implied by the same individual both gambling and buying insurance has led several authors[26] to suggest that the marginal utility of income may be increasing over some ranges and decreasing over others, i.e., that utility functions contain inflection points. Four specific utility of return functions (illustrated in Figure 3) are examined below with regard to their implications for distributions of returns from investment. Two of these functions contain inflection points and one of them changes functional form at some value of R.[27]

The first of the functions to be examined, function (a), is a quadratic of the form

$$U(R) = aR^2 + (a + 1)R$$

where

$$-1 < a < 0 \text{ and } R < \frac{a + 1}{-2a}.$$

Function (b), a variation on the quadratic, is

$$U(R) = \begin{cases} aR^2 + (a + 1)R \text{ for } R < b' \\ ab'^2 + (a + 1)R \text{ for } R \geq b', \end{cases}$$

where

$$-1 < a < 0.$$

---

[25] For example:

let

$$U(W) = AW^2 + BW, \qquad A < 0 < B, W < \frac{-B}{2A},$$

Then

$$U(R) = A(1 + R)^2 W_1^2 + B(1 + R)W_1 - AW_1^2 - BW_1$$
$$= AW_1^2 R^2 + (2AW_1^2 + BW_1)R,$$

where

$$(1 + R) < \frac{-B}{2AW}.$$

[26] M. Friedman and L. Savage, "The Utility Analysis of Choices Involving Risk," *Journal of Political Economy*, Vol. LVI, No. 4 (August, 1948), pp. 279–304; H. Markowitz, "Utility of Wealth," *Journal of Political Economy*, Vol. LX, No. 2 (April, 1952), pp. 151–58; G. Archibald, "Utility, Risk and Linearity," *Journal of Political Economy*, Vol. LXVII, No. 5 (October, 1959), pp. 437–450.

[27] All these functions are arbitrarily scaled so that $U(0) = 0$ and $U(-1) = -1$. Such arbitrary scaling is required since the utility functions implied by the underlying axioms of rationality are defined only up to a linear transformation. In some instances, a limiting relationship is also required between the range of R and the coefficients of the utility function in order to insure that marginal utility is positive for all R.

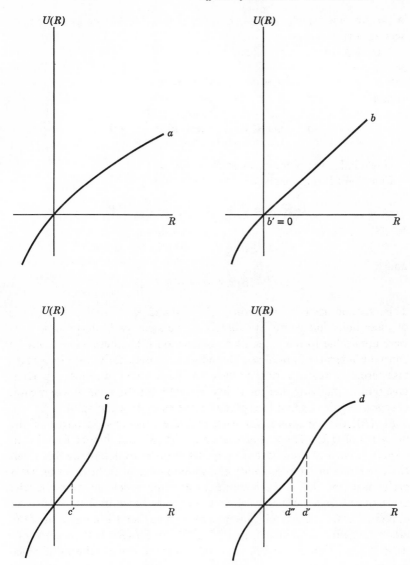

Figure 3 Utility functions.

This function changes form at point b'. If it is assumed that the utility of percentage returns is derived from a utility of wealth function, b' may be defined as a constant in terms of dollars of wealth and may, therefore, change in terms of percentage return when the initial value of wealth changes. Alternatively b' may be defined as a constant in terms of percentage returns implying that the corresponding parameter of the utility of wealth function changes as wealth changes. The former interpretation seems more plausible.

Function (c) is a cubic of the form

$$U(R) = aR^3 + bR^2 + (1 - a + b)R$$

where

$$a > 0, b < 0, (1 - a + b) > \frac{b^2}{3a} > 0.*$$

A single inflection point exists at $R = -b/3a$.

Function (d) is a quartic of the form

$$U(R) = aR^4 + bR^3 + (a - b + 1)R$$

where

$$-1 < a < 0, \qquad 0 < b < 1$$

and

$$(4aR^3 + 3bR^2 + a - b + 1) > 0.*$$

This function has two inflections, at $R = 0$ and $R = -b/2a$. The values of these inflection points are subject to the same two interpretations as were applicable to the value of b' in function (b). These values may be constant in terms of initial wealth and may, consequently, vary in percentage terms as wealth varies, or they may be constant in terms of percentage returns implying that the utility of wealth function changes as wealth changes. Again the first interpretation seems more meaningful.

$E[U(R)]$ can be found, for each of these functions, in terms of the moments of $f(R)$. The first derivative of $E[U(R)]$ can then be found with respect to each of the relevant moments in order to determine for which characteristics of the probability distribution of returns the investor has a preference (the derivative is positive) and for which an aversion (the derivative is negative). Implicit in each utility function there is also an indifference map. Each relevant moment can be found as a function of the other moment (or moments) and $E[U(R)]$. If $E[U(R)]$ is then held constant, this function can be differentiated to find the shape of the indifference curves.

Use of this analysis shows that, for each of the illustrated functions, the expected value of utility increases, *ceteris paribus*, as the mean return, M_R, increases. For function (a) utility decreases as V_R (the variance of return, which can be considered a measure of risk) increases, implying that

---

* These illustrations are not perfectly general; there are other cubic and quartic functions which would fit the requirement that marginal utility be positive for all R.

the slope of the corresponding indifference curves, dM_R/dV_R, is positive.[28]
In function (b), $S_R \left[= \int_{-100}^{b'} R^2 f(R) \, dR \right]$ is the appropriate measure of risk
(instead of V_R) and dM_R/dS_R is a positive constant.[29] This measure of risk
is sensitive to differences in skewness of distributions as well as to differences in dispersion. Since taxes tend to reduce the dispersion of the distribution of returns by a greater amount in the positive range than in the
negative range, there is an intuitive advantage for tax analysis in measuring
risk by S_R. On the other hand, if b' is interpreted as being constant in
terms of the dollar value of initial wealth, b' becomes smaller as wealth
increases, implying a greater willingness to take risk at higher levels of
wealth. This assumption can be questioned. Furthermore, it may be
questioned whether the absence of an income effect, which is implied by
the constant value of dM/dS, is plausible.

The cubic illustrated in function (c) describes an investor whose utility
increases with variance of returns if the mean expected return is above
the inflection point c', and declines with larger variances if the mean is
below c'. His utility is also reduced by negative values of the third moment
about the mean, a measure of skewness which is negative if the distribution
of R has a tail to the left.

This preference pattern seems intuitively plausible, implying as it does
that if expected return is below some value, c', the possibilities of greater

---

[28] The expected value of utility equals

$$a(M_R{}^2 + V_R) + (a + 1)M_R.$$

Differentiating with respect to V_R gives

$$0 = 2aM_R \left(\frac{dM_R}{dV_R} \right) + a + (a + 1) \left(\frac{dM_R}{dV_R} \right)$$

or

$$\frac{dM_R}{dV_R} = \frac{-a}{2aM_R + a + 1}$$

which is positive and constant for any given value of M_R. Thus, the indifference curves
are parallel at any given mean.

[29] The expected value of utility equals

$$aS_R + (a + 1)M_R$$

Differentiating with respect to S_R gives

$$0 = a + (a + 1)\frac{dM_R}{dS_R}$$

or

$$\frac{dM_R}{dS_R} = \frac{-a}{a + 1}.$$

Thus, the indifference curves are parallel straight lines.

losses associated with larger variance are not compensated by the possibilities of greater gains. If expected return is higher, it becomes more worthwhile to run the risk of large losses, if this risk is associated with significant possibilities of large gains, i.e., if the dispersion is not predominantly in the negative direction.

Indifference curves relating the mean and negative values of the third moment about the mean (taxes introduce negative skewness into symmetrical before-tax distributions) therefore indicate that, at a given level of utility, a larger negative third moment (T_R) must be compensated for by a larger mean expectation (M_R). Such indifference curves shift depending on the value of V_R and, for different values of V_R, cross each other at the value of M_R equal to c'. Hence, while a cubic function may seem intuitively plausible, it is more difficult to derive general conclusions from such an initial assumption.

This same conclusion applies to a quartic utility function such as (d). If such a function were unbounded, it would imply an aversion to variance if M_R is *above* the upper inflection point d', and a preference for variance if M_R is below d', the reverse of the preference pattern implied by a cubic function. Utility is also *increased* by negative skewness if the mean is above d' (the point of inflection in the marginal utility function) and decreased if the mean is below d'. Such an intuitively implausible pattern of preferences probably results from ignoring the upper bound which is necessary for such a function to define utility. It does serve to indicate, however, the necessity of making additional restricting assumptions about the parameters of more complicated utility functions if useful results are to be derived from them. In the absence of more extensive empirical information about utility functions, such assumptions would have to be completely arbitrary.

Therefore, in this study, the analysis is based on the assumption that investors' utility functions are either of form (a) or of form (b), as described above. It is further assumed that, if an investor's utility function is quadratic (function a), the probability of R exceeding the upper bound is so small that this bound can be ignored and, if an investor's utility function is of form b, b' equals zero. This implies that the characteristics of probability distributions relevant to the investor's choice are the mean (M_R) and either the variance (V_R) or the "semi-variance" (S_R).

Determination of the Optimum Portfolio

It has been assumed thus far: (1) that the investor's problem or goal can be defined as maximization of his expected utility of returns from invested wealth over a single planning period; (2) that the investor has a given set of expectations about the asset market which can be described by defining the subjective joint probability distributions of returns from the assets which may be held in the portfolio; and (3) that the investor achieves his goal by choosing the optimum M_R-V_R or M_R-S_R pair from a set of pairs which differ depending on the proportion of the portfolio held in the various different assets. From the assumption that, *ceteris paribus*, the investor's utility increases as M_R increases, it follows that his choice is one of those portfolios for which M_R is a maximum, given the value of V_R or S_R. Such M_R-V_R (or M_R-S_R) pairs constitute the opportunity locus. This locus is piece-wise parabolic or elliptical;[30] its slope depends generally on the sign of the correlation between the means and variances of the component assets. (That is, if the investor thinks that those assets with higher expected return are more risky, it follows that, as the proportion of risky assets in the total portfolio increase, both the expected return and the variance, or semi-variance, of the total portfolio increases.) The particular M_R-V_R (or M_R-S_R) point which the investor chooses is determined by the highest tangency or intersection of this opportunity locus with his indifference map.

Taxes shift the investor's opportunity locus—each tax in a different way—and consequently shift his optimum portfolio. Richter[31] assumes a quadratic utility function and derives from the definition of the optimum portfolio the changes induced by various taxes in the means and variances associated with the optimum portfolio. The change in the variance of total returns, however, does not necessarily indicate a corresponding change in the demand for riskier assets. In order to attack the problem of demand for risky assets, this study sacrifices mathematical generality and argues from arithmetic example. It postulates sets of parameters which, it is hoped, might describe a representative investor's expectations fairly realistically. From these parameters, derived from empirical data, estimates are made of the investor's opportunity locus. Tax-induced shifts in this opportunity locus are estimated, and are used, in combination with the information about the contour of his indifference map which is derived from the assumed form of his utility function, to estimate the possible range of resulting changes in portfolio composition.

TYPES OF ASSETS

A precise picture of the range of opportunities confronting the investor can be obtained only by considering *all* available assets. Since our central

---

[30] For proof, see H. Markowitz, "Portfolio Selection," *Journal of Finance*, Vol. VIII (March 1952), pp. 77–89, especially p. 87.
[31] Richter, *op. cit.*

purpose, however, is to explore the question of discrimination against relatively riskier investment, our range of vision can be safely limited to diversification among major asset categories. For the purposes of the model, it is assumed that a quite limited number of financial instruments are available. Each of these hypothetical instruments is defined in terms of characteristics corresponding to those of a major category of the financial assets actually in existence. Indexes of returns from major asset categories can then be used to derive the historical frequency distribution of returns. This in turn may indicate the general magnitudes of the parameters of a representative investor's probability distribution of expected returns.

Characteristics of Financial Assets

In order to define these hypothetical financial instruments, it is necessary to analyze those characteristics of financial assets which are generally considered by investors.

Marketability is one such characteristic. This criterion immediately separates savings bonds and accounts with savings institutions into a special category. Instead of being marketable, such assets are convertible (nominally, after a brief time lag) into cash at a specified price. Because of this characteristic, such assets have no capital value risk.

Among legally marketable assets, there are also sharp differences in the perfection of the market among certain asset types at the other end of the risk spectrum, in particular between mortgages and bonds regularly traded by recognized brokers or dealers. While these two assets are similar in that they both bear a fixed interest return and have senior claims on property, they differ sharply in their degree of "product standardization" and, therefore, in the ease and speed with which a buyer can be found for the particular asset in question.

Between these extremes, there are degrees of marketability, or market perfection, attaching to various assets depending on the number of buyers and sellers regularly in the market, and measured by the average number of units traded daily or by the average spread between bid and ask prices. Although such differences in marketability may be quite important for the institutional investor with some degree of monopoly (or monopsony) power, they are unlikely to be very important for the private individual investor.[32] It is assumed in this study that all assets are readily marketable except for the savings instruments mentioned above and that these markets are perfectly competitive.

---

[32] For a corroborating opinion, see Benjamin Graham and David L. Dodd, *Security Analysis* (3rd ed.; New York: McGraw-Hill, 1959), p. 32.

Another common and clear-cut distinction is the legal one between debts and equities. Several important distinguishing characteristics among debt instruments are length of maturity, degree of default risk, and call or convertibility provisions. It is necessary, first of all, to separate those debt instruments with time to maturity less than the length of the investment period from those with longer maturities. In the former case, there is no capital value risk; hence, as is implied by the concept of near-money, these bonds or bills may well be classed with savings bonds or accounts although there is some uncertainty about the yield at which the funds can be reinvested. In the latter case, the amount of price variation resulting from changes in money-market yields usually varies directly with the time to maturity.

Default risk depends, of course, on the issuer of the bond. It is non-existent on Federal Government issues and is measured for other issues by their ratings. These ratings appear to influence not only the level of interest returns on bonds but also the amount of fluctuation in yield to which bonds are subject.[33] Therefore, for the individual investor, expectations about the level and range of price variation reflect, in part, the rating of the bond as well as its maturity. It is also possible that the most likely direction of price fluctuation of a bond in any period reflects its rating. As one author[34] has pointed out, it was thought in investment circles prior to the 1930 depression that yields on issues other than Federal Government bonds should *rise*—and prices should fall—during business recessions since the default risk would then increase. It is shown, however, that yields on most high grade bonds have tended, in the past twenty or thirty years, to reflect movements in yields on Federal Governments (thus usually falling during business recessions) rather than to reflect severe swings in investors' confidence. It is assumed in this study that private investors' bond holdings are most likely to be issues of the Federal Government or very high-grade issues, primarily of state and local governments.[35]

Finally, it should be mentioned that call provisions have been an important factor in recent decades in limiting investors' capital gains from the frequent declines in bond yields. Call provisions have apparently tended to affect interest rates on bonds[36] and may affect price fluctuations, but

---

[33] One study which develops evidence for this proposition in regard to local issues is Charlotte D. Phelps, "The Impact of Tightening Credit on Municipal Capital Expenditures," *Yale Economic Essays*, Vol. 6, No. 2 (Fall, 1961), pp. 275–321.

[34] H. C. Sauvain, "Changing Interest Rates and the Investment Portfolio," *Journal of Finance*, Vol. XIV, No. 2 (May, 1959), p. 230.

[35] Graham and Dodd, *op. cit.*, go so far as to suggest that the only rational bond investments for private individuals are savings bonds or tax-exempt State and local issues (p. 52 ff).

[36] See Phelps, *op. cit.*

little conclusive evidence has been developed on this point. Thus the major effect of a call provision would be to introduce skewness into investor's expectations. Since there are few other reasons to deal with skewed before-tax expectations, call provisions are ignored in this study.

Thus, monetary policy and other money-market influences are assumed to be the most significant elements in investors' expectations about returns from bonds. This seems to suggest that, in some periods at least, fluctuations in prices of bonds and equities from year to year might be in opposite directions. This effect would be augmented to the extent that money which moves out of the stock market during periods of decline is likely to flow into the bond or bill market[37] or vice versa.

Among equities, there are many classifications which appear to be used by investment analysts and advisors. One categorization suggested by the research department of a large investment trust and advisory firm,[38] and apparently widely used, characterizes common stocks as "investment," "growth," "cyclical" or "low-priced." These categories are not necessarily either exhaustive or mutually exclusive. In general, investment quality stocks are those of large, established firms with good records of price and earning stability. Cyclical stocks are those of firms in industries which react sharply to periodic fluctuations in general business activity. Firms with low-priced stocks may exhibit any of a variety of characteristics, such as speculative capital structure, high fixed or operating costs, or the experience of some set-back which has been sharply compensated for by the market. Growth stocks are those with recognized potential for capital appreciation which is usually associated with large retained earnings, high price-dividend ratios, expanding market opportunities, and rapid product innovation.

There is obviously some fuzziness along the borders of these categories. Cyclical and low-priced stocks share some attributes; in particular, their profitability to the investor depends to a substantial degree on accuracy of prediction of future developments for a particular industry or firm. Because of the greater risk which this entails, such stocks generally sell at lower price earnings ratios. (In periods of very low earnings or deficits, however, the price-earnings ratio may be fairly high suggesting either that the price is determined by the book value of the firm or contains a large speculative component.) The particular size of the ratio usually depends on the size of dividend payments, the size of the firm, the availability of

---

[37] See Harold B. Elsom, "Common Stocks and the Short-Term Interest Rate," *Financial Analysts Journal* (March-April, 1961), p. 21.

[38] Because confidential data pertaining to activities of this firm are used later in this study, the name of the firm must be withheld and the generous assistance of one of its officers can be acknowledged only anonymously.

current assets, and the amount of instability of earnings, i.e., on the numerous specific factors which affect the riskiness of the investment.[39] There is also some overlapping between growth and investment stocks. Some growth firms are large enough, and have sufficiently imposing records of earnings and dividends, to warrant classification of their stocks as investment stocks. Such stocks are generally thought to have good defensive characteristics. In general, however, the higher price-earnings ratios of growth stocks do *not* imply less risk but rather the capitalization by the market of future expansion of earnings. This implies greater risk, since the market may, in the future, re-evaluate and reduce the capitalization ratio. It also suggests that some investors have less pressing current income requirements and may, therefore, plan over a longer horizon.

One final consideration is purchasing power variation as measured by movements in the consumer price index. The generally, though moderately, inflationary atmosphere of the post-World War II years is frequently thought to be a major factor stimulating investment in equities. As pecuniary earnings should, theoretically, reflect price level changes, and as stocks have an open-ended possibility for capital appreciation, it is natural that stocks should be thought of as an inflation hedge. In practice it appears, first, that only some stocks have this quality and, second, that there are significant differences in timing, in the short run, between movements in stock prices and in the consumer price index (see Figure 4). This implies little more for the short run planning of the individual investor than the fact that those investments which have the largest returns in current dollars also have the largest returns in constant dollars. Therefore, plans can be made in terms of current-dollar returns; returns are based on current dollars in this study.

Hypothetical Assets

On the basis of the observations made above, four hypothetical assets are to be defined. The first (subscript 1) is a nonmarketable "savings instrument" bearing a fixed (i.e., certain) return. The second (subscript 2) is a marketable "bond" with time to maturity longer than the planning period. It bears a fixed interest return (all returns are measured as a per cent of purchase price) and in addition has the possibility of yielding a capital gain or loss. The third (subscript 3) is an equity of investment

---

[39] These observations, suggested in a qualitative way by discussions and writings of security analysts (for instance, Graham and Dodd, *op. cit.*) are seemingly corroborated by regression analyses such as those by Haskel Benishay ["Variability in Earnings-Price Ratios of Corporate Equities," *American Economic Review*, Vol. LI, No. 1 (March, 1961), p. 81 ff] and M. J. Gordon ["Dividends, Earnings, and Stock Prices," *Review of Economics and Statistics*, Vol. 41, No. 2 (May 1959), p. 99 ff].

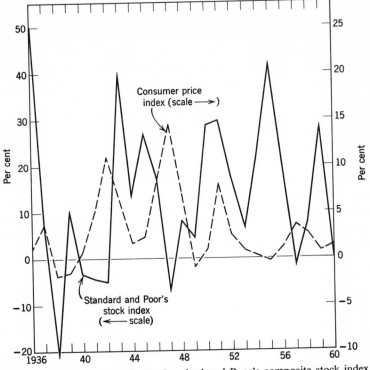

Figure 4 Percentage changes in the Standard and Poor's composite stock index and the consumer price index, 1936 to 1960.

quality which is assumed to yield a fixed dividend (an obvious simplification) and an uncertain capital gain or loss. (The difference between the growth-oriented investor and the income-oriented investor—apart from the difference in willingness to assume risk—can be taken into consideration by varying the proportion of dividend to expected capital gain on this asset; the growth oriented investor is assumed to hold those safe equities which yield larger capital gains relative to dividends.) The fourth (subscript 4) is a "risk-equity." Its expected dividend return is a smaller proportion of expected total return than is the case for the "investment equity" and the expected capital gain is less certain.

Analysis of portfolio diversification among these four assets illustrates the extent of tax-discrimination against risk by showing the effects of various taxes on willingness to hold equities. It takes into account the role of assets intermediate in riskiness and assets which may have negative covariances. The implications of differential taxation of capital gains and of interest can also be considered.

It is assumed that the investment period equals one calendar year and, hence, that returns on each asset equal the dividend or interest income plus capital gain or loss accrued over that period, as a per cent of the opening price. Large investors, of course, probably make changes in their portfolios much more frequently than once a year, but shifts among basic asset classes are likely to be minor. The annual computation of income taxes, moreover, forces estimation of the year's proceeds and provides a convenient period for analysis.

Expected Returns from the Hypothetical Assets

As mentioned before, investors' expectations of developments in the markets for assets and in the total economy determine the parameters of the subjective joint probability distribution of returns on the available assets. These parameters consist of the means (m_i) and the variances and covariances $(v_{i,j})$, of the distributions of returns on the four assets. Legal and institutional factors mentioned above limit the range of variation of these parameters. Thus, it is likely that the expectations of almost all investors would fall within the following constraints.

1. $m_4 > m_3 > m_2$.
2. $v_{4,4} > v_{3,3} > v_{2,2} > v_{1,1} = 0$.
3. $v_{2,3} \gtrless 0$; $v_{2,4} \gtrless 0$; $v_{3,4} > 0$.
4. $v_{1,2} = 0$; $v_{1,3} = 0$; $v_{1,4} = 0$.

Furthermore it seems quite likely that the historical behavior of returns from various assets has considerable bearing on individuals' expectations. This is not to say that individuals expect "history to repeat itself" in any specific sense, or that they are unconcerned, while forming their expectations, with current information on variables which might influence returns. Certainly, however, the recent history of returns from any broad category of assets indicates how such returns are likely to respond to various circumstances and how accurate predictions are likely to be. The theory of regression analysis provides a formalization of this concept. Thus, it might be assumed, for example, that past returns from various assets constitute a sample of draws from a universe of joint events, $r_1, r_2, r_3, r_4, t, y_1, y_2, \ldots,$ where t is time in investment-period units and the y's are the corresponding values of such variables as GNP, productivity, corporate profits, etc. which investors expect to influence their earnings. Expectations of returns in any investment period are then described by the conditional probability distribution which is determined by the value of t and the other predetermined independent variables. Assume further that some r_i with a large historical variance is used as a dependent variable in a regression. It then follows from this model (1) that r_i is significantly correlated with a volatile independent variable, or (2) that a large number of independent variables are needed to explain the fluctuations of r_i. If the investor knew the values of the variables needed to predict r_i, his best estimate of r_i would be the value derived from the regression equation; the variance of his subjective probability distribution of r_i would be smaller than the historical variance. On the other hand, if an investor is unable to predict successfully the value of the independent variables in this regression, then the historical mean of r_i constitutes his best estimate of the mean of the conditional distribution which describes his current expectations, and the large variance of r_i would indicate that his subjective probability distribution should have a large variance.

In general, efforts to predict returns from investment have not been highly successful. Indeed, the unpredictability of the stock market is legendary. This seems to suggest that investors' forecasts vary widely and that not all investment behavior is very rational. It also suggests that the parameters of the historical frequency distributions of returns should have some bearing on expectations of most rational investors.

It is possible, of course, that investors who are confronted with highly unpredictable situations are not rational Savage-men but may react to this uncertainty by "slanting" their subjective probabilities in such a way that their sum is not 1.[40] This reaction to uncertainty is not taken into consideration in our model since it is assumed to have the same effect on the probability distributions of all assets at any one time. If investors actually do react in such a way to uncertainty and investors' uncertainty changes from time to time, the "slanting" effect does imply that investors' utility functions shift over time. Without more detailed knowledge of such shifts it is impossible to say what effect, if any, they have on the shape of the utility functions.

Assuming then that historical experience does play an important role in the formation of investors' expectations, it follows that the historical behavior of indices of prices and yields of various classes of assets would give some assistance in finding reasonably representative values for the parameters of the probability distributions of returns from our hypothetical assets. Several such indices exist, including Moody's indices of prices and dividends for growth stocks and for income stocks, and Standard and Poor's indices of prices of high-grade stocks and of municipal and long-term U.S. bonds. These indices and an index of prices and yields of low-priced stocks specially compiled for this study were used in constructing Tables 1, 2, and 3. The values of the parameters of the historical frequency distributions given in Table 2.1 are used most extensively in the subsequently

---

[40] W. Fellner, "Distortion of Subjective Probabilities as a Reaction to Uncertainty," *Quarterly Journal of Economics*, Vol. 75, No. 4 (November 1961), pp. 670–689.

Table 1 Historical Returns from Various Classes of Assets (Computed Returns, in Per cent[a])

Year	Moody's Growth Stocks[b]	A Group of Low-Priced Stocks[c]	A Combination of Growth and Low-Priced Stocks	Moody's Income Stocks[b]	Standard and Poor's High-Grade Stocks[a]	Standard and Poor's Index of Municipal Bonds[a]	Standard and Poor's Index of Long Term U.S. Bonds[a]
1953–54	45.5	34.3	39.9	14.8	24.6	8.4	7.8
1954–55	38.3	38.0	36.2	15.5	24.2	1.0	−0.6
1955–56	25.2	7.7	16.5	6.8	18.0	−2.3	−0.1
1956–57	16.9	−15.8	0.6	−0.9	10.0	−5.6	−1.9
1957–58	26.8	38.0	32.4	21.9	19.7	4.3	6.2
1958–59	59.8	53.7	56.8	18.6	24.7	−1.6	−6.7
1959–60	28.8	−4.9	11.9	−3.1	16.5	7.2	4.7

[a] Computed returns equal the percentage change in annual average prices plus annual dividend or interest return.
[b] Moody's price and dividend indices are obtained from *Moody's Stock Survey*, September 4, 1961 and subsequent issues.
[c] The index of low-priced stocks was compiled (on the basis of one share each) from Moody's quotations for a list of low-priced stocks used by a large trust company.
[a] Standard and Poor's indices of high-grade stock and bond prices are obtained from their *Trade and Securities Statistics*. The bond indices are for a municipal bond with a 4 per cent coupon and 20 years to maturity and a U.S. government bond with a 3 per cent coupon and 15 years to maturity. A dividend yield of 4 per cent was arbitrarily imputed to the high-grade stock series.

Table 2 Parameters of Distribution of Returns on Hypothetical Assets (Derived from Historical Returns Shown in Table 1)

1. $m_1 = 3\%$ $v_{1,1} = 0$	$m_2 = 1.7^a$ $v_{1,2} = 0$ $v_{2,2} = 25.0$	$m_3 = 10.5^b$ $v_{1,3} = 0$ $v_{2,3} = +8.31$ $v_{3,3} = 81.40$	$m_4 = 27.7^c$ $v_{1,4} = 0$ $v_{2,4} = +23.78$ $v_{3,4} = 136.64$ $v_{4,4} = 317.38$
2. $m_1 = 3\%$ $v_{1,1} = 0$	$m_2 = 1.34^d$ $v_{1,2} = 0$ $v_{2,2} = 22.52$	$m_3 = 10.5$ $v_{1,3} = 0$ $v_{2,3} = +0.75$ $v_{3,3} = 81.40$	$m_4 = 27.7$ $v_{1,4} = 0$ $v_{2,4} = -13.84$ $v_{3,4} = 136.64$ $v_{4,4} = 317.38$
3. $m_1 = 3\%$ $v_{1,1} = 0$	$m_2 = 1.7$ $v_{1,2} = 0$ $v_{2,2} = 25.0$	$m_3 = 19.7^e$ $v_{1,3} = 0$ $v_{2,3} = +11.81$ $v_{3,3} = 24.10$	$m_4 = 27.7$ $v_{1,4} = 0$ $v_{2,4} = +23.78$ $v_{3,4} = 83.16$ $v_{4,4} = 317.38$
4. $m_1 = 3\%$ $v_{1,1} = 0$	$m_2 = 1.34^f$ $v_{1,2} = 0$ $v_{2,2} = 22.52$	$m_3 = 19.7^g$ $v_{1,3} = 0$ $v_{2,3} = +0.85$ $v_{3,3} = 24.10$	$m_4 = 27.7$ $v_{1,4} = 0$ $v_{2,4} = -13.84$ $v_{3,4} = 83.16$ $v_{4,4} = 317.38$
5. $m_1 = 3\%$ $v_{1,1} = 0$	$m_2 = 2.68^h$ $v_{1,2} = 0$ $v_{2,2} = 9.19$	$m_3 = 9.65^i$ $v_{1,3} = 0$ $v_{2,3} = 16.90$ $v_{3,3} = 131.15$	$m_4 = 19.50^j$ $v_{1,4} = 0$ $v_{2,4} = 27.18$ $v_{3,4} = 67.71$ $v_{4,4} = 216.99$
6. $m_1 = 3\%$ $v_{1,1} = 0$	$m_2 = 0.68^k$ $v_{1,2} = 0$ $v_{2,2} = 5.87$	$m_3 = 24.74^l$ $v_{1,3} = 0$ $v_{2,3} = -10.10$ $v_{3,3} = 153.84$	$m_4 = 32.72^m$ $v_{1,4} = 0$ $v_{2,4} = -27.48$ $v_{3,4} = 168.68$ $v_{4,4} = 341.48$

[a] Derived from computed returns on municipal bonds.
[b] Derived from computed returns on Moody's index of income stocks.
[c] Derived from computed returns on the combined growth-low-priced group.
[d] Derived from computed returns on U.S. government bonds.
[e] Derived from Standard and Poor's high-grade stock series.
[f] Derived from returns from U.S. government bonds.
[g] Derived from returns from Standard and Poor's high-grade stocks.
[h] Derived from computed returns from U.S. government bonds in the years 1947, 1948, 1950, 1952, 1953, 1954, 1957, 1958, and 1960 which were indicated as non-boom years by a value of the diffusion index of leading indicators, compiled by the National Bureau of Economic Research, which was below 60 per cent in June of the preceding year.
[i] Derived from computed returns from Standard and Poor's composite stock index (500 stocks) in non-boom years.
[j] Derived from computed returns from the combined low-priced and growth-stock index in non-boom years. For years prior to 1954, this index was constructed as a multiple of the composite stock index.
[k] Derived from computed returns from U.S. Government bonds in the years 1949, 1951, 1955, 1956, 1959, indicated as boom years by the National Bureau of Economic Research index.
[l] Derived from Standard & Poor's composite stock index in boom years.
[m] Derived from the growth-low-priced index in boom years.

Table 3 Separation of Mean Returns into Capital Gain and Interest or Dividend Components

U.S. Government bonds:	interest return = 3.2%
	mean capital gain = 1.6
U.S. Government bonds (non-boom years):	interest return = 3.0
	mean capital gain = −0.32
U.S. Government bonds (boom years):	interest return = 3.00
	mean capital gain = −3.68
Municipal bonds:	interest return = 3.5
	mean capital gain = −1.8
Moody's income stocks:	dividend return = 5.1
	mean capital gain = 6.3
Standard and Poor's high-grade stocks:	dividend return = 4.0
	mean capital gain = 15.7
Growth-low priced:	mean dividend return = 3.5
	mean capital gain = 24.2
Standard and Poor's composite stock index (non-boom years):	dividend return = 5.3
	mean capital gain = 4.4
Standard and Poor's composite stock index (boom years):	dividend return = 5.7
	mean capital gain = 19.0

described calculations. The values given in Table 2.5 and 2.6 are based upon the assumption that investors have some idea of whether the forth-coming year will be generally a "good" year or a "bad" year for business. Given this assumption, previous "good" or "bad" years constitute the relevant basis for forming expectations. In compiling Table 2.5 and 2.6 the diffusion index of leading indicators (compiled by the National Bureau of Economic Research) in the middle of the preceding year was used as an index of "good" or "bad" years.

THE BASIC EFFECTS OF SPECIFIC TAX PROVISIONS

The investment opportunities confronting an individual can be illus-trated by an opportunity locus which is shifted, depending on the structure of the tax applying to investment returns. Before examining these shifts, however, it is necessary to consider the mechanics of constructing the approximation to the investor's opportunity locus, which is to be used in this paper, and the nature of the specific tax provisions which may be a part of any given tax structure.

It has been assumed that the parameters of the probability distributions of total returns which are relevant to an investor's choice of portfolio are the mean, M_R, and either the variance, V_R, or the semi-variance, S_R, of the truncated distribution. Thus, if there is no tax on investment returns,

$$M_R = \int_{-100}^{\infty} Rf(R) \, dR$$

$$V_R = \int_{-100}^{\infty} R^2 f(R) \, dR - M_R^2$$

$$S_R = \int_{-100}^{\infty} R^2 f(R) \, dR$$

where

$$R = \sum x_i r_i$$

$$f(R) = \frac{C}{\sigma_R \sqrt{2\pi}} \, e^{-\frac{1}{2}\left(\frac{R - \mu_R}{\sigma_R}\right)^2}, \; -100 \le R < \infty$$

$$\mu_R = \sum x_i r_i$$

$$\sigma_R = \sqrt{\sum_i \sum_j x_i x_j v_{i,j}}$$

Formulae can be derived for evaluating the definite integrals of $Rf(R) \, dR$ and $R^2 f(R)$. Both formulae are functions of the parameters of $f(R)$, the limits (-100%, 0 and ∞ in the equations above), and the areas and ordinates of the unit normal curve. In the numerical calculations described below the upper and lower limits were always taken as $(\mu_R + 3\sigma_R)$ and $(\mu_R - 3\sigma_R)$ respectively; $(\mu_R - 3\sigma_R)$ was always greater than -100 per cent and thus the symmetry of the before tax distribution was preserved. Figure 5 contains an approximation of the investor's opportunity locus, assuming that returns from investments are not taxed and that the investor's expectations are described by Table 2.1. In order to compute the points illustrated in this chart fifty-six portfolios were chosen from the infinite number available to the investor. Four of these fifty-six portfolios consist entirely of one asset; others are fairly evenly diversified.[41] M_R, V_R, and S_R were computed for each of these portfolios. Of the fifty-six M_R-V_R points and fifty-six M_R-S_R points, those points with minimum V_R for M_R within a given interval are plotted in Figure 5(a) and those with minimum S_R for M_R within a given interval are plotted in Figure 5(b). These points suggest the position and shape of the opportunity locus. The

---

[41] The fifty-six portfolios used for these and the following computations are all those portfolios in which the proportion invested in any asset is either zero or an even multiple of 0.2 (except for the portfolio in which $x_1 = 1.0$, $x_2 = 0$, $x_3 = 0$, $x_4 = 0$ for which the portfolio $x_1 = 0.9$, $x_2 = 0.1$, $x_3 = 0$, $x_4 = 0$ was substituted).

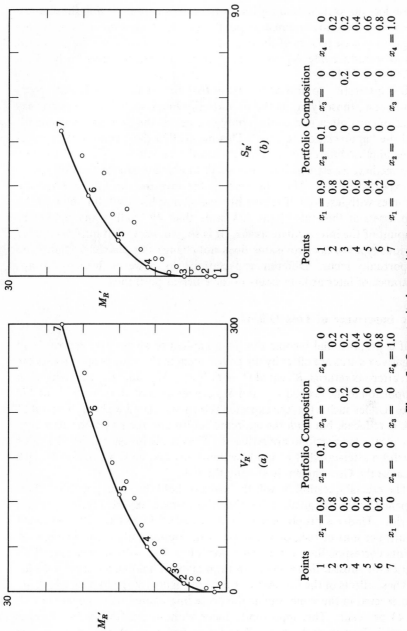

Figure 5 Opportunity locus without tax.

lists of portfolios (defined by the proportion in each asset) on or very near these loci (as sketched) are given in the tables accompanying the figures. Obviously the limited number of points and their scatter make it impossible to give a precise picture of the opportunity loci. The taxes to be examined below introduce effects gross enough in most cases, however, to be illustrated by this device.

It is interesting to note at this point that almost all the "efficient" portfolios—i.e., those lying on the opportunity locus—are linear transformations of each other and contain only two assets, the "savings instrument" and the "appreciation equity." This means that the given set of expectations implies differences in risk between the most risky asset and the two intermediate assets which are too small to compensate for the differences in expected return. Thus, in general, the investor can limit the risk he assumes with less loss of return by diversifying his portfolio between the two assets at the ends of the risk scale than by holding any significant amount of the intermediate assets. It is shown below that introduction of various types of tax provisions does not change this characteristic of the opportunity locus. Different expectations do, however, lead to the appearance of intermediate assets in the efficient portfolios.

The Importance of Loss Offsets

If a proportional income tax (t) is applied to all positive returns, and negative returns are offset by the government in the same proportion as the tax, after-tax returns, R', equal $(1 - t) \sum x_i r_i$, $M_{R'}$ and $D_{R'}$ are reduced in proportion to the tax and $V_{R'}$ and $S_{R'}$ are reduced by the square of the tax rate. Under such a tax, the expected return associated with any amount of risk is reduced, but *both* the expected return and the risk associated with any particular portfolio are reduced. Thus if the investor holds the same portfolio after-tax that he holds without any tax, he is assuming less risk because the Government is sharing the risk.

The crucial question is, will the investor hold the same portfolio. This depends on the marginal, rather than the average, expected return per unit of risk. Under a proportional tax with perfect loss-offsets, the marginal return per unit of risk, or the slope of the opportunity locus, is *larger* at points corresponding to the same portfolio, than without any tax. This causes the substitution effect to work in favor of holding more risky assets.

These effects of the tax are illustrated in Figures 6(*a*) and 6(*b*), which are constructed in the same way as the preceding figures, assuming a tax rate of 43 per cent. The opportunity locus without tax (the dashed line) is superimposed in each chart. The lower positions of the after-tax loci illustrate the reduction in expected return per unit of risk. The shifts in

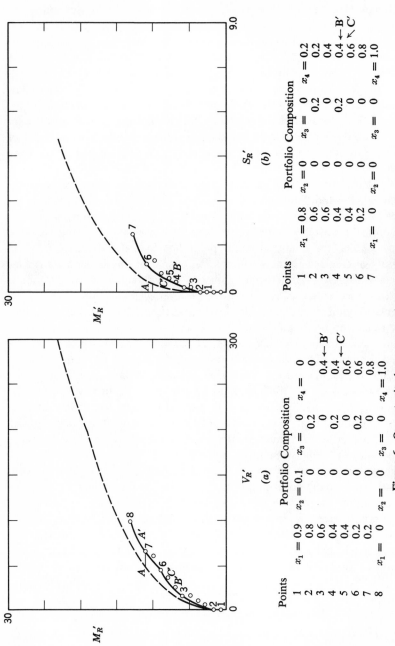

(a)

Portfolio Composition

Points	$x_1 =$	$x_2 =$	$x_3 =$	$x_4 =$	
1	0.9	0.1	0	0	
2	0.8	0	0.2	0	
3	0.6	0	0	0.4	← B'
4	0.4	0	0.2	0.4	← C'
5	0.4	0	0	0.6	
6	0.2	0	0.2	0.6	
7	0.2	0	0	0.8	
8	0	0	0	1.0	

(b)

Portfolio Composition

Points	$x_1 =$	$x_2 =$	$x_3 =$	$x_4 =$	
1	0.8	0	0	0.2	
2	0.6	0	0.2	0.2	
3	0.6	0	0	0.4	
4	0.4	0	0.2	0.4	← B'
5	0.4	0	0	0.6	← C'
6	0.2	0	0	0.8	
7	0	0	0	1.0	

Figure 6 Opportunity locus-proportional tax with perfect loss offsets.

each figure from points A to points B', which correspond to the same portfolio, illustrate the reduction in both M_R and V_R resulting from the tax. In the vicinity of points C', the slopes of the after-tax loci are approximately equal to the slopes of the no-tax loci at points A. (This construction cannot be accurate without exact calculation of the locus by some quadratic programming technique such as that of Markowitz;[42] direct analytical derivation of the slope of the locus proves it to depend in a complicated way on the values of the parameters.) Since the slopes of the opportunity loci generally decline to the right, the positions of points C' to the right of points B' indicate the increased marginal return per unit of risk resulting from the tax.

If the investor's utility function is such that risk is measured by semivariance, the indifference curves are positively sloped, parallel straight lines (as previously shown). Therefore, if the no-tax equilibrium point is at point A, the after-tax equilibrium is at the highest point having the same slope. Thus, the composition of portfolios indicated by points in the vicinity of C' gives a general impression of the shift in demand for riskier assets which results from the tax. Since the indifference curves corresponding to measurement of risk by variance are curvilinear, the slope at the after-tax equilibrium point is not the same as that at the no-tax equilibrium. The range can be found, however, within which the after-tax equilibrium occurs, since the indifference curves are parallel at points having the same mean (see p. 67) and become less steeply sloped at points having smaller means. Therefore, if the after-tax locus is more steeply sloped at or above point A' than the before-tax locus at point A, the new equilibrium will be at a higher $M_{R'}$ than the old one. If the new locus is less steeply sloped at and above A', the new equilibrium must be at a lower value of M_R. Furthermore, it must, in this case, be above the highest point C' (which has the same slope as A).

Thus, the positions of points C' to the right of point B' also indicate that sharing by the government in risk as well as return has the effect of increasing the incentive to hold risky assets.

A very different tax is one under which the government shares only in gains, leaving losses unaffected. Calculation of $M_{R'} - V_{R'}$ and $M_{R'}\text{-}S_{R'}$ points under such a tax requires computation of the parameters of a distribution of total returns which is not a continuous function. Thus,

$$R' = \begin{cases} R, & -100 < R \leq 0 \\ (1 - t)R, & 0 < R < \infty \end{cases}$$

---

[42] H. Markowitz, *Portfolio Selection-Efficient Diversification of Investments* (Cowles Foundation for Research in Economics at Yale; New York: John Wiley, 1959), Appendix A.

A distribution divided into segments in this way is illustrated in Figure 1. The effects of such a tax can be derived analytically as follows:[43]

$$M_R' = \int_{-100}^{0} Rf(R)\, dR + \int_{0}^{\infty} (1 - t)Rf(R)\, dR$$

$$= M_R - t\int_{0}^{\infty} Rf(R)\, dR$$

$$V_R' = \int_{-100}^{0} R^2 f(R)\, dR + \int_{0}^{\infty} (1 - t)^2 R^2 f(R)\, dR - \left(M_R - t\int_{0}^{\infty} Rf(R)\, dR \right)^2$$

$$= V_R - (2t - t^2)\int_{0}^{\infty} R^2 f(R)\, dR + (2tM_R)\int_{0}^{\infty} Rf(R)\, dR$$

$$- t^2\left(\int_{0}^{\infty} Rf(R)\, dR \right)^2$$

$$S_R' = \int_{-100}^{0} R^2 f(R)\, dR = S_R$$

Both $M_{R'}$ and $V_{R'}$ are affected by the impact of the tax on positive returns, but $M_{R'}$ is reduced by more than it was in the case of a tax with perfect loss offsets, and $V_{R'}$ is reduced by less; $S_{R'}$ is not affected. Thus, under a proportional tax without loss offsets, the mean return associated with any amount of risk is reduced by slightly more than in the case of perfect loss-offsets, and the variance of any particular portfolio by slightly less. Point B', the point corresponding to the same portfolio as A on the no-tax locus, is moved to the left by a smaller amount than in the former tax-case. The slope of the locus with no loss-offset is also generally somewhat flatter than in the preceding case, meaning that point C' may be moved farther to the left. As long as C' is above B', there is no possibility of any tax-induced reduction in demand for riskier assets. This situation is illustrated by the points B_2' and C_2' in Figure 7(a). As illustrated by points B_1' and C_1' in the same figure, however, it is possible under this tax for points B' and C' to be very close together or even for C' to be to the left of B'.[44] This

---

[43] They can be derived alternatively from the after-tax distribution which is defined:

$$f(R') = f(R), \qquad -100 < R' \le 0$$

$$f(R') = \frac{1}{\sqrt{2\pi}\sigma_{R'}} e^{-\frac{1}{2}\left(\frac{R' - \mu_{R'}}{\sigma_{R'}} \right)^2}, \qquad 0 < R' < \infty$$

where $R' = (1 - t)\mu_R$ and $\sigma_R' = (1 - t)\sigma_R$.

[44] The error in plotting of these graphs is equal to the size of the discrete intervals to which the data are scaled by the computing machine. This is 5 percentage points along the horizontal axis and 1.17 percentage points along the vertical axis. In Figure 7(a), C' is actually to the left of B' after allowing for the plotting error in B'.

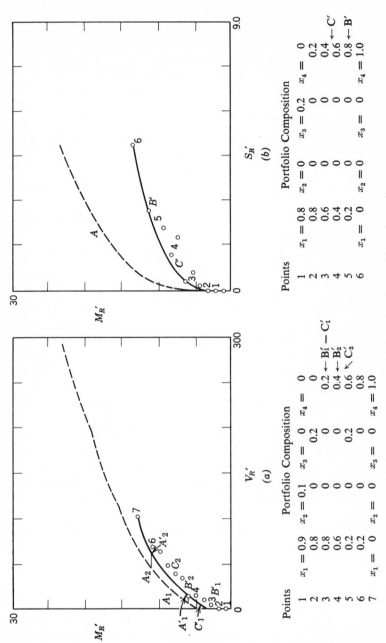

Figure 7 Opportunity locus-proportional tax with no loss offset.

(a)

Points	\multicolumn{4}{c}{Portfolio Composition}	
	$x_1 = 0.9$	$x_2 = 0.1$	$x_3 = 0$	$x_4 = 0$	
1	0.9	0.1	0	0	
2	0.8	0	0.2	0	
3	0.8	0	0	0.2	← B'₁ — C'₁
4	0.6	0	0	0.4	← B'₂
5	0.2	0	0.2	0.6	↖ C'₂
6	0.2	0	0	0.8	
7	$x_1 = 0$	$x_2 = 0$	$x_3 = 0$	$x_4 = 1.0$	

(b)

Points	\multicolumn{4}{c}{Portfolio Composition}	
	$x_1 = 0.8$	$x_2 = 0$	$x_3 = 0.2$	$x_4 = 0$	
1	0.8	0	0.2	0	
2	0.8	0	0	0.2	
3	0.6	0	0	0.4	← C'
4	0.4	0	0	0.6	← C'
5	0.2	0	0	0.8	← B'
6	$x_1 = 0$	$x_2 = 0$	$x_3 = 0$	$x_4 = 1.0$	

possibility exists for portfolios with low M_R relative to V_R, i.e., for portfolios which already contain relatively small proportions of risky assets.

Turning to the opportunity locus of the individual for whom risk is measured by semi-variance [Figure (7b)], it can be seen that the risk associated with any portfolio is *not* affected by the tax. The marginal return per unit of risk is, none-the-less, reduced by the tax, thus pushing C' to the left. For such individuals a tax without loss offsets does lead to a reduction in demand for riskier assets.

The conclusion implied by these two cases is that there is no disincentive to risk-taking as a result of a tax, as long as the Government shares in losses as well as gains. If the Government does not do so, the existence of a disincentive effect depends on the form of individuals' utility functions— whether they dictate measurement of risk by variance, semi-variance or some other statistic—and whether or not individuals would hold substantial proportions of their portfolios in risky assets without any tax.

Various Kinds of Partial Loss-Offsets

A government which is seriously concerned about possible tax-induced disincentives to risk-taking might be prompted by this conclusion to incorporate complete loss-offsets into the tax structure. Such provisions, however, are generally considered difficult to administer. They also raise the question whether it is equitable to ask the public at large to compensate individuals who may take obviously foolish risks either out of ignorance or a love of gambling. For these reasons, various compromise measures in the form of partial loss-offsets are frequently found in tax structures.

The simplest example of a partial loss offset provision is one requiring compensation of current losses up to some specified amount at a rate equal to the tax rate. If we take as an example an investor with an investment balance of \$100,000, a maximum loss offset of \$1,000 means that the government will offset, at a rate equal to the tax rate, losses up to 1 per cent. Letting k equal this maximum loss offset,

$$R' = R + tk, \qquad -100 < R \leq -k$$
$$R' = (1 - t)R, \qquad -k < R < \infty$$

A simple variation on this tax is a tax including the possibility of a limited loss carry-back. This is equivalent to an increase in the size of the effective current loss-offset at times when returns were positive in the preceding investment period.

The effect of introducing a current loss offset of 1 per cent into a tax which had no offset is to increase $M_{R'}$ by a small amount and to reduce

$V_{R'}$ and $S_{R'}$ by a small amount.[45] These changes in $M_{R'}$, and $V_{R'}$ and $S_{R'}$ have the dual results of shifting the C''s to the right and the B''s to the left, thus slightly reducing any disincentive, or increasing any tax incentive to hold riskier assets.

An additional opportunity for at least partial loss offset may be introduced through a loss carry-forward. If we assume that the investor in the previous example had a loss in the preceding investment period which exceeded the maximum current loss offset by an amount equal to, or greater than, a maximum loss carry-forward of l (if the maximum carry-forward was \$1000, l would equal 1 per cent), the probability distribution of returns on any portfolio in the current planning period would consist of four segments:

$$R' = R + tk, \qquad -100 < R \le -k$$
$$R' = (1 - t)R, \qquad -k < R \le 0$$
$$R' = R, \qquad 0 < R \le l$$
$$R' = (1 - t)R + tl, \qquad l < R < \infty$$

If the period over which an investor maximizes expected utility is equal to the investment period, there can be no effect from a carry-forward, except in periods following one in which a loss occurred. Following a period in which a loss did occur, the carry-forward provision reduces the effective tax rate on positive returns (l is defined as greater than zero) and, hence, redresses by a very small amount the asymmetry in treatment of

---

[45] $M_{R'}$ (partial loss offset) $= M_{R'}$ (no loss offset) plus

$$\left(tk \int_{-100}^{-k} f(R)\, dR - t \int_{-k}^{0} Rf(R)\, dR \right).$$

Both terms are greater than zero. $V_{R'}$ (partial loss offset) $= V_{R'}$ (no loss offset) plus

$$+2tk \int_{-100}^{-k} Rf(R)\, dR + t^2 k^2 \int_{-100}^{-k} R^2 f(R)\, dR - 2tkM_R$$

$$\times \int_{-100}^{-k} f(R)\, dR + 2t^2 k \int_{-100}^{-k} f(R)\, dR \int_{-k}^{\infty} Rf(R)\, dR - t^2 k^2 \left[\int_{-100}^{-k} f(R)\, dR \right]^2$$

$$+ (t^2 - 2t) \int_{-k}^{0} R^2 f(R)\, dR + (2tM_R) \int_{-k}^{0} Rf(R)\, dR - t^2 \left[\int_{-k}^{0} Rf(R)\, dR \right]^2.$$

Each term other than the second and fourth, and the sum, is less than zero. $S_{R'}$ (partial loss offset) $= S_{R'}$ (no loss offset) plus

$$2tk \int_{-100}^{-k} Rf(R)\, dR + t^2 k^2 \int_{-100}^{-k} f(R)\, dR + (t^2 - 2t) \int_{-k}^{0} R^2 f(R)\, dR.$$

Each term other than the second is less than zero.

losses and gains. If the utility period is longer than the investment period, the possibility that losses incurred in one investment period will be offset in a subsequent period may mitigate any disincentive to risk-taking in both periods. This effect is not equivalent, however, to enlarging the current loss offset by amount *l* for two reasons: first, the offsetting of a loss depends on the subsequent occurrence of a gain and second, the post-ponement of the offset means that a loss is likely to affect the size of the investment balance in following periods.

The mitigating effects of both of these provisons are very small relative to the effect of the tax without any loss offsets (they are too small to be illustrated graphically but are shown in Table 5). Thus it appears that partial loss offsets and carry-forwards, when limited to the amounts specified in the current tax codes, *may* be too small to have any real effect on investment incentives. Their primary significance would seem to be on the equity of the treatment of very small investors. Since the effects of those provisions depend on their magnitude in percentage terms, while they are defined in dollar terms, their strength declines as the size of the invest-ment balance increases.

Progressivity in the Rate Structure

A progressive tax is characterized by its taking increasingly large per-centages out of higher incomes. If such a tax applies to positive returns from investment and losses are not offset at all, a disincentive to risk taking may result similar to that which might occur under a proportional tax without loss provisions. This is illustrated in Figures 8(*a*) and 8(*b*).

These figures are constructed on the assumption that the progressive tax rate in the first bracket is equal to 43 per cent (the same as the proportional tax rate used in the previous figures) but that returns above 3 per cent are taxed at a marginal rate of 47 per cent, returns above 11 per cent are taxed at a marginal rate of 53 per cent, and returns above 25 per cent are taxed at a marginal rate of 59 per cent. This rate structure is generally similar to the appropriate three brackets of the Federal income tax[46] under the additional assumptions given in Table 4 and assuming that the nominal rates are actually applicable.

Use of brackets in the tax structure applied to positive returns segments the probability distribution of returns as follows:

$$R' = R, \qquad -100 < R \le 0$$
$$R' = (1 - t_1)R, \qquad 0 < R \le 3$$
$$R' = (1 - t_i')R + (t_i' - t_i)b_i, \qquad b_i < R \le b_{i+1}$$

---

[46] Prior to the 1964 income tax reduction.

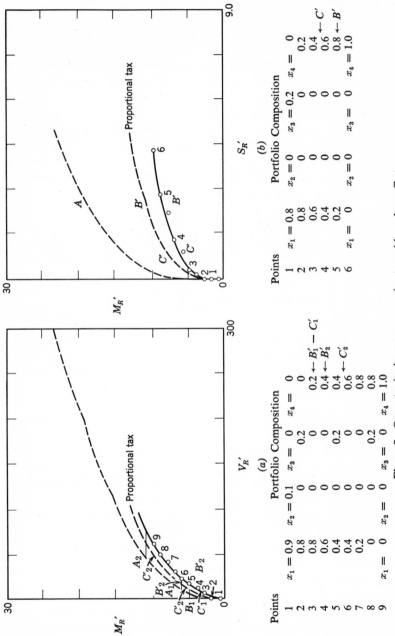

(b)

Portfolio Composition

Points	x_1	x_2	x_3	x_4	
1	0.8	0	0.2	0	
2	0.8	0	0	0.2	
3	0.6	0	0	0.4	
4	0.4	0	0	0.6	← C'
5	0.2	0	0	0.8	← B'
6	0	0	0	1.0	

(a)

Portfolio Composition

Points	x_1	x_2	x_3	x_4	
1	0.9	0.1	0	0	
2	0.8	0	0.2	0	
3	0.8	0	0	0.2	← B_1' — C_1'
4	0.6	0	0	0.4	← B_2'
5	0.4	0	0.2	0.4	
6	0.4	0	0	0.6	← C_2'
7	0.2	0	0	0.8	
8	0	0	0.2	0.8	
9	0	0	0	1.0	

Figure 8 Opportunity locus—progressive tax with no loss offsets.

Table 4 Schedules of Tax Rates

Progressive Tax Brackets	Schedule I		Schedule II	
	Average Rate	Marginal Rate	Average Rate	Marginal Rate
0 to 3%	$t_1 = 0.43$	$t_1' = 0.43$	$t_1 = 0.30$	$t_1' = 0.30$
3% to 11%	$t_2 = 0.43$	$t_2' = 0.47$	$t_2 = 0.30$	$t_2' = 0.34$
11% to 25%	$t_3 = 0.46$	$t_3' = 0.53$	$t_3 = 0.33$	$t_3' = 0.38$
25% and above	$t_4 = 0.50$	$t_4' = 0.59$	$t_4 = 0.36$	$t_4' = 0.42$

Loss Brackets				
−1% to 0	$t_{-1} = 0.43$		$t_{-1} = 0.30$	
−5% to −1%	$t_{-m} = 0.38$		$t_{-m} = 0.25$	
or −25% to −1%	$t_{-m} = 0.20$			

Assume: *a.* The proportional tax rate = 0.43.

      b. The investor has an investment balance of $100,000.

      c. The maximum loss offset, k, = $1000, or 1%.

      d. The maximum loss carry-forward, l, = $1000, or 1%.

      e. The investor has $25,000 taxable, noninvestment income (e.g., $30,000 less $1800 personal exemptions and $3200 deductions), and files a joint return.

      f. Capital gains are taxed at the same nominal rates as other income; alternatively, total gains, $\frac{1}{2}$, or $\frac{1}{10}$ of gains are subject to tax.

where

$$i = 2, \quad 3 < R \leq 11$$
$$i = 3, \quad 11 < R \leq 25$$
$$i = 4, \quad 25 < R < \infty$$

and

    $t_i' \equiv$ the marginal tax-rate in the *i*th bracket

    $t_i \equiv$ the average tax-rate at the lower limit of the *i*th bracket

    $b_i \equiv$ the lower limit of the *i*th bracket

It can be seen from Figure 8(*a*) that introduction of progressivity into the tax structure further reduces the return for a given amount of risk, the return and variance associated with any portfolio, and the slope of the opportunity locus. Thus points B' and C' (indicating, respectively, the portfolio with the same composition as A and the point with the same slope as A) are moved farther to the left than under a proportional tax. At points with low return relative to variance, C' may be below B', implying the possibility of a disincentive to holding risky assets. The major effect of this particular rate structure, applied to this particular set of expectations, however, is to reduce both the mean and variance associated with any given portfolio.

The effect of a progressive tax without loss provisions on the $M_{R'}\text{-}S_{R'}$ opportunity locus is also very similar to that of the comparable proportional income tax. The semi-variance of the portfolio is unaffected by the tax but the means are reduced substantially. Under such a tax a significant disincentive to risk taking exists as illustrated in Figure 8(b).

Redressing the asymmetrical treatment of losses and gains is difficult under a progressive tax because of the problem of developing a manageable scheme to offset losses at rates comparable to those applied to gains. If losses are offset against current noninvestment income, they may be offset at lower rates than those applicable to gains. Furthermore, if losses are large enough to affect investors' tax brackets, the rate of offset *decreases* while the opposite is true of the tax rates applying to positive returns. Much the same thing is true of loss carry-backs. This means that partial current loss offsets (or carry-back provisions) in a progressive tax may have a smaller effect on the risk associated with any particular portfolio than they have in a proportional tax.

Losses which are carried forward, however, are offset at the same rates at which gains are taxed. Therefore, the loss carry-forward has a stronger power to increase mean returns in a progressive tax than in a proportional tax. It also causes a reduction in the variance of returns, in distinction to the increase in variance which results from a carry-forward provision in a proportional tax. These effects of the partial offset and carry-forward provisions combined are too small, when their magnitudes are limited to 1 per cent, to be graphically illustrated. Some idea of their impact within proportional and progressive taxes can be gleaned, however, from Table 5.[47] This table suggests that, within the structure of a progressive tax, partial loss offset and carry-forward provisions increase both the average and marginal expected return per unit of risk, measured by variance, and consequently reduce any disincentive to risk-taking which might otherwise result from the tax. The effects of partial loss offsets and carry-forward

---

[47] Adding these loss provisions to a progressive tax breaks the probability distribution into the following segments:

$-100 < R \leq -k$: $R' = R + t_{-1}k$ (where t_{-1} is the rate applicable to losses)

$-k < R \leq 0$: $R' = (1 - t_{-1})R$

$0 < R \leq l$: $R' = R$

$l < R \leq b_i + l$: $R' = (1 - t_i)R$

$b_i + l < R \leq b_{i+1} + l$: $R' = (1 - t_i')R + (t_i' - t_i)b_i + t_i l.$

Table 5 Effects of Partial Loss Offset and Carry-Forward Provisions on Expected Return and Risk

Portfolio[a]	Proportional Tax				Progressive Tax			
	No Loss Provisions		With Loss Provisions		No Loss Provisions		With Loss Provisions	
	M_R	V_R	M_R	V_R	M_R	V_R	M_R	V_R
1	1.64	0.08	1.64	0.08	1.64	0.07	1.89	0.07
2	4.52	4.01	4.52	4.09	4.35	3.54	4.61	3.69
3	7.30	16.63	7.70	16.88	6.67	13.32	7.10	13.01
4	10.07	38.18	10.46	38.56	8.89	29.86	9.47	28.78
5	12.84	68.70	13.05	69.30	11.16	50.34	11.68	48.57

Portfolio 1. $x_1 = 0.9$ $x_2 = 0.1$ $x_3 = 0$ $x_4 = 0$
Portfolio 2. $x_1 = 0.8$ $x_2 = 0$ $x_3 = 0$ $x_4 = 0.2$
Portfolio 3. $x_1 = 0.6$ $x_2 = 0$ $x_3 = 0$ $x_4 = 0.4$
Portfolio 4. $x_1 = 0.4$ $x_2 = 0$ $x_3 = 0$ $x_4 = 0.6$
Portfolio 5. $x_1 = 0.2$ $x_2 = 0$ $x_3 = 0$ $x_4 = 0.8$

[a] The M_R-V_R points corresponding to these portfolios are on or near the opportunity locus of each of the taxes under consideration.

provisions on the semi-variance of portfolios are much more substantial.[48] Thus, as Figure 9 shows, the shift in the M_R-S_R locus is even more favorable to risk-taking.

Special Treatment of Capital Gains

Despite the voluminous controversy concerned with taxation of capital gains, this tax has not been analyzed in detail in terms of its effects on risk. Since most of the fluctuation in returns from investment results from capital gains and losses, it appears that their treatment should be particularly crucial. Under U.S. tax laws, only a part of capital gains are subject to tax which has the effect of reducing the applicable tax rate.

Under the assumptions of this model, all the variance of the probability distribution of total returns is attributed to the capital gain or loss component. Hence R equals D—the certain dividend and interest component —plus G—the uncertain capital gain or loss, and V_G must equal V_R. If it

---

[48] This substantial effect occurs for two reasons: first, the loss carry-forward provision increases the area of the positive tail of the distribution relative to the negative tail and, second, the effect of the loss offset is not "diluted" by its inability to reduce positive dispersion.

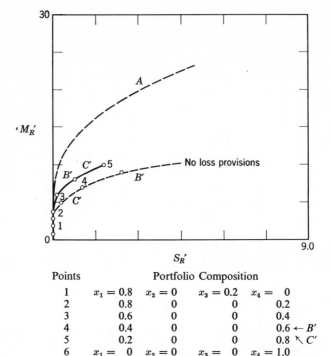

Points | Portfolio Composition
| | | | |
1 | $x_1 = 0.8$ | $x_2 = 0$ | $x_3 = 0.2$ | $x_4 = 0$
2 | 0.8 | 0 | 0 | 0.2
3 | 0.6 | 0 | 0 | 0.4
4 | 0.4 | 0 | 0 | 0.6 ← B'
5 | 0.2 | 0 | 0 | 0.8 ↖ C'
6 | $x_1 = 0$ | $x_2 = 0$ | $x_3 = 0$ | $x_4 = 1.0$

Figure 9 M_R'-S_R' locus-progressive tax with loss provisions.

is assumed that the progressive tax structure already discussed applies to total interest and dividend returns $(\sum x_i d_i)$, and that the fraction of gains $(\sum x_i g_i)$ subject to the same tax is $1/a$, $(a > 1)$, this is equivalent to taxing gains at $1/a$ times the rate applicable to other income. If the tax structure also contains loss offset and carry-forward provisions, the probability distribution of returns on any portfolio is divided into the segments defined in Table 6.

From this table, it can be seen that the capital gains provision affects only the right tail of the distribution of returns. Thus, the effect of the

Table 6 Segments of the Probability Distribution of Returns Under a Progressive Income Tax with a Special Capital Gains Provision

$$R' = R + t_{-1}k, \qquad -100 < R \leq -k$$
$$R' = (1 - t_{-1})R, \qquad -k < R \leq 0$$
$$R' = (1 - t_i')R + (t_i' - t_i)b_i, \qquad 0 < R \leq D \quad \text{and} \quad b_i < R \leq b_{i+1}$$
$$R' = (1 - t_i')D + (t_i' - t_i)b_i + G, \qquad D < R \leq D + l \quad \text{and} \quad b_i < R \leq b_{i+1}$$
$$R' = (1 - t_i')D + [1 - (t_i'/a)]G + (t_i'/a)l + (t_i' - t_i)b_i,$$
$$D + l < R \quad \text{and} \quad a(b_i - D) + D + l < R < a(b_{i+1} - D) + D + l$$

provision, in comparison to the same tax without it, is to cause a smaller reduction in both the mean return and risk associated with any portfolio [see Figures 10(a) and 10(b)]. The change in the slope of the $M_{R'}$-$V_{R'}$ locus is negligible, and thus point C' (having the same slope as A) is shifted very little, except at the upper end of the locus. Point B' (the same portfolio as A) is shifted significantly rightward. This implies the possibility of a *reduction* in willingness to hold risky assets—a surprising conclusion. At the upper end of the locus (above A), however, the incentive to hold risky assets is increased. The slope of the $M_{R'}$-$S_{R'}$ locus, on the other hand, is significantly increased (compare higher with lower solid line in Figure 10(b)) shifting C' to the right. Therefore, the capital gains provision leads to an increased willingness to hold risky assets on the part of investors for whom semi-variance is the appropriate measure of risk, while the opposite *may* be true of investors who are concerned with the entire variance.

The apparent ambiguity of the results of introducing a capital gains provision, for investors whose utility of returns functions are quadratic (i.e., where $M_{R'}$-$V_{R'}$ analysis is used), does not imply ambiguity about whether investors are made "better off" by the tax provision. As long as the marginal utility of positive returns is positive, the tax provision makes investors better off, if they hold any portfolio which may yield positive returns.

It would seem that the capital gains provision should produce a disincentive to risk-taking only if there is a significant "income effect," since it leaves investors unaffected or better off at all possible outcomes of their investing venture. The crucial question, as mentioned above, is not whether the investors are made better off, however, but the effects of a change in the marginal relationship of $M_{R'}$ and $V_{R'}$ on the investors' portfolio selection. Our analysis shows that the capital gains provision considered here raises the $V_{R'}$ associated with each portfolio, as well as the $M_{R'}$, and reduces the marginal relationship of $M_{R'}$ to $V_{R'}$ for some portfolios. This mathematical translation of an extension of the *right* tail of the distribution of returns into an increase in "risk" illustrates the possible inadequacy of variance as a proxy for risk in analyses where the skewness of the distribution of returns varies.

Summary

From this analysis of the impact of various tax provisions, it is possible to draw several preliminary generalizations. First, a tax may create a disincentive to risk-taking if it does not allow for sharing in losses by the government. Second, the extent of any disincentive to risk-taking depends significantly on the measure of risk relevant for investors and, possibly,

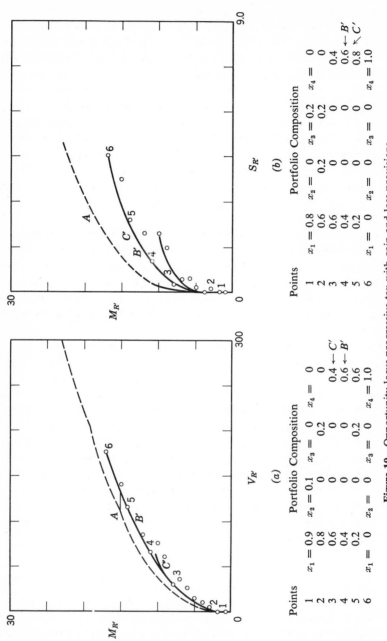

(a)

Points	Portfolio Composition			
	$x_1 = 0.9$	$x_2 = 0.1$	$x_3 = 0$	$x_4 = 0$
1	0.9	0.1	0	0
2	0.8	0	0.2	0
3	0.6	0	0	0.4 ← C'
4	0.4	0	0	0.6 ← B'
5	0.2	0	0.2	0.6
6	0	0	0	1.0
	$x_1 = 0$	$x_2 = 0$	$x_3 = 0$	$x_4 = 1.0$

(b)

Points	Portfolio Composition			
	$x_1 = 0.8$	$x_2 = 0$	$x_3 = 0.2$	$x_4 = 0$
1	0.8	0	0.2	0
2	0.6	0.2	0.2	0
3	0.6	0	0	0.4
4	0.4	0	0	0.6 ← B'
5	0.2	0	0	0.8 ↖ C'
6	0	0	0	1.0
	$x_1 = 0$	$x_2 = 0$	$x_3 = 0$	$x_4 = 1.0$

Figure 10 Opportunity locus-progressive tax with gain and loss provisions.

also on their willingness to assume risk in a tax-free situation. Third, a progressive rate structure does play a major role in any disincentive to investment in risky assets. A capital gains provision which reduces the progressivity of a rate structure in the higher brackets *may* counteract much of the effect of the progressivity, depending on the nature of preferences. Fourth, some kinds of special loss provisions which fall short of complete loss offsets may be fairly effective in limiting any disincentive to risk-taking otherwise implicit in the tax structure. The apparent effectiveness of a loss carry-forward (the effectiveness depends, of course, on the length of investors' planning horizons and their time preference) suggests that some kind of income-averaging should be seriously considered by taxing authorities.

COMPARISON OF EFFECTS ON RISK-TAKING OF SEVERAL TAX STRUCTURES

In the preceding discussion, several specific tax provisions were examined, either independently or in fairly simple combinations. This led to some conclusions concerning their effects on individuals' willingness to hold risky assets. In today's economy, tax structures are not simple, however, and changes in such structures are unlikely to be as gross as the comparisons made in the previous part. Therefore, in this part, "marginal" changes in tax structure are considered in comparison with the progressive structure with gain and loss provisions discussed in the last part.

More on Loss-Offsets

The first situation to be examined is one in which the maximum loss offset permitted by the tax code is 5 per cent instead of the 1 per cent maximum considered above. It is assumed that the progressive rate structure specified in Table 4 (schedule I) applies, and that losses larger than 1 per cent reduce the investor's tax bracket and, therefore, are offset at a lower rate. As might be expected from the preceding comparison of a progressive tax with and without special loss provisions, moderate expansion of the loss provision does not have a marked effect on the $M_{R'}$-$V_{R'}$ opportunity locus. Portfolio means are raised slightly and variances are reduced slightly, but these effects are limited to the general magnitudes of 1.0 and 1.5 per cent (too small to illustrate graphically). The M_R-S_R locus is shifted significantly, however, by the reduction in the dispersion in negative tails of the distributions of returns [see Figures 11(a) and 11(b)]. Thus, moderate variation in the treatment of current losses may or may not be significant, depending on investors' basic attitudes toward losses.

A similar conclusion applies to the effects of quite large increases in loss offsets on the $M_{R'}$-$V_{R'}$ locus. Extension of the maximum loss offset to 25 per cent, coupled with a substantial, but proportionately smaller, reduction in the offset rate (as shown in Table 4) changes the M_R's and V_R's

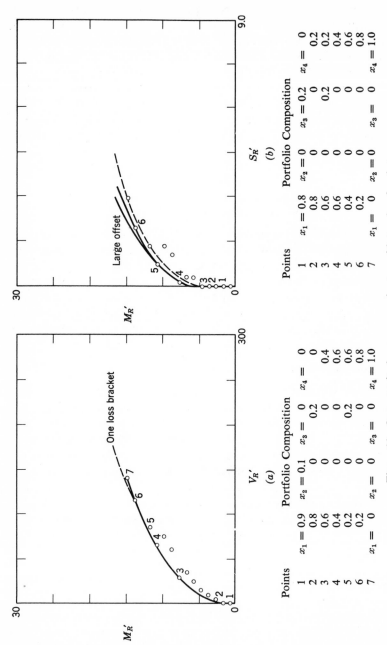

Figure 11   Opportunity locus-progressive tax with two loss brackets.

of portfolios near the locus by about 0.3 per cent and 1.6 per cent respectively. The $M_{R'}$-$S_{R'}$ locus, on the other hand, is shifted at its upper end [see Figure 11(b)], corresponding to portfolios with the largest risk. Thus, for investors who might, under favorable tax conditions, hold substantial proportions of risky assets, an increase in the maximum loss offset could be significant. It should also be noted that if investors' expectations were considerably more pessimistic than those being considered, the significance of an increase in the maximum loss offset would be greater with either measure of risk. This suggests that such a tax measure might be a useful counter-cyclical tool. Its obvious rationalization would be that the government stood ready to compensate investors for losses incurred at times when aggregate economic phenomena were likely to have disproportionate effects on capital values.

The Importance of the Progressive Tax Rate

Reduction in tax rates, illustrated by the substitution of schedule II (Table 4) for schedule I appears, in Figure 12(a), to induce a relatively small shift in the $M_{R'}$-$V_{R'}$ locus, suggesting that investors' equilibrium points on the two loci would not be very far apart. The lesser slope of the lower-tax locus moves point C' (having the same slope as point A on the higher-tax locus) to the left for any A above point 3. This reduction in the risk associated with the new equilibrium position implies an even greater reduction in holdings of risky assets because the lower tax rates have the effect of shifting B' (corresponding to the same portfolio as A) slightly to the right. Thus, as indicated in the table accompanying the figure, there may actually be a reduction in demand for risky assets as a result of a change from the higher to the lower rate schedule. While such a result could be rationalized in terms of the "income effect," it occurs here because of the effect on the variance of the distribution of returns of an extension of the right tail. A similar anomaly was discussed previously in relation to the introduction of the capital gains provision.

The shift in the $M_{R'}$-$S_{R'}$ locus, on the other hand, is not only more pronounced but also more auspicious for the holding of risky assets. Most of the shift in the locus is attributable to the higher expected return from any portfolio, resulting from the lower tax rates. Some of the shift also occurs, however, from a *reduction* in risk associated with any portfolio. This results from the difference in the relative weights of the negative and positive tails of the distribution under the two taxes; the negative tail of the distribution has a smaller weight under the lower tax.

The efficacy of the lower rate schedule in causing an advantageous shift of the $M_{R'}$-$S_{R'}$ locus raises the question of the relative merits of lowering rates or increasing loss offsets. As shown in Figure 12(b), the lower rate schedule not only makes people better off than does the 25 per cent loss

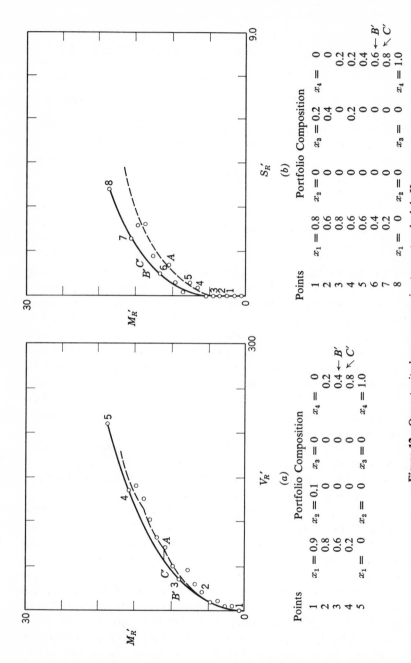

Figure 12 Opportunity locus-progressive tax, rate schedule II.

offset, but may be more effective in inducing them to invest in risky assets. Thus the tax authority considering changes in the tax code for the purpose of encouraging risk-taking is confronted with a dilemma: are investors concerned only with the negative dispersion of returns or with the entire dispersion? If they are concerned only with negative dispersion (or, as seems most probable, with statistics closely related to it), a reduction in the rate schedule may be a useful instrument and easier to administer than the large loss offset provision which would be needed to match it in effectiveness. But, if investors are concerned with the entire dispersion, a reduction in the rate schedule might have an adverse effect. In either case, an increase in the loss offset would presumably be a cheaper tool, in terms of revenue loss, to accomplish this limited purpose.

Variation in the Size of the Capital Gains Exemption

An alternative way of reducing the effective tax rate is to increase the proportion of capital gains exempted from tax. This has a somewhat smaller effect on $M_{R'}$ than a general reduction in rates, but it increases $V_{R'}$, as did a rate reduction. Thus the implied adverse effect of such a measure on willingness to hold risky assets is greater at most points along the locus. The problem of interpreting this "fluky" result has been discussed earlier.

As Figure 13(a) illustrates, the lower capital gains rate results in a general flattening of the opportunity locus; consequently, at most points (particularly at the lower end) C' is pushed to the left. Simultaneously, an increase in the variance associated with any portfolio pushes B' to the right. At a few points, however, where pieces of the locus intersect, this disincentive effect does not appear. In contrast to the effect on the $M_{R'}$-$V_{R'}$ locus, the $M_{R'}$-$S_{R'}$ locus is favorably shifted as might be expected [see Figure 13(b)].

In considering such a change in the tax code, the empirical question of the nature of investors' preferences is again crucial. Two other considerations not introduced into this theoretical model, however, must also be borne in mind. The first is that the amount of tax paid out of capital gains is particularly likely to affect the size of an individual's investment balance. Thus, investors who have been successful in one risky venture have more funds available to them for the next such venture, the lower the capital gains rate. The second consideration is that of the timing of tax payments. If the possibility exists of deferring tax payments on gains (a possibility which is not built into our model), more funds may be available for risky investment. On the other hand, it is also possible that funds will be "frozen" into ventures which were once, but are no longer, risky. Thus, a lower tax rate applicable to gains, coupled with "constructive realization" of unrealized capital gains for tax purposes, might be preferable to a higher rate with payments deferred.

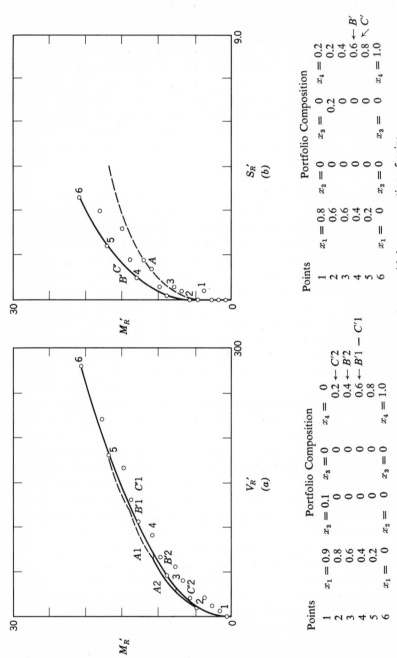

(a)

Points	Portfolio Composition			
1	$x_1 = 0.9$	$x_2 = 0.1$	$x_3 = 0$	$x_4 = 0$
2	0.8	0	0	0.2 ← $C'2$
3	0.6	0	0	0.4 ← $B'2$
4	0.4	0	0	0.6 ← $B'1 - C'1$
5	0.2	0	0	0.8
6	$x_1 = 0$	$x_2 = 0$	$x_3 = 0$	$x_4 = 1.0$

(b)

Points	Portfolio Composition			
1	$x_1 = 0.8$	$x_2 = 0$	$x_3 = 0$	$x_4 = 0.2$
2	0.6	0	0.2	0.2
3	0.6	0	0	0.4
4	0.4	0	0	0.6 ← B'
5	0.2	0	0	0.8 ← C'
6	$x_1 = 0$	$x_2 = 0$	$x_3 = 0$	$x_4 = 1.0$

Figure 13 Opportunity locus-progressive tax with large exemption of gains.

Tax-Exemption of Interest from Bonds

The tax-exemption of interest on state and local bonds, which is a notable feature of the U.S. tax code, exists in part for institutional rather than economic reasons. It has usually been thought, however, that it also serves as a boon to local communities and, thus, might have adverse implications for risk ventures. Our analysis suggests that, at the lower end of the locus, some portfolios containing bonds become desirable under this tax provision which would not be so without it. There is virtually no effect, however, on the upper end of the locus and, thus, no effect on those individuals most likely to hold risky assets.

Alternative Expectations

Expectations differ, of course, among individuals and, for the same individual, over time. Therefore, it is important to have some inkling of how sensitive the composition of individuals' portfolios may be to their expectations. Figures 14(*a*) and 14(*b*) illustrate the opportunity loci, without tax and under a progressive tax (schedule I with one loss bracket and capital gains taxed at the higher rate) for two different sets of expectations. The first set (the dashed lines) is the set which has been used for the preceding figures. The second set is derived from four "boom" years and is described in Table 2.6. It is characterized by higher expected returns from both types of equities coupled with larger variances of possible returns. The variance of returns from income equities (asset 3) is also very slightly larger, relative to that of appreciation equities, than in the first set of expectations. The expected return from bonds is negative in the second set and bond returns are negatively correlated with returns from equities.

The $M_{R'}$-$V_{R'}$ locus corresponding to the second set of expectations lies above that for the first set and is, generally, more steeply sloped. The difference in slope is much greater in the middle range than at the upper end. Thus, individuals who are relatively unconcerned about risk are not induced by more optimistic expectations to increase their already large holdings of risky assets, but they do substitute "income equities" for cash in their portfolios. For individuals preferring to assume only moderate risk, more optimistic expectations result in increasing the equity share of their portfolios and diversifying it between income and appreciation equities, rather than holding primarily appreciation equities and cash. Thus, more buoyant expectations do not have the result, which might be expected, of shifting a large amount of funds into the riskiest assets. The larger total holdings of both types of equities, induced by more optimistic expectations, do, however, imply behavior consistent with the experience of rising prices on all types of stocks during boom periods.

One caveat seems necessary, however, in interpreting these conclusions. The second set of expectations under consideration allows for larger

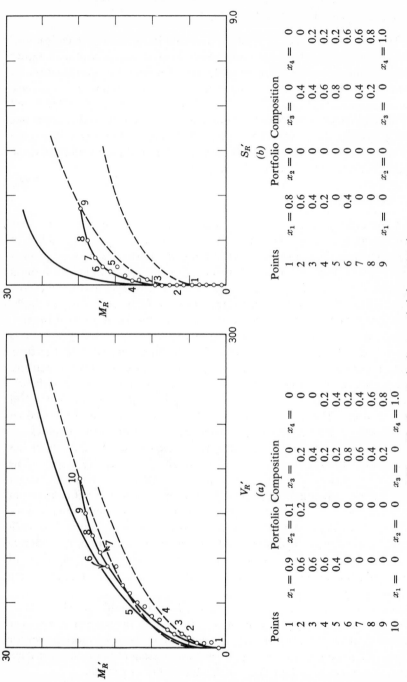

Figure 14 Opportunity locus–optimistic expectations.

variances of returns from equities, relative to the first set, as well as larger mean returns. Although, in terms of the recent history of boom periods, such parameters seem justified, it is likely that unsophisticated investors may not recognize the many uncertainties existent in the boom situations.

The $M_{R'}$-$S_{R'}$ loci in Figure 14(*b*) are seen to reflect more dramatically the differences in expectations. When risk is measured by semi-variance, the effect of more optimistic expectations is to reduce risk, despite the somewhat larger dispersion of the probability distribution of returns. This means that portfolios with relatively low risk, given the first set of expectations, have negligible risk, given the second set. Thus, with more optimistic expectations, there is a much greater incentive to hold some income equity instead of holding as large a proportion of the portfolio in savings instruments. At the upper end of the locus, however, there is slightly less incentive to hold large amounts of appreciation equity.

Turning to the implications of different expectations for the effects of various taxes, there does not appear to be any qualitative difference in the reaction to the progressive tax (with gain and loss provisions) as a result of differing expectations. There seems little reason to believe that the relative effects of various tax provisions depend in any crucial way on individuals' expectations within some fairly wide range of variation, with the exception of the greater effect of loss offset provisions when expectations are pessimistic.

THEORETICAL AND EMPIRICAL FINDINGS

Theoretical Summary

In summarizing our conclusions, it is useful to consider three types of possible behavior which have been separated by our analysis. The first belongs to individuals for whom measurement of risk by variance of the distribution of returns is appropriate and whose preferences are such that they hold a relatively small proportion of their portfolio in equities, i.e., less than 40 per cent, given the expectations described in Table 2.1. A second type of behavior belongs to those individuals for whom variance is the appropriate measure of risk but who are more willing to take risk. A third pattern of behavior is that of individuals for whom semi-variance is the appropriate measure of risk.

The difference between the first and the second type of behavior reflects the kind of difference in preferences frequently discussed, i.e., variations in the shapes of indifference curves deriving from differences in the *parameters* of the underlying utility functions. The distinction between the third type of behavior and the other two depends upon difference in the *functional form* of underlying utility function. The importance of these distinctions for policy purposes—if our model has any relevance at all—is highlighted in this study. It also appears from the analysis on pp. 63–68 that distinctions between the possible functional forms of investors' utility functions might be testable by some sort of systematic observation of attitudes towards variance, skewness, etc., of probabilities. This should be somewhat easier than efforts to measure the parameters of utility functions, and might even be amenable to a questionnaire approach.

Our analysis suggests that, for the first type of individual, proportional taxes without loss offsets and progressive taxes reduce the already small incentive to hold risky assets. Introduction of a capital gains provision, which reduces the progressivity of the tax, or moderate lowering of the rate schedule coupled with some reduction of its progressivity have only slight effectiveness in reducing the tax-induced disincentive to risk-taking. The only measure which might be expected to have a significant effect appears to be a substantial increase in the maximum permissible loss offset.

The second type of investor may be induced to hold more risky assets by a progressive tax. This behavior might, therefore, be considered to be dominated by the "income effect" rather than the "substitution effect" of the tax; this is analogous to the possibility that an income tax would increase the supply of labor. If investors' expectations were particularly pessimistic (i.e., if the mean expectations associated with riskier portfolios were lower relative to the variances), limitation of loss offsets might, however, have an adverse effect. Given the expectations which have been assumed in this study, the impact of the tax on positive returns is the over-bearing consideration. For such investors, reduction of tax rates may actually have an adverse effect on the incentive to hold risky assets, and the effects of a capital gains provision is ambiguous. Again, expanded loss offset provisions can be expected to have the most beneficial effect. The difficulties associated with applying mean-variance analysis where the skewness of the distribution of returns is not constant must be borne in mind, however, in considering this "type" of investor.

The third type of investor views the distribution of anticipated returns as having, essentially, two separate parts. The negative tail of the distribution measures the risk for which he has an aversion, while it is primarily the positive tail which determines the inducement to invest. The effects of taxes can, therefore, be considered in terms of their impact on these two parts of the distributions. From this analysis, it can be seen that, given the size of the limited loss offset provision, the tax which reduces expected returns by the largest proportion has the greatest adverse effect on investment incentives. Reduction of the level of rates and expansion of capital gains exemptions consequently reduce the disincentive effect because their impact on mean returns is greater at higher levels of mean return. Approaching the disincentive effect from the other side, however, increasing the compensation for losses also reduces the tax disincentive to holding risky assets. Thus, there is the possibility of a trade-off between provisions affecting one tail of the distributions of returns and provisions affecting the other.

Empirical Evidence

The empirical evidence relevant to our problem is sparse. To be conclusive, such evidence would have to consist of both cross-section and time-series data on individuals' income, wealth, asset holdings, etc. Such information is difficult and expensive to obtain.

The best existing data of which this author is aware are those collected by Butters, Thompson, and Bollinger[49] for their study on the effects of taxation on individuals' investments. These were derived from a sample survey of 746 active investors who were contacted in 1949 through 60 investment banking firms. Of these 746 investing units, 535 were in the top 5 per cent of the population with respect to income, having incomes above $7500, and 353 had incomes of $12,500 and over. These investors answered detailed questions about their financial status and investment attitudes.

The findings from this survey suggest, first of all, that investors generally fall into two categories, income- and security-minded, and appreciation-minded. The majority of investors in each income class were income- and security-minded, but the proportion of appreciation-minded investors increased with income. The proportion of investors who showed a significant awareness of taxes also increased with income.

Among income- and security-minded investors, there seemed to be a clear indication that risk was conceived of as the possibility of loss and, to the extent that tax awareness existed, these individuals were concerned about the reduction in return for risk-taking. In general, this led such investors to report that taxes caused them to hold fewer risky investments. Appreciation-minded investors, on the other hand, were concerned primarily with the tax-advantages from receiving returns in the form of capital gains, and were reportedly induced by the tax to hold more risky assets.

In some respects, these conclusions suggest that investors fall into two categories similar to our first and second investor types. Butters *et al.* stress, however, that it is only the capital gains provision in the current tax code which induces "appreciation-minded" investors to increase their holdings of risky assets. This does not very clearly corroborate our finding that the second type of investor may not, theoretically, respond favorably to an easing of the capital gains provision and might hold more risky assets under a progressive tax than under a proportional one. An alternative

---

[49] J. K. Butters, L. E. Thompson, and L. L. Bollinger, *Effects of Taxation on Investment by Individuals* (Cambridge: Harvard University, Graduate School of Business Administration, 1953). New relevant data may emerge from survey work currently (1964–65) being undertaken at the University of Wisconsin.

interpretation is that investors' behavior is more adequately described by analysis using semi-variance. (Analysis which used more complicated utility functions might be even better, of course. For instance, it is possible that the semi-variance analysis should actually be interpreted as an inadequate proxy for analysis using a cubic utility function.) If this interpretation is accepted, Butters' evidence, *in general*, corroborates our theoretical conclusions.

The portfolios of investors in the two classes differed in the ways implied by their investment goals and reports of tax effects. It must be noted, however, that the measurement of tax effects in this study consisted only of reports of tax-effects and cross-section comparisons of portfolio composition. Thus, it is impossible to discriminate between the effects of taxes and of preferences in determining portfolio composition, or to differentiate among the effects of various tax provisions. It is estimated by the authors that the tax-induced changes in portfolio composition in either direction were probably not larger than 10 per cent of total wealth. It is also estimated that the larger number of observations of tax disincentives slightly outweighed the larger dollar volumes of the portfolios positively affected by taxes. Thus, on balance, they estimate that tax-induced disincentives to risk-taking might have affected the form in which about 5 per cent of the total wealth of surveyed individuals was invested.

The types of assets considered in the investigation by Butters *et al.* encompassed a wider range than those considered in our theoretical study. It is, therefore, particularly interesting to note their finding that, to the extent that investment motives are dominant, the attitude of appreciation-minded investors toward riskier marketable securities carries over to new issues and closely held ventures. Indeed, in many instances such investors held fewer readily marketable equities than income-minded investors. They held more of the equity component of their portfolio in new ventures and closely held firms in extraction industries or agriculture in order to take advantage of various specially favorable tax provisions.

Another source of data pertinent to our study is a series of interviews which the author had with the senior officer in the research department of a large New York trust company. Impressions gathered from these interviews reinforced the conclusion that investors' goals differ and are important in planning their portfolios. They also suggested that risk is viewed primarily as the possibility of actual loss and that tax considerations do play a role in planning a portfolio. In summarizing the factors considered in managing an account, this officer mentioned cash withdrawal requirements, the earned income and debt of the account owner, and the owner's tax bracket.

For investors in high tax brackets and without large cash needs, the general policy was described as investment in tax-exempt securities and equities likely to provide capital gains. He stated that the capital-gains tax leads to more risk-taking. In the view of this highly sophisticated analyst, capital-gain possibilities may occur as often from cyclical stocks as from some of the recognized, and therefore over-capitalized, growth stocks. (He admitted substantial holdings, however, of a few "over-capitalized growth stocks.") The implication that a substantial proportion of investors' portfolios was held in risk equities is consistent with our analysis.

He also reported that the bond component of portfolios was generally held in fairly short-term bonds because of the risk of capital loss, and that shares in public utilities frequently served as substitutes for bonds. This point substantiates the conclusion from our theoretical analysis that bonds alone should play a negligible role in the diversification of most portfolios, except where the tax exempt feature is important.

Some information on the aggregate portfolio of investment management (i.e., not trust) accounts was also made available. This aggregate portfolio was valued at about $445 million in January, 1959. Two thirds of the assets in this fund belonged to individuals in the 50 per cent, or higher, tax brackets, and a "good proportion" were "up in the 80 per cent region." Approximately 95 per cent of the fund was in accounts which were diversified, in some proportions, among four categories of assets. These categories were: (1) cash and fixed-value assets; (2) bonds, preferred stocks, and shares of public utilities; (3) stable income and growth stocks; (4) cyclical stocks. Examination of the actual, aggregate portfolio over a period of 10 years reveals that its composition fluctuated cyclically (as might be expected for professionally managed portfolios) but that, on the average, the diversification among the four asset categories was approximately 3 per cent, 39 per cent, 16 per cent and 42 per cent, respectively.

This information does not shed light directly on the questions of tax effects but does provide a basis for evaluating some of the structure of our theoretical model.

Conclusions

This study concludes by accepting as valid the concern of many individuals about the effects of taxes on the availability of risk capital but rejecting their line of reasoning as incomplete. It reinforces the views of Simons and Lerner[50] that loss-offsets and other structural provisions might be combined to make a tax code consistent with several goals. Indeed, it is suggested that expansion of loss-offsets be used as a counter-cyclical weapon. Accurate use of tax provisions as tools of economic policy will require, however, a more detailed knowledge of investors' attitudes. Thus, finally, the necessity is stressed of discovering the way in which investors conceptualize risk.

---

[50] Henry C. Simons, *Personal Income Taxation* (Chicago: University of Chicago Press, 1938); A. P. Lerner, "Functional Finance and the Federal Debt," *Social Research*, Vol. 10, No. 1 (February, 1943).

5

Stock Market Indices: A Principal Components Analysis*

GEORGE J. FEENEY and DONALD D. HESTER

This chapter investigates a widely quoted stock market index, the Dow Jones Industrial Average (hereafter DJI), and constructs some alternative indices. Their performances are compared to the DJI. The question of applying the indices to problems of portfolio selection is explored when investors' utility functions are quadratic in the rate of return. By constructing indices from data collected in different time periods, some conclusions are drawn about the constancy of price and rate of return covariance and correlation matrices of the 30 Dow Jones industrial stocks over time.

I

In evaluating indices it is necessary to examine the purpose for which an index is to be used. As investors are concerned with earning a high rate of return, it is perplexing to find that the most quoted indices are price indices, not indices of rate of return.[1] Investors of course are concerned with price

---

* The authors are respectively employed by the General Electric Company and Yale University. We are indebted to the Cowles Foundation and the RAND Corporation for supporting this research and to James Keaton for research assistance. In part this paper reports on research carried out under a grant from the National Science Foundation. The paper was presented at the TIMS meeting in Pittsburgh, March, 1964.
[1] Specifically, the rate of return is defined to be a stock's quarterly dividend plus change in price over a quarter divided by the stock's previous quarter closing price, all figures adjusted for stock dividends or splits.

appreciation which serves to increase the rate of return. Perhaps more plausible explanations for emphasis on prices derive from low marginal rates of taxation of capital gains and from interest on the part of brokerage houses in encouraging trading commissions. This chapter reports indices of both prices and rates of return.

What do investors seek from a stock market index? One possibility is that investors desire to know the values of their portfolios. In this view the best index will have weights equal to the percentage of an investor's portfolio in each stock; a second portfolio requires a second index. Unless investors agree to restrict their asset bundles to a small set of alternatives, there is little hope of constructing an optimal set of weights.

A second possibility is that investors desire information about alternatives to their portfolio or "the market." This information may be viewed as a norm by which to evaluate the performance of their portfolios. If, in addition, investors implicitly agree to view a set of common stocks as describing the market, a basis exists for constructing an optimal price index. No pretense of sampling is made. For purposes of the present paper we adopt this interpretation.

Historians may have good reason for specifying *a priori* a set of weights to apply to their ideal index. For example, Cowles Commission indices weight stock prices by the volume of shares outstanding in order to portray the experience of the representative investor at different points in time.[2] The present purpose of constructing a norm makes no appeal to such arguments; *a priori* weights are not of interest. The weights will be seen instead to depend on which of a number of naive theories best describes investors' desired information about the market.

Stock price indices have a notoriously unsophisticated past. Failures to adjust for stock splits, stock dividends, and warrants, naive sampling schemes, and highly arbitrary and undefended sets of weights are conspicuous examples.[3] The DJI is an excellent representative of this tradition. The index may be thought of as a weighted average of prices of 30 widely held common stocks. All stock prices are weighted equally; weights are changed only when (*a*) a large stock dividend or split occurs or (*b*) a new stock is substituted for one of the 30. The principle for determining weights is simply continuity; if a split occurs, the weight of each price increases so that the previous day's closing DJI will be unchanged if the implied post-split price is used.[4] Of course, many other sets of weights exist which will

---

[2] Alfred Cowles, *Common Stock Indices*, 1871–1937, Bloomington: Principia Press, Inc., 1938.
[3] *Op. cit.*, pp. 33–50.
[4] *Basis of Calculation of the Dow-Jones Averages*, a short description published by Dow Jones and Co., Inc., 1963.

assure continuity. The defense for the present procedure appears to be computational simplicity. In the day of the computer, do such arguments apply?

The Dow Jones' weighting scheme implies that when a stock splits it is of less consequence to investors; at least it will be given a smaller voice in the average. If stocks split only when they are rising relative to other stocks, the DJI will exhibit a downward bias. While we know of no investigation of corporate share splitting policy, this appears to be the practice. Further, by ignoring minor stock dividends, the average incorporates a downward bias over time. A more sophisticated stock price index seems to be called for.

What criteria should be employed in constructing an index? To develop these criteria consider a one dimensional index a. In this index investors are believed to measure the market by movements in stock prices (adjusted only for splits and stock dividends) or rates of return. An index which reports this information is assumed to be a (linear) combination of, for example, adjusted prices. The index will be most sensitive (informative) if weights are assigned in a way which captures the maximum variance of the set of reference stock prices over time. An algebraic technique for obtaining an index with this property is the extraction from a covariance matrix of stock prices of the largest characteristic root, or the principal component.[5] The value of its associated vector, normalized in some arbitrary manner, is the index $\bar{a}$. Symbolically, investors wish an index which reports the maximum variance in some $(N \times 1)$ column vector of N stock prices X_t over time. For T periods, successive vectors define a $(N \times T)$ matrix M. The largest λ solving the determinantal equation $|MM' - \lambda I| = 0$ is the variance of the index $\bar{a} = \sum \bar{a}_i x_{it}$ when $\sum \bar{a}_i^2 = 1$. For purposes of exposition, here the normalization is $\sum \alpha_i^2 = \lambda$. This normalization implies that the resulting α_i's are the correlation coefficients between index a and the corresponding stock price or rate of return.

A number of objections can be raised against index a. Suppose two stocks each fall one point. An investor may well not regard these two pieces of news as being equally informative. Perhaps one of the stocks is high priced; a one point reduction may reflect considerably different

[5] For discussion see: (1) H. Theil, "Best Linear Index Numbers of Prices and Quantities," *Econometrica*, Vol. 28, No. 2 (April 1960), pp. 464–480, (2) M. G. Kendall, *A Course in Multivariate Analysis* (New York: Hafner Publishing Co., 1957), pp. 10–36, (3) T. W. Anderson, "Asymptotic Theory for Principal Component Analysis," *Annals of Mathematical Statistics*, Vol. 34, pp. 122–148, and (4) H. Hotelling, "Analysis of a Complex of Statistical Variables in Principal Components," *Journal of Educational Psychology*, September–October, 1933.

percentage declines in the two stock prices. If investors are concerned with percentage declines, rates of return are the best representation of stocks; they are studied below. An alternative to rates of return is a component analysis of logarithms of stock prices.[6]

Second, one of the stocks may have a much larger variance in its price movements; an investor may subjectively adjust for this stock's behavior when evaluating the informational content of the market news. We might therefore transform the stock price into a standardized variate with zero mean and unit standard deviation. In terms of the discussion above we have another time dated column vector of stocks Y_t having elements related to their corresponding elements in X_t by the simple rule

$$y_{it} = \frac{x_{it} - \bar{x}_i}{s_i}$$

where $\bar{x}_i$ is the stock's mean price and s_i is an estimate of its standard deviation. Index b is constructed by extracting characteristic roots from the $N \times N$ correlation matrix corresponding to MM'.

Third, is the investor likely to view equal positive and negative movements of a stock price, standardized or raw, as being equally informative? In view of the long history of rising stock prices, we believe downward movements are likely to be recorded as more informative. More precisely, investors may extrapolate a past price trend and view equal movements of standardized variables about this trend as conveying equivalent amounts of information. That is, an index c is constructed by the technique described above from a vector Z_t having element

$$z_{it} = \frac{x_{it} - \bar{x}_i}{s_i} - bt$$

In each of these three indices we make a guess about what conveys the most information to decision makers, the investors. We know of no study which allows an investigator to consider any one of them as most useful, although such research is elemental in the construction of an optimal index. This problem (having to guess) can be viewed differently. Investors have a set of beliefs at time $\hat{t}$ about the future stream of returns from the market. How, if at all, are investors' beliefs changed by having perceived certain price movements in an interval after $\hat{t}$? If the set of beliefs remain unchanged, we infer that price movements in the interval conveyed no

---

[6] The *Value Line* 1100 *Stock Average* is a geometric average of stock prices.

information.[7] What transformation of stock prices best describes changes in investor beliefs?

Fourth, in order that indices constructed in this framework be equally informative in different time periods, it is necessary that investors assume that the "structure" of stock prices remains constant over time; each index makes a different, but obvious, assumption about the structure of prices. This means that similar movements in the index at different dates cause the same change in investor beliefs. Alternatively, investors may derive information only from movements in linear combinations of stock prices; deviations in the observed correlations of prices are strictly ignored. In Section IV some evidence about the stationarity of the relevant correlation and covariance matrices is presented.

Fifth, a stock price may move, but contain no information about the market. This would happen if a conspicuous explanation for the movement exists, e.g., news of an impending strike or failure of a company sponsored legal action.[8]

Finally, a stock price movement may result from a stock's going ex dividend. This movement clearly conveys no information; it will not affect rates of return.

The criterion for constructing an ideal index is, therefore, not surprisingly the information which investors plan to derive from it. Indices are estimated by extracting characteristic roots from an appropriate covariance matrix or more familiarly by the method of principal components.

One question remains; precisely how many numbers should be used to describe the movements of a set of N stocks? So far we have spoken about only one number, the value of a vector associated with the largest λ; this is a one dimensional representation of stock prices. Most price indices are one dimensional. If individuals do subjectively represent information in more than one dimension, there is reason to report the value of vectors associated with other λ's. Of course, if individuals subjectively represent information in N dimensions there is little point in constructing an index.

---

[7] The reader should recognize that movements of stock prices may convey no information. In this case, beliefs are a function of income statements and other data collected from outside the stock market. This suggests that descriptions of stock market action permit one to say nothing about future stock prices. The observable similarity of opening and closing prices of stocks would appear to contradict this view; surely one can make probability statements about the range of a stock's closing price on the basis of its opening that morning.

[8] In a factor analysis of a set of stock prices, adjustment for this fifth consideration is the estimation of communalities. In future studies, perhaps independent estimates of communalities can be constructed. Research in progress by J. Bossons at the Carnegie Institute of Technology may provide the raw material for this further extension of the present study.

We suggest that this is highly unlikely; investors can evaluate only a very few numbers at one time. In the next section indices *a*, *b*, and *c* are each reported in two dimensions.

II

Data utilized in this study were collected from standard sources, *The New York Times*, *The Wall Street Journal*, *Standard and Poor's Stock Guide*, etc. They include cash and stock dividends, end of quarter closing prices, and stock splits for the 30 stocks in the DJI on December 31, 1961. The period covered includes 50 consecutive quarters subsequent to December 31, 1950.[9]

The data were adjusted for stock dividends and splits prior to calculations. Thus, if a stock splits 3 for 1, its price is weighted in the postsplit period by the factor 3, etc. Individual stocks were normalized, so that after adjustment their second quarter 1963 price used in the calculations was the observed second quarter price.

Table 1 reports weights estimated for the three stock price indices from data from all 50 quarters. Index *a* computed from raw price data is perhaps the closest to the spirit of the DJI. Its first component (dimension) accounts for 76 per cent of the generalized variance of the 30 stocks; its second component explains 14 per cent.[10] Not surprisingly, stocks which were high priced in 1963 tend to be weighted heavily, i.e., duPont, General Foods, AT & T, Eastman Kodak, Owens-Illinois, and Union Carbide. Other securities which for various reasons are highly erratic during the period also carry large weights, e.g., U.S. Steel and General Electric. While the DJI makes no effort to exploit the observed variance of individual stocks, it is heavily influenced by high price stocks as is index *a*. A comparison of the weights of index *a* with those of the DJI is not illuminating; the latter are time subscripted. Index *a* has been normalized to have the same mean and variance as the DJI in Figures 1 and 2. The high correlation between the first component of *a* and the DJI in Figure 1 confirms the suspicion that their similar emphasis on high price securities makes the two very similar. To put it differently, the DJI weighting scheme

---

[9] Stock substitutions were made in the DJI stocks during the 1950's; no adjustment is attempted in the present study. End of quarter price quotations refer to closing prices on the last trading day in March, June, and September. Fourth quarter price quotations are the closing prices on the last trading day prior to Christmas. This different treatment is intended to avoid noise resulting from investors realizing capital gains or losses before the year's end.

[10] "Generalized variance" refers to the trace of the corresponding covariance or correlation matrix.

Table 1 Weights for First Two Components of Price Indices *a*, *b*, and *c*.

	a		b		c	
	(1)	(2)	(1)	(2)	(1)	(2)
Allied Chemical	0.137	0.039	0.820	−0.251	0.837	−0.049
Alcoa	0.405	0.308	0.757	−0.596	0.424	−0.851
American Can	0.067	0.035	0.647	−0.399	0.895	0.340
AT & T	0.361	−0.272	0.800	0.559	−0.773	0.013
American Tobacco	0.123	−0.081	0.792	0.498	0.485	0.487
Anaconda	0.101	0.168	0.423	−0.734	0.911	−0.164
Bethlehem	0.217	0.104	0.849	−0.416	0.761	−0.566
Chrysler	−0.042	0.025	−0.305	−0.199	0.765	0.493
duPont	0.951	0.217	0.931	−0.235	−0.255	−0.865
Eastman Kodak	0.587	−0.231	0.900	0.334	−0.779	−0.505
General Electric	0.376	0.047	0.932	−0.141	−0.015	−0.896
General Foods	0.391	−0.254	0.841	0.511	−0.841	−0.126
General Motors	0.236	0.009	0.922	−0.080	0.510	−0.405
Goodyear	0.222	−0.012	0.958	0.044	0.562	−0.453
International Harvester	0.123	−0.051	0.836	0.326	0.636	0.390
International Nickel	0.297	−0.061	0.927	0.159	−0.123	−0.465
International Paper	0.156	0.054	0.917	−0.335	0.943	−0.156
Johns-Manville	0.150	−0.004	0.872	−0.001	0.732	0.008
Owens-Illinois	0.374	−0.012	0.943	0.025	−0.104	−0.811
Procter and Gamble	0.342	−0.238	0.823	0.532	−0.733	−0.030
Sears	0.319	−0.185	0.845	0.455	−0.694	−0.030
Standard Oil (Cal.)	0.195	0.007	0.863	−0.089	0.646	−0.075
Esso	0.198	0.068	0.793	−0.334	0.680	−0.270
Swift	0.037	0.019	0.344	−0.194	0.813	0.360
Texaco	0.251	−0.090	0.889	0.271	−0.371	−0.024
Union Carbide	0.422	0.131	0.903	−0.286	0.193	−0.910
United Aircraft	0.186	0.155	0.636	−0.592	0.721	−0.321
U.S. Steel	0.407	0.136	0.866	−0.283	0.207	−0.886
Westinghouse	0.145	0.004	0.670	−0.006	0.585	−0.016
Woolworth	0.175	−0.124	0.786	0.537	0.117	0.348
Percent variance	75.76	13.93	65.67	13.70	39.90	23.20

is a very informative index if investors are concerned with raw stock prices; virtually it is the best price index available!

Index *b* is estimated from standardized stock prices and thus will not necessarily accord high weights to stocks simply because they carry a high price tag. Inspection of the weights suggests that time trends dominate the weights. Stocks which had a low rate of price appreciation during the twelve year period, Chrysler, Swift, United Aircraft, American Can, Anaconda, and Westinghouse, have low weights. All other stocks are weighted more or less equally. The first component accounts for 66 per cent of the generalized variance. Figures 3 and 4 show plots of index *b*

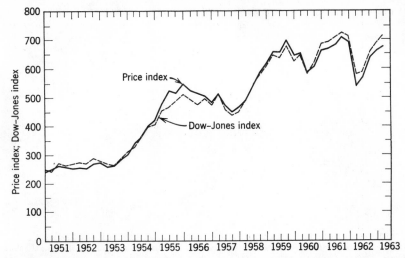

Figure 1 Index *a* component 1, *R* = .992. *R* denotes the correlation between the component and the Dow-Jones Index.

against the DJI. It is a bit surprising to find that the largest component of the normalized index *b* also correlates highly with the DJI.

One would expect differences between index *b* and index *a* (and the DJI) unless variances of individual stock prices are identical. Variances are not identical; Table 2 reports means and variances of end of quarter adjusted prices and of quarterly rates of return of the 30 DJI stocks over the 50

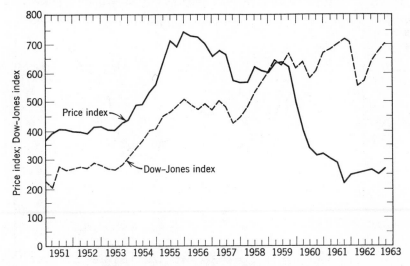

Figure 2 Index *a* component 2, *R* = −.111.

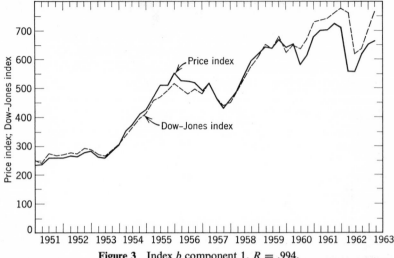

Figure 3 Index *b* component 1, *R* = .994.

quarter period. The trend in end of quarter prices is also reported in this table. The weights of index *a* and *b* differ greatly but the principal component of each is highly correlated with the DJI. It is tempting to conclude that a large number of positive weighted indices would correlate well with the DJI; nevertheless, for the period studied, the DJI is again nearly a best price index for individuals who subjectively adjust for stock variances.

The reason that both first components are positive (except Chrysler) is the strong positive trend in stock prices over the 50 quarter period. As

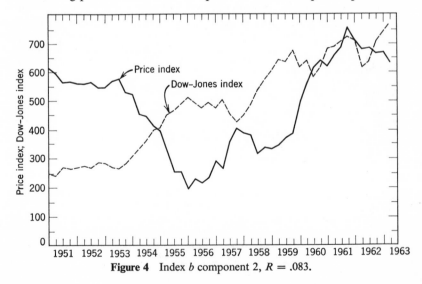

Figure 4 Index *b* component 2, *R* = .083.

Table 2 Means, Standard Deviations, and Trends of Adjusted End of Quarter Prices and Quarterly Rates of Return

	$\bar{P}(\$)$	$\sigma_p\,(\$)$	$\dfrac{dP}{dt}\left(\dfrac{\$}{\text{quarter}}\right)$	$\bar{R}(\%)$	$\sigma_R\,(\%)$
Allied Chemical	45.12	9.47	0.387	2.34	9.09
Alcoa	62.32	29.55	1.163	4.75	14.68
American Can	40.62	5.83	0.238	2.37	7.37
AT & T	73.62	25.97	1.557	3.11	6.19
American Tobacco	23.05	9.05	0.503	2.96	8.46
Anaconda	51.65	13.26	0.114	2.79	12.41
Bethlehem	33.04	14.28	0.687	3.90	11.77
Chrysler	33.46	8.40	−0.198	3.12	14.22
duPont	177.44	56.28	3.182	3.60	8.64
Eastman Kodak	59.21	36.70	2.374	5.00	9.78
General Electric	55.38	22.50	1.359	4.52	11.39
General Foods	37.13	26.59	1.670	5.38	8.24
General Motors	38.71	14.27	0.879	4.77	10.17
Goodyear	23.55	13.11	0.819	5.73	12.78
International Harvester	39.12	8.40	0.466	2.81	8.42
International Nickel	42.46	18.33	1.127	4.23	10.18
International Paper	26.02	9.50	0.500	3.50	10.74
Johns-Manville	44.54	9.99	0.505	2.70	9.25
Owens-Illinois	66.67	22.33	1.315	2.82	8.54
Procter and Gamble	38.02	23.95	1.451	4.23	8.89
Sears	38.93	21.45	1.341	4.66	9.44
Standard Oil (Cal.)	39.18	12.65	0.771	3.97	8.39
Esso	42.69	13.91	0.740	4.51	8.31
Swift	40.02	6.04	0.066	1.96	8.32
Texaco	31.50	15.96	1.054	5.41	8.77
Union Carbide	100.25	26.23	1.322	2.50	9.12
United Aircraft	42.72	16.32	0.609	4.42	15.22
U.S. Steel	53.39	26.39	1.283	3.84	12.94
Westinghouse	33.55	12.12	0.480	3.10	14.61
Woolworth	53.49	12.86	0.698	2.39	8.22

economists are all too frequently aware, time series variables or indices with trends tend to be highly correlated. The high correlations between first components of indices *a* and *b* and the DJI probably are mostly owing to this trend.

The second components of *a* and *b* and the first component of *c* also have an interpretation. As the components are unique only up to linear transformations we may reverse the signs of the second component of index *b* without loss of information. Then the reader may verify that stocks in all three components having substantial negative signs are AT & T, Eastman Kodak, General Foods, Procter and Gamble, and Sears. Woolworth has large negative signs in two of the components. These are perhaps the most consumer oriented of the Dow Jones stocks; apparently these components discriminate between producer and consumer goods industrial stocks. An explanation for this might be that profits of producer goods firms and consumer goods firms reach peaks at different points in a business cycle. A simple accelerator model might yield such a result. In

Table 3 Weights for Rate of Return Indices *a*, *b*, and *c*

	a		*b*		*c*	
	(1)	(2)	(1)	(2)	(1)	(2)
Allied Chemical	0.455	−0.095	0.783	0.041	0.780	0.046
Alcoa	0.663	0.023	0.628	0.369	0.599	0.404
American Can	0.185	−0.044	0.422	0.026	0.414	−0.001
AT & T	0.184	−0.108	0.529	−0.457	0.538	−0.473
American Tobacco	0.176	0.097	0.373	−0.581	0.375	−0.591
Anaconda	0.648	0.096	0.776	0.205	0.773	0.215
Bethlehem	0.597	0.151	0.723	0.200	0.706	0.225
Chrysler	0.478	0.264	0.466	0.158	0.494	0.130
duPont	0.438	0.0	0.780	0.159	0.780	0.153
Eastman Kodak	0.399	−0.164	0.636	−0.038	0.633	−0.033
General Electric	0.475	−0.322	0.619	0.106	0.605	0.121
General Foods	0.217	−0.108	0.455	−0.573	0.462	−0.575
General Motors	0.489	0.221	0.715	0.207	0.716	0.198
Goodyear	0.637	−0.076	0.748	0.076	0.732	0.100
International Harvester	0.389	0.039	0.712	−0.047	0.724	−0.061
International Nickel	0.491	0.076	0.736	−0.082	0.730	−0.071
International Paper	0.548	−0.117	0.793	0.142	0.785	0.153
Johns-Manville	0.385	−0.097	0.646	−0.141	0.638	−0.133
Owens-Illinois	0.360	−0.097	0.685	−0.267	0.682	−0.264
Procter and Gamble	0.313	−0.105	0.580	−0.589	0.592	−0.582
Sears	0.378	0.046	0.645	−0.368	0.658	−0.372
Standard Oil (Cal.)	0.302	0.032	0.579	0.405	0.576	0.381
Esso	0.305	0.052	0.557	0.586	0.544	0.576
Swift	0.306	−0.161	0.585	−0.156	0.583	−0.165
Texaco	0.411	−0.020	0.744	0.206	0.745	0.193
Union Carbide	0.477	−0.102	0.798	0.131	0.790	0.145
United Aircraft	0.398	0.651	0.335	0.065	0.313	0.075
U.S. Steel	0.738	0.097	0.842	0.072	0.830	0.099
Westinghouse	0.348	−0.600	0.338	−0.092	0.331	−0.087
Woolworth	0.251	−0.002	0.530	−0.461	0.538	−0.470
Percent total	41.23	8.67	41.10	8.77	40.69	8.92

order for this explanation to hold, it must also be assumed that stock prices are closely related to current earnings.

That trend is largely responsible for the signs of weights in the first components of a and b can be seen by examining the largest component of index c which is adjusted for trend. One third of its weights are negative and the component accounts for only 40 per cent of the generalized variance. Allied Chemical, American Can, Anaconda, Bethlehem, Chrysler, International Paper and Swift enter the index with strong positive weights. These securities would seem to support only weakly the accelerator argument suggested above. Perhaps in the case of this component variations in individual stock trends about the market trend mask the accelerator relation. The seven securities above have a comparatively slow rate of price appreciation over the twelve year period. The consumer stocks with the exception of Woolworth tended to have much higher rates of price appreciation.

One final point should be made about price indices. In Section I, it was argued that there were reasons to expect that the DJI had a downward bias over time. Inspection of Figures 1 and 3 lend no empirical support to this view. If a downward bias exists, it is of small consequence over the recent decade.

In Table 3 the first two components of a, b, and c rate of return indices are reported. The first two components of index a account for much smaller fractions of the generalized variance, 41 per cent and 9 per cent, than was the case for prices. A major reason for this is the absence of any sharp trend in rate of return during the period under study. All stocks are positively correlated with the index; Alcoa, Anaconda, Bethlehem, Goodyear, International Paper, and U.S. Steel have the largest correlations with the component. For purposes of comparison we have constructed an index of rates of return for Dow Jones stocks.

$$RI = \frac{DJI_t - DJI_{t-1}}{DJI_{t-1}} + \sum \frac{DJI_t}{DJI_{t-1}} \cdot \frac{D_{i,t-1}}{P_{i,t-1}}$$

where:

$P_{i,t-1}$ is the adjusted price of the ith stock at the beginning of period $t - 1$.

$D_{i,t-1}$ is the amount of dividends paid by the ith stock during period $t - 1$.

This pseudo DJ return index is plotted against the first two components of index a in Figures 5 and 6. The correlation between this index and our first component is again very high, 0.931.

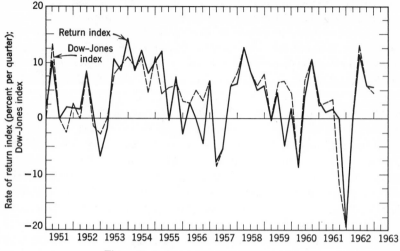

Figure 5   Index *a* component 1, $R = .931$.

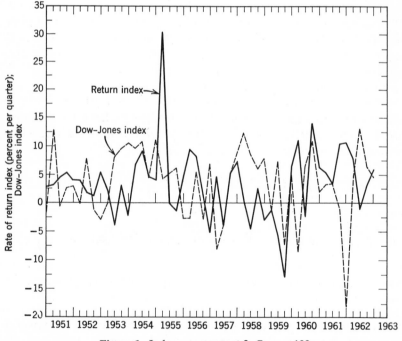

Figure 6   Index *a* component 2, $R = -.100$.

The first two components of index *b*, which refer to standardized rate of return data, account for the same amount of the generalized variance as index *a*, 41 per cent and 9 per cent respectively. All stocks are again positively correlated with the first component. Allied Chemical, Anaconda, duPont, International Paper, Union Carbide, and U.S. Steel have correlations exceeding 0.75. The correlation between the first component and the pseudo index is 0.952.

As can be seen from Table 3, the weights of index *b* and *c* are virtually identical owing to the absence of trend in rate of return.

The following comments summarize this section. The first component of stock price indices is much better in representing information about the 30 Dow Jones stock prices than the first component of the rate of return index in representing their rates of return. This is due to a strong positive postwar trend in stock prices. Once this trend is removed from stock prices the first component accounts for about 40 per cent of the generalized variance. The first component of any of the rate of return indices also accounts for about 40 per cent of the generalized variance.

The first components of the three rate of return indices are defined by positive vectors.[11] This pattern might be expected if the "attitude of the market" really is the most important determinant of stock price movements. Apparently then movements of individual stock prices are dominated by the tone of the market over the 50 quarter period. The significance of this observation for investors choosing portfolios is suggested in the next section.[12]

Finally, the DJI is highly correlated with the first components of indices *a* and *b*. In a sense it is a very good and informative index; whether it will retain its properties in periods where the strong trend is absent is hypothetical. Judging from the methods used in calculating it, an equivalent performance in a trendless world is dubious. Once trend is removed, the weighting of stocks in the largest component bears very little resemblance to those used in calculating the DJI. No evidence of a downward bias in the DJI was detected.

---

[11] Of course components are only unique up to a multiplicative constant, which may be positive or negative. A more accurate description of the vectors would be that they are isosign; that is, their elements are either nonnegative or nonpositive. Rather than apply novel terminology we suffer the inaccuracy in the text. It is trivial to demonstrate that a correlation matrix which contains no negative elements has a largest characteristic vector which is isosign. Other correlation matrices, like the matrix of Dow Jones stock rates of return, which have a few small negative elements may also have isosign largest characteristic vectors if their ranks exceed two.

[12] A similar observation has been made by K. Borch, "Price Movements in the Stock Market," mimeographed Econometric Research Program Paper No. 7, Princeton University, April 30, 1963.

III

In this section the relation between the computed indices and the problem of portfolio selection is examined. It is assumed that the utility function of investors is quadratic in the rate of return, i.e.,

$$u = f(r, \sigma_r^2), \qquad \frac{\partial u}{\partial r} > 0, \qquad \frac{\partial u}{\partial \sigma_r^2} < 0.^{13}$$

It is convenient also to view the 30 Dow Jones industrials as constituting the universe of available assets.

Inspection of the utility function indicates that rate of return, not price, components will be of interest in this section. However, owing to higher marginal rates of taxation on dividend income than capital gains, the utility function of high marginal tax rate investors is probably better viewed as a quadratic function of $(P_t - P_{t-1})/P_{t-1}$. The reader is cautioned that we have not used this argument in our calculations; strictly speaking, our conclusions apply only to investors whose behavior is independent of the tax structure.

Investors will be concerned with the components of covariance matrices; they will find little of interest in the components of correlation matrices, indices *b* and *c*. This is because components are not invariant to change in units of variables, except in the trivial case of a scalar multiplication of elements of a covariance matrix. Consequently this section refers only to components of index *a*.

It is worth noting that these elementary observations have been totally ignored in a recently published study of portfolio behavior of mutual funds. We restrict comments to Farrar's empirical work.[14]

In Chapter 2, he correctly specifies Markowitz's utility function.[15] In Chapter 3 he states:

> In order to reduce the population to feasible dimensions, therefore, a good deal of aggregation is immediately necessary. Despite its obvious shortcomings, the absence of a practicable alternative serves to justify aggregation according to industry and asset groupings. The presence of convenient and reliable Standard and Poor's price indices for such classifications is also a non-negligible factor in the choice.[16]

---

[13] Portfolio selection has been analyzed previously in this framework by H. M. Markowitz, *Portfolio Selection*, New York: John Wiley and Sons, Inc., 1959, and J. Tobin, "Liquidity Preference as Behavior Towards Risk," this volume, Chapter 1.

[14] D. E. Farrar, *The Investment Decision Under Uncertainty* (Englewood Cliffs: Prentice-Hall, Inc., 1962), Chs. 2–4.

[15] *Ibid.*, p. 27.

[16] *Ibid.*, p. 39.

Using monthly industrial stock price indices he extracts principal components from a 47 × 47 matrix of correlation coefficients. Although he professes to be concerned with reducing "redundancy" or "collinearity," a legitimate objective of principal components analysis, Farrar inappropriately applies factor analytic techniques which assume the existence of a particular *model*.[17] He finds that the 47 × 47 correlation matrix of indices is nearly represented by three nonorthogonal vectors. These vectors along with other pseudo assets or assets are assigned rates of change of prices based on a set of expectations assigned to the 23 mutual funds studied. Using a quadratic programming algorithm, Farrar estimates a risk return efficiency locus and concludes that the funds are behaving reasonably efficiently.[18]

Three points deserve mention. First, it is difficult to justify making a factor analysis of stock prices, rather than rates of return or at least percentage change in stock prices. Farrar has used a different variable than the rate of return, the argument of Markowitz's quadratic utility function. Second, when estimating principal components, he extracted roots from the correlation, not the covariance, matrix. It seems likely that considerable differences in the variance of different industrial stock indices exist, to say nothing about stocks used in constructing the indices. For both reasons Farrar's vectors are not appropriate for studying the Markowitz model.

Finally, the power of Farrar's evaluation of the efficiency of mutual fund portfolios appears to be extremely low; for common stocks nearly all the variance and the highest return is associated with his largest industrial factor in which most widely held common stock groups receive a heavy weight. All funds' portfolios lie relatively close to his estimated efficiency frontier because all of the following are nearly on it and on a straight line from the origin of the risk-return axes; cash, the two largest bond components, a utility stock index, and the largest common stock factor. These assets or pseudo assets probably account for over 90 per cent of the investments eligible for mutual funds. Farrar's random portfolio selection test does not take this last consideration into account.

Returning to the main argument, there are two important reasons for applying quadratic utility functions to problems of portfolio selection: (1) diversification is a reasonable form of behavior and (2) the problem, in principle, can be solved. Quadratic programming routines exist for large digital computers; these routines with a set of expected rates of return and a known covariance matrix should reduce the problem of

---

[17] Kendall, *op. cit.*, p. 37.
[18] Markowitz, *op. cit.*, p. 20.

portfolio selection to an uninteresting manipulation. Why then should this problem be reconsidered here?

If risk avoidance is very important to investors an illuminating representation of a perceived covariance matrix is simply its set of characteristic roots and vectors. Elsewhere one of us has argued that, in a risky world, if the covariance matrix is singular and short sales are permitted, then a riskless portfolio with nonnegative return always exists.[19] Further, even if the covariance matrix is not singular, a minimum risk portfolio is a

Table 4   A Representation of Six Securities in Three Dimensions

Security	Component 1	Component 2	Component 3	$E(R)$
x_1	0	0	0	0.05
x_2	1.00	0	0	0.08
x_3	0.25	0.25	−0.5	0.06
x_4	1.0	0	0	0.04
x_5	0.42	−0.75	0	0.04
x_6	0.5	0.5	0.25	0.05
λ	2.49	0.88	0.31	

weighted average of normalized characteristic vectors, where weights are reciprocals of the associated characteristic roots. In the present study we did not find that the covariance matrix is singular, although the smallest root was very small indeed.

Do investors really have well formulated expectations about future returns to an asset? This question cannot be studied with our data. Is a covariance matrix constant over time? This question is investigated in the next section; in the present section the answer is assumed to be affirmative. To what extent do investors perceive the covariance matrix? A covariance matrix for the Dow Jones industrials is, of course, a 30 dimensional vector space. We believe it to be highly unlikely that ordinary mortals can have very strong convictions about each of the 435 covariances among these stocks, to say nothing about the universe of available assets. They must somehow simplify their beliefs about the covariation of a set of assets. We propose that in effect investors summarize the covariance matrix in the largest few principal components.

It would be neat to demonstrate that investors actually thought in terms of components of covariance matrices; we don't try. However, investors

---

[19] Hester, D., "Efficient Portfolios with Short Sales and Margin Holdings," in this volume, Chapter 3.

or at least financial newspapers do reveal a set of beliefs about the structure of the covariance matrix of rates of return. We will demonstrate that these beliefs have empirical substance.

First, Table 4 suggests how a set of beliefs about six securites might be viewed in a three dimensional vector space. Table 5 reports the first five components of the rate of return covariance matrix of the 30 Dow Jones industrials.

Table 5 Weights for the Five Largest Components of Index *a*

	Component 1	Component 2	Component 3	Component 4	Component 5
Allied Chemical	0.455	−0.095	−0.038	0.015	−0.050
Alcoa	0.663	0.023	0.128	0.462	0.209
American Can	0.185	−0.044	−0.033	−0.004	−0.056
AT & T	0.184	−0.108	−0.071	−0.163	−0.037
American Tobacco	0.176	0.097	−0.242	−0.315	0.022
Anaconda	0.648	0.096	−0.090	0.108	−0.104
Bethlehem	0.597	0.151	0.025	0.074	0.094
Chrysler	0.478	0.264	0.473	−0.108	−0.527
duPont	0.438	−0.000	−0.012	0.038	−0.126
Eastman Kodak	0.399	−0.164	−0.114	0.011	0.095
General Electric	0.475	−0.322	0.146	0.092	0.149
General Foods	0.217	−0.108	−0.083	−0.266	0.036
General Motors	0.489	0.221	0.028	0.019	−0.195
Goodyear	0.637	−0.076	−0.144	0.015	0.111
International Harvester	0.389	0.039	−0.003	−0.081	−0.084
International Nickel	0.491	0.076	−0.091	−0.117	0.025
International Paper	0.548	−0.117	−0.155	0.114	−0.007
Johns-Manville	0.385	−0.097	−0.006	−0.101	0.050
Owens-Illinois	0.360	−0.097	−0.180	−0.078	0.044
Procter and Gamble	0.313	−0.105	−0.019	−0.366	0.097
Sears	0.378	0.046	−0.062	−0.268	−0.103
Standard Oil (Cal.)	0.302	0.032	−0.194	0.178	−0.136
Esso	0.305	0.052	−0.063	0.268	−0.094
Swift	0.306	−0.161	0.043	−0.087	−0.045
Texaco	0.411	−0.020	−0.150	0.093	−0.030
Union Carbide	0.477	−0.102	0.000	0.074	0.026
United Aircraft	0.398	0.651	0.330	−0.176	0.463
U.S. Steel	0.738	0.097	−0.040	−0.013	0.006
Westinghouse	0.348	−0.600	0.561	−0.138	0.063
Woolworth	0.251	−0.002	−0.216	−0.243	−0.018
Cumulative Percent of Variance	41.23	49.90	56.90	63.59	68.79

The coefficients in Table 4 are rough subjective estimates of the correlation between each of the components and the individual securities. All assets are assumed to have the indicated expected rates of return and identical variances. Perhaps the components can be interpreted as (1) the market, (2) the defense sector, and (3) the farm sector, respectively, all of which are believed to be orthogonal. Although knowledge of the structure of the covariance matrix is crude, it is not without value. A portfolio of a risk averting investor might include x_1, x_2, and x_3. Such a portfolio will capture a considerable amount of uncorrelated variation (which of course is invaluable in reducing portfolio variance!), while earning a good rate of return. If short sales are allowed, then a riskless portfolio with positive rate of return is holding x_2 and selling x_4 short. If x_3 were not available, x_6 would appear more attractive, for it would serve to capture uncorrelated variation in components 2 and 3. A more subtle investor might recognize that x_5 and either x_3 or x_6 make attractive pairs; by suitably purchasing from the set of securities much of the variance of the second component can be eliminated from the portfolio. Similarly, holding x_3 and x_6 together will serve to eliminate variance of the third component.

Assuming that investors represent the Dow Jones industrials in five dimensions we may draw some conclusions about stocks which would have been useful in reducing portfolio variance during the 50 quarter period. We shall not venture to name these components. From Table 5, one may see that stocks whose rate of return was either relatively uncorrelated with any of the components or was highly correlated with any of the last four components are attractive; most stocks were highly correlated with the first component. Likely candidates from the 30 are Alcoa, American Can, AT & T, Chrysler, United Aircraft, and Westinghouse. Whether or not these securities will prove useful for purposes of diversification in future years depends upon whether the covariance matrix is unchanging over time. Evidence concerning this issue is presented in the next section.   .

While we do not presume to summarize the vast literature concerning the New York Stock Exchange or the 30 Dow Jones industrials, one common theme is evident in this material: individual stocks are frequently summarized by industries. The suggestion is that rates of return of stocks in an industry are positively correlated; this is a hypothesis about the structure of the covariance matrix. It is by no means obvious that this hypothesis is valid. If GM is having a good year is that because all automotives are doing well or is it because GM is cutting into sales by Ford, American Motors, and/or Chrysler? A test of whether it is useful to aggregate into industries is whether firms in the same industry enter different components of the market with similar weights.

A null hypothesis is that the correlations of two stocks with a component will be of the same sign with probability 0.5. By examining the frequency with which a pair of stocks have the same sign of correlation coefficient with a number of different components we may test the hypothesis underlying the aggregation of stocks into industry classifications. The meaning of acceptance of the hypothesis for portfolio selection is clear. If stocks of the same industry have highly correlated rates of return, unless one of the stocks is sold short, there is no advantage to having a position in more than one. Rejection of the hypothesis implies that portfolio risk is reduced by spreading out one's automotive holdings among the different firms.

Table 6 reports the frequency of same sign component correlations for 13 pairs of stocks for arbitrarily defined industries. While the distribution

Table 6 Number of Industry Similar Signs among the Largest 5 and the Largest 10 Rate of Return Components 1951–1963

Industry and Firm	Largest 5	Largest 10
Automobiles		
Chrysler and GM	4	6
Chemicals		
duPont and Allied	5*	7
Electricals		
GE and Westinghouse	4	6
Foods		
Swift and General Foods	3	5
Nonferrous Metals		
Anaconda and Alcoa	3	6
Anaconda and International Nickel	3	8*
Alcoa and International Nickel	3	6
Oils		
Esso and Standard Oil (Cal.)	5*	9*
Esso and Texaco	4	7
Texaco and Standard Oil (Cal.)	4	5
Packaging		
American Can and Owens-Illinois	4	6
Retailing		
Sears and Woolworth	4	8*
Steels		
U.S. Steel and Bethlehem	3	8*
Actual (sum)	49	88
Expected	32.5	65
Standard deviation	4.0	5.7
	Significant	Significant

* The asterisk indicates significance at .05 in the binomial approximation.

of some signs is not binomial, a rough test can be applied by assuming that they are binomially distributed. Tests are performed roughly at the 0.05 level for each pairwise comparison and for a pooled sum of the 13 pairwise comparisons. The results appear to support the hypothesis rather impressively. In all 13 cases signs of correlations of firm stock rates of return with either the first five or the first ten components are more often similar than not. In 5 of the 13 industry groupings one or both of the pairwise comparisons were significant. The pooled sum of similar signs in pairwise comparisons is overwhelmingly significant.

Finally we note that although the "industries" representation of the market has empirical support, it may not be too useful a representation for investors. Different industries may move together; a portfolio of an automotive stock and a steel stock may not afford much greater protection against risk than an alternative consisting of GM and Ford, assuming no short sales. Alternatively, orthogonality may be a useful property to impose on representations of covariance matrices.

In summary, the Dow Jones rate of return covariance matrix is not singular; there is considerable variation about the first or market component which accounts for only 40 per cent of the generalized variance. The variance explained by the next four components individually is 9%, 7%, 7%, and 5% of the generalized variance. Many opportunities existed during 1951–63 for portfolio diversification by risk averting investors among these 30 stocks, even when short sales were outlawed. Second, to think that investors really do think in terms of 30 dimensional vector spaces seems a trifle unreasonable. We suggest that a compression of beliefs about covariance matrices into a much smaller number of dimensions is more likely to approximate their evaluation of a portfolio's risk. A very rough example suggests how such compressed information might be utilized.

Finally, we noted that investors or rather the financial press often refers to groups of stocks, firms in an industry, when discussing portfolio selection problems. This appears to reflect a belief about the structure of the covariance matrix, i.e., stocks of the same industry have positively correlated rates of return over time. We reported evidence which strongly supports this belief about the covariance matrix, but observed that this representation may not be too helpful to investors.

IV

In this section intertemporal constancy of indices, the correlation matrix, and the covariance matrix are studied by breaking the 50 quarter period in half, January 1951 to December 1956 and January 1957 to June

1963. Calculations are restricted to *a* and *b* indices; index *c* is not sufficiently interesting to justify the expense of further calculations. A number of different comparisons are made for both price and rate of return indices. First, are the weights associated with indices the same when indices are estimated from each of the subperiods? Second, is the percentage of the generalized variance explained by components estimated from each of the subperiods the same? Third, do components estimated in the early period accurately describe stock price movements in the second period? Of more interest to problems of portfolio selection is the degree to which rate of return covariance matrix components retain their property of orthogonality. Finally, is the popular view of structure, intra-industry similarity of movements in rates of return, empirically valid in subperiods?

Table 7 reports correlations between the largest components of price indices *a* and *b* and adjusted prices of each of the 30 Dow Jones industrials. The indices are estimated from each of the two subperiods. The correlation between the weights of the two estimated first components of indices *a* and *b* were respectively −0.086 and +0.063. The structure of both the covariance and the correlation matrices of stock prices was quite different in the two subperiods. This result should prove very discouraging to advocates of stock price indices.

Table 8 reports correlations between the largest components of rate of return indices *a* and *b* and rate of return of each of the 30 stocks. The correlation between the weights of the two estimated first components of the two indices were respectively +0.561 and +0.552; both differ significantly from zero using Fisher's z transformation. Although changes in the weights are undeniable, apparently some constant structure exists in both the covariance and the correlation matrices so far as the first components go. Examination of the signs of weights in the second through fifth components does not provide support for a hypothesis that these weights are constant as well. Approximately half the weights changed signs between the two subperiods for both indices. Evidently the structure of the rate of return matrices did in fact change between the two periods; some further details about the nature of the change are presented below. At least as far as the first component goes, there does seem to be some hope for constructing an interesting rate of return index.

Table 9 summarizes a different, not independent, comparison of the structure of the covariance and correlation matrices of the two subperiods. The percentage of the generalized variance explained by the five largest components is shown for each index, for both price and rate of return in each subperiod. Both price indices changed markedly between the two periods. In the early subperiod, the first component accounted for a very large proportion of the generalized variance. Partly this was owing to the

Table 7   First Components of Price Indices Estimated from Subperiods

Stock	Index *a*		Index *b*	
	1951–1956	1957–1963	1951–1956	1957–1963
Allied Chemical	0.159	0.173	0.937	0.780
Alcoa	0.575	−0.158	0.945	0.052
American Can	0.093	−0.015	0.807	−0.173
AT & T	0.062	0.861	0.918	0.806
American Tobacco	0.026	0.268	0.723	0.777
Anaconda	0.274	−0.054	0.888	0.142
Bethlehem	0.221	−0.045	0.953	0.115
Chrysler	0.019	0.015	0.216	0.001
duPont	0.982	0.661	0.965	0.699
Eastman Kodak	0.173	0.837	0.967	0.879
General Electric	0.284	0.185	0.950	0.586
General Foods	0.080	0.800	0.949	0.829
General Motors	0.209	0.210	0.968	0.575
Goodyear	0.115	0.189	0.957	0.847
International Harvester	0.044	0.264	0.685	0.870
International Nickel	0.200	0.390	0.913	0.804
International Paper	0.165	0.062	0.969	0.559
Johns-Manville	0.119	0.194	0.907	0.760
Owens-Illinois	0.227	0.370	0.951	0.825
Procter and Gamble	0.071	0.752	0.946	0.814
Sears	0.111	0.671	0.942	0.785
Standard Oil (Cal.)	0.168	0.088	0.963	0.117
Esso	0.226	−0.044	0.943	−0.294
Swift	0.087	0.132	0.659	0.836
Texaco	0.119	0.331	0.966	0.604
Union Carbide	0.385	0.231	0.962	0.610
United Aircraft	0.331	−0.195	0.936	−0.622
U.S. Steel	0.321	0.088	0.942	0.379
Westinghouse	0.073	0.153	0.625	0.495
Woolworth	0.034	0.464	0.629	0.903

larger trend component in stocks in that period. The DJI rose from 248 in March 1951 to 499 in December 1956; at the end of June 1963 it was 707. This difference is not sufficient to explain the variation. A more important consideration is that the market had no major slumps in the first period of the magnitude of those in 1957–1958 or 1962. This changed structure reinforces the previous conclusion about the lack of any stationary structure in the price matrices.

Table 8 First Components of Rate of Return Indices Estimated
from Subperiods

Stock	Index *a*		Index *b*	
	1951–1956	1957–1963	1951–1956	1957–1963
Allied Chemical	0.277	0.460	0.711	0.808
Alcoa	0.521	0.514	0.576	0.677
American Can	0.131	0.152	0.366	0.517
AT & T	0.057	0.257	0.486	0.632
American Tobacco	0.036	0.257	0.057	0.575
Anaconda	0.527	0.524	0.800	0.748
Bethlehem	0.550	0.422	0.723	0.772
Chrysler	0.302	0.514	0.478	0.480
duPont	0.348	0.376	0.796	0.750
Eastman Kodak	0.271	0.394	0.553	0.669
General Electric	0.345	0.415	0.606	0.610
General Foods	0.083	0.290	0.264	0.613
General Motors	0.439	0.389	0.737	0.693
Goodyear	0.469	0.554	0.705	0.768
International Harvester	0.273	0.395	0.706	0.772
International Nickel	0.292	0.487	0.589	0.793
International Paper	0.419	0.466	0.804	0.769
Johns-Manville	0.216	0.397	0.536	0.687
Owens-Illinois	0.253	0.338	0.722	0.663
Procter and Gamble	0.304	0.284	0.784	0.560
Sears	0.315	0.368	0.637	0.714
Standard Oil (Cal.)	0.227	0.250	0.589	0.551
Esso	0.200	0.256	0.493	0.588
Swift	0.165	0.338	0.514	0.628
Texaco	0.304	0.370	0.679	0.785
Union Carbide	0.269	0.490	0.648	0.854
United Aircraft	0.549	0.146	0.365	0.318
U.S. Steel	0.570	0.639	0.766	0.894
Westinghouse	0.283	0.326	0.532	0.241
Woolworth	0.143	0.298	0.469	0.610

The story differs considerably for rates of return; the first five components appear to explain similar percentages of the generalized variance in the two periods. This statement is more accurate with respect to index *a* which concerns the covariance matrix. The explanation for the failure of signs of weights for components two through five to remain unchanged in rate of return indices is not a change in the proportion of variance which the components individually explain. Covariance and correlation matrices of rates of return thus appear to exhibit a second intertemporal constancy.

What do these intertemporal constancies of the first component of the rate of return index mean for risk averting investors? If investors only wish to reduce variation in the rate of return of these portfolios relative to the generalized variance of the 30 stocks, they could have done so in period two by purchasing stocks with low weights in the first period's

Table 9 Percent of Variance Explained by First Five Components of Indices *a* and *b*

	Price				Rate of Return			
	a		*b*		*a*		*b*	
Component	1951– 1956	1957– 1963	1951– 1956	1957– 1963	1951– 1956	1957– 1963	1951– 1956	1957– 1963
1	91	57	78	42	41	43	38	45
2	3	23	7	16	14	11	12	10
3	2	9	5	14	9	10	8	7
4	1	4	3	6	7	7	6	6
5	1	1	1	3	5	5	5	5
First 5	98	94	94	81	76	76	69	73

principal component. However, they would have no assurance that a portfolio so selected would be particularly immune to variance of the rate of return absolutely! If investors had knowledge about the path of the generalized variance, these constancies would be of more interest. Incidentally the generalized variance of rate of return index *a* increased 30 per cent in the second subperiod over its value in the first subperiod.

Figure 7 shows the first component of price index *a* plotted against the DJI when the component has been estimated from data in the first subperiod. Figure 8 shows the corresponding rate of return index plotted against our pseudo DJ rate of return index. The high correlation between the first component of the price index and the DJI no doubt is largely attributable to the considerable trend component. The explanation for the high correlation between the rate of return indices is apparently owing to the fact that the principal component and the DJ index have captured the constancy of the covariance matrix. Investors would have obtained a roughly equivalent description of the market whether they were thinking in terms of a covariance or a correlation matrix in the first subperiod.

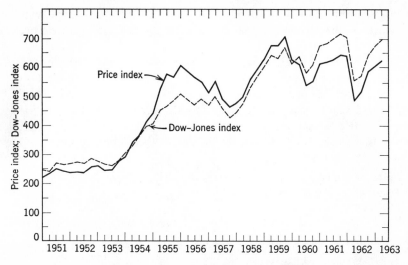

Figure 7 Index *a* component 1, $R = .946$.

A property of principal components is that they are orthogonal. If components are estimated in a subperiod, they need not retain this property over the whole period of observations. It would be convenient for portfolio selection if at least the large components of a return index estimated from a subperiod retained this property. Table 10 reports the correlation matrix in the second period of the five largest components of index *a*

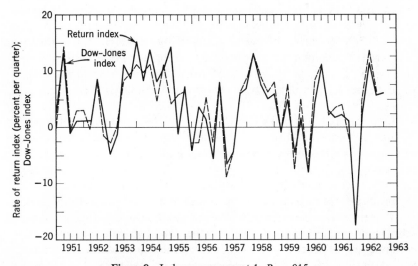

Figure 8 Index *a* component 1, $R = .915$.

estimated from the first subperiod. It is evident that the change in the structure of the covariance matrix between the two periods destroyed orthogonality.

Finally, in Section III evidence was found which supported a popular hypothesis about the structure of the covariance matrix, i.e., that rates of return of stocks of firms in an industry are positively correlated. Would this hypothesis be accepted in each of the subperiods? Table 11 reports the relevant information; it is analogous to Table 6. Evidence in favor of the hypothesis is conspicuously weaker in the second subperiod. In

Table 10 Correlation Matrix in Subperiod 2 of the Largest Five Components of Index a Estimated in Subperiod 1

	c_1	c_2	c_3	c_4	c_5
c_1	1				
c_2	−0.534	1			
c_3	−0.504	0.156	1		
c_4	−0.061	−0.034	0.484	1	
c_5	0.265	−0.168	0.286	0.026	1

the first 24 quarters 6 of 13 pairwise comparisons are significant in one or both of the sets of components; only two are in the second period. In 11 of the 13 comparisons the number of similar signs declined. One of the two exceptions, steel, was undoubtedly influenced considerably by the tumultuous clash between the industry and the White House in 1962. The sums of the 13 pairwise comparisons are highly significant during the first 24 quarters; only one of the two sums is significant in the second period (and it is barely so at that). The structure of the covariance matrix changed so that rates of return of stocks of firms in an industry were much less strongly correlated.

An interpretation is that during the buoyant first subperiod all firms in an industry were profiting by expanding industry sales. In the second subperiod, profits of firms were more at the expense of rivals in an industry. In a sense, the situation changed from a "seller's" market to a "buyer's" market. In the seller's market, products of firms were being disposed of in rapidly increasing quantities; the principal determinant of firms' profits and the related rate of return on their stock was the rate of growth in industry sales. In the buyer's market, although the rate of growth of industry sales continued to influence firm profits, it was joined by a second determinant, the extent to which firms were able to cut in on rivals' sales. In view of the

Table 11 Number of Industry Similar Signs among Largest 5 and Largest 10 Components of Index *a*, Estimated from Subperiods

Industry-Firm	First 24 Quarters		Last 25 Quarters	
	of 5	of 10	of 5	of 10
Automobiles				
Chrysler and GM	4	6	2	5
Chemicals				
duPont and Allied	4	7	3	5
Electricals				
GE and Westinghouse	5*	8*	3	5
Foods				
Swift and General Foods	5*	7	3	6
Nonferrous Metals				
Anaconda and Alcoa	4	7	3	5
Anaconda and Intnl. Nickel	4	8*	3	7
Alcoa and Intnl. Nickel	3	5	1	4
Oils				
Esso and Standard Oil (Cal.)	5*	9*	4	8*
Esso and Texaco	5*	8*	3	6
Texaco and Standard Oil (Cal.)	5*	9*	3	6
Packaging				
American Can and				
Owens-Illinois	3	5	2	4
Retailing				
Sears and Woolworth	3	5	4	6
Steels				
U.S. Steel and Bethlehem	4	6	5*	10*
Actual sum	54	90	39	77
Expected sum	32.5	65	32.5	65
Standard deviation	4.0	5.7	4.0	5.7
Deviation	Significant	Significant	Nonsignificant	Significant

* The asterisk denotes significance at the 0.05 level in the binomial approximation.

fact that similar signs of weights slightly exceeded the null hypothesis expectation, we infer that the first determinant was slightly stronger than the second in the second subperiod. For portfolio selection, the conclusion is that in the second subperiod investors could diversify to a greater extent by investing in different firms in an industry.

V

We conclude this chapter with a few suggestions for future research. First, serious efforts to describe empirically investors' portfolio behavior will need to make explicit the set of information which investors have on hand. An interesting experiment would be to invite a sample of investors to make estimates of the covariance between various securities. We hypothesize that the resulting subjective covariance matrix could be essentially represented in a very small number of dimensions—say, three.

Second, a formal analysis of how investor beliefs are related to news in the market is necessary if the approach of this chapter is to be carried further. What data are important or significant in the minds of investors? The Dow Theory and other such constructs argue that some information is contained in past performance of aggregative indices. An alternative theory is that information is acquired only by studying income statements, balance sheets, and the rate of growth of firms. The relative informational value of these two sources can only be appraised by studying a sample of investors.

Third, from our investigation of a 50 quarter period we believe that an informative one dimensional index of rate of return may be constructed. Further sophistication of this index requires that noise owing to situations peculiar to a particular firm be eliminated from the index. This means that some attempt must be made to estimate communalities, before extracting the largest root of the covariance matrix. Alternatively some technique must be devised by which the informational content (for the market) of a stock's rate of return movements can be separated from its total rate of return variance. We do not think that simple (linear) stock price indices are as promising a guide for investors, because weights of even the largest components appear to change considerably over relatively short periods of time.

Finally, the conspicuous weakening in the "all firms in an industry move together" hypothesis deserves more extensive investigation. Can it be shown that changes in either firms' profits or sales were more at the expense of rivals in the second subperiod than in the first? What can be said about the sensitivity of rates of return to such changes in current profits or sales, if true? In particular, what rate of discount of an earnings stream is implied by the seeming sensitivity of stock rates of return to earnings? Both the formulation and testing of these questions is a major research endeavor; its returns may well justify the investment.

6

The Accumulation of Risky Capital: A Sequential Utility Analysis*

EDMUND S. PHELPS

This paper investigates the optimal lifetime consumption strategy of an individual whose wealth holding possibilities expose him to the risk of loss. The vehicle of analysis is a stochastic, discrete-time dynamic programming model that postulates an expected lifetime utility function to be maximized. All wealth consists of a single asset, called capital.

The problem described belongs mainly to the theory of personal saving. Models of saving behavior thus far have been entirely deterministic [4, 7, 8, 11, 12, 13],[1] whereas, in fact, the saver is typically faced with the prospect of capital gain or loss. So it seems appropriate to determine whether the results of the conventional theory carry over or have to be qualified upon admitting capital risk into the theory.[2] The question also arises as to the effect of capital risk itself upon the level of consumption. This neglected factor may play a role in the explanation of certain inter-group differences in saving behavior.

---

* For helpful discussions on this subject I am grateful to T. N. Srinivasan and S. G. Winter.
[1] An exception is a Cowles Foundation Discussion Paper by Martin Beckmann [2]. That paper (which deals with wage rather than capital uncertainty) uses a technique similar to the one here.
[2] The model below resembles Ramsey's more than contemporary models [7, 11] so that it is largely his results that are modified.

These questions are easier to raise than to answer, and this paper is frankly an exploratory effort. No generality or definiteness is claimed for the results obtained. A brief outline of the paper and sketch of some of these results follow.

In the first two sections, a utility function and a stochastic capital growth process are postulated and discussed. Subsequently, the "structure" of the optimal consumption policy, that is, the way in which consumption depends upon the individual's age and capital, is established. One's expectations, based on existing "deterministic" theory, are confirmed: Optimal consumption is an increasing function of both age and capital. Little else appears deducible without further restrictions upon the utility function.

Thereafter attention is confined to certain monomial utility functions. These special cases cannot yield general theorems but they do have the function of providing counter-examples to conjectures and of serving to suggest other hypotheses for empirical test.

For example, it is shown that the classical phenomenon of "hump saving" [8, 12] need not occur, quite apart from reasons of time preference, if capital is risky. Instead a low-capital "trap" region is possible in which it is optimal to maintain or decumulate capital, no matter how distant the planning horizon.

These utility functions all make consumption linear homogeneous in capital and permanent nonwealth income, and linear in each of these variables. But the straight-line classroom consumption function is not really upheld: Consumption cannot be expressed as a function of aggregate expected income because expected wage income (treated as certain) and expected capital income have different variances, whence different impacts upon the level of consumption. The marginal propensity to consume out of risky income is smaller than out of sure income. This result may help to explain why households which depend primarily upon (risky) capital income (e.g., farmers, wealthy heirs) are comparatively thrifty.

Finally, we consider the effect upon the consumption level of variations in the riskiness and in the expected rate of return of capital (given capital and nonwage income). Not surprisingly, the direction of effect of both are unpredictable without knowledge of the type of utility function; the familiar conflict between substitution and income effects applies as much to risk as to the rate of return. Two closely related utility functions give opposite results. But it is interesting that risk always "opposes" return. Where increase of the rate of return raises (reduces) the propensity to consume, an increase in risk reduces (raises) it; and where return has no effect, neither does risk.

THE BEHAVIOR OF CAPITAL

Capital is treated as homogeneous in the sense that each unit of the asset experiences the same rate of return.[3]

The individual's consumption opportunities occur at discrete, equally spaced points in time. These points divide the lifetime of the consumer into N periods. The state of the system at the beginning of each period, $n = 1, 2, \ldots, N$, is described by the variable x_n, the amount of capital then on hand. At this time the individual chooses to consume some amount c_n of this capital.

The unconsumed capital is left to grow at a rate which is not then known. In addition to the capital growth, the individual receives an amount, y, of nonwealth income at the end of the period. This income is the same each period. Consequently the amount of capital available for consumption in the next period is given by the difference equation

$$x_{n+1} = \beta_n(x_n - c_n) + y, \qquad x_1 = k, \tag{1}$$

where $\beta_n - 1$ is the rate of return earned on capital in the nth period.

We shall assume that the random variables β_n are independent and drawn from the same probability distribution. There are m possible rates of return, $0 \leqslant \beta_i$, $i = 1, 2, \ldots, m$. The probability of the ith rate of return will be denoted by p_i (the same from period to period). In addition we shall assume that $\bar{\beta} = \sum_1^m p_i \beta_i > 1$ so that the consumer expects capital to be productive. However, $\sum_1^m p_i(\beta_i - \bar{\beta})^2 > 0$, and so the realized return may differ from the expected one.

THE UTILITY FUNCTION

This model postulates a consumer who obeys the axioms of the von Neumann-Morgenstern utility theory. His consumption strategy (or policy) can therefore be viewed as maximizing the expected value of utility, which is determined up to an increasing linear transformation.

Second, we suppose that the lifetime utility associated with any consumption history is a continuously differentiable function of the amount consumed at the beginning of each period.

The lifetime utility function is assumed to be of the independent and additive form

$$U = \sum_{i=1}^{N} \alpha^{n-1} u(c_n), \qquad 0 < \alpha \leq 1. \tag{2}$$

---

[3] Alternatively, capital might have been envisioned more like identical female rabbits. In any short time period, some units of the asset would multiply while others would not. This might be termed subjective or *ex ante* homogeneity.

The implications of this functional form are several. Preferences for the consumption "chances" or distributions of any period are invariant to the consumption levels befalling the individual in other periods (separability). Preferences among consumption subhistories in the future are independent of the age of the individual (stationarity). Preference for a consumption strategy is independent of or unaffected by any serial correlation in the random consumption sequence associated with that strategy (independence).[4]

The same axioms which yield the von Neumann-Morgenstern utility indicators also imply that $U(c_1, \ldots, c_N)$ is bounded from above and below.[5] Consequently $u(c_n)$ is also a bounded function. Let $\bar{u}$ and $\underline{u}$ denote the upper and lower bounds of $u(c_n)$, respectively.

Finally, we postulate that the individual strictly prefers more consumption to less (monotonicity) and that he is strictly averse to risk (concavity). The latter means that for every pair of consumption histories $(c_1, \ldots, c_N)$ and $(c_1{}^o, \ldots, c_N{}^o)$ to which he is not indifferent, he will strictly prefer the certainty of the compromise history $\theta c + (1 - \theta)c^o$ to the mixed prospect offering him the history c with probability θ and the history c^o with probability $1 - \theta, 0 < \theta < 1$. It follows trivially that $u(c_n)$ is a strictly increasing and strictly concave function.

DERIVATION OF THE FUNCTIONAL EQUATIONS

We seek the consumption strategy (or, equivalently, policy)—denoted by the sequence of functions $\{c_n(x)\}$ for $x \geqslant 0$, $n = 1, 2, \ldots, N$—which maximizes expected lifetime utility:

$$J_N(c) = \exp_{\beta} U \qquad (3)$$

subject to the relation of equation 1. Notice that the optimal c_n, $n = 1, \ldots, N$, will be a stochastic rather than a predetermined function of n.

To treat this variational problem we turn to the technique of dynamic programming [3]. Observing that the maximum expected value of lifetime utility depends only upon the number of stages in the process and the

---

[4] However the necessary and sufficient conditions for independence of utilities when choice takes place under uncertainty have yet to be investigated. The independence of utilities when choice takes place in an environment of certainty has been axiomatized by Debreu [6]. The meaning of additivity with a variable utility discount factor and an infinite number of periods has also been investigated by Koopmans [9].

[5] A proof of boundedness may be found in [1] and [5]. The proof uses the "continuity axiom" and a generalization of the St. Petersburg game, the idea for which Arrow [1] credits to K. Menger.

initial capital, k, we define the function

$$w_N(k) = \max J_N(c) \tag{4}$$

where the maximum is taken over all admissible policies. The function defined may be interpreted as the utility-of-wealth function of the optimizing consumer having N periods of life remaining.

Next one reduces the problem with N decision variables to a sequence of N problems, each involving only one policy variable, the decision which must be taken at the current moment. This approach leads to the following functional equations:[6]

$$w_N(x) = \max_{0 \le c \le x} \left\{ u(c) + \alpha \sum_{i=1}^{m} p_i w_{N-1}[\beta_i(x - c) + y] \right\}, \qquad N \ge 2, \tag{5}$$

and

$$w_1(x) = \max_{0 \le c \le x} u(c) \tag{6}$$

which defines the utility of wealth in the single stage process. Without a subscript, the symbol c shall always denote the value of consumption in the first period of the (not necessarily original) multistage process. Similarly x shall denote capital at the start of whatever process is being considered.

PROPERTIES OF THE OPTIMAL CONSUMPTION POLICY

A number of standard results follow from this model: First, the optimal consumption strategy is unique; the optimum value of c_n is a unique function of x_n for every n.

The proof consists of showing that the utility of wealth function is strictly concave if the utility of consumption function is strictly concave; therefore the maximand in each period is a strictly concave function of current consumption, whence the maximizing consumption level is unique.[7]

---

[6] The argument starts with the observation that with the elapse of each period the individual is confronted with another multistage decision problem which differs only in having one less stage and, in general, a different initial capital. By the "principle of optimality" [3], if the individual's consumption strategy is optimal for the original N-stage process then that part of the strategy relating to the last N-1 stages must also constitute a complete optimal strategy with respect to the new N-1 stage process. This principle, equation 1, the additive utility function of equation 3 and the definition of equation 4 combine to yield the sequence of equations in the unknown utility of wealth functions in equations 5 and 6.

[7] Readers who are unfamiliar with this type of proof may wish to consult [3]. Proofs of the result above and of the other results stated but not proved in this section can be found in an earlier version of this paper (same title) by the author, published as Cowles Foundation Discussion Paper No. 109.

Second, consumption is an increasing function of capital and age. The latter result depends upon the further assumption made now that $\alpha \bar{\beta} > 1$. It will become clear that this inequality is also a necessary condition for positive accumulation of capital.

The proof is rather involved and is omitted here. It can be shown that if $\alpha \bar{\beta} > u'(0)/u'(y)$ then, with $N \geq 2$ periods remaining, consumption is the following function of capital:

$$c = \begin{cases} 0, & 0 \leq x \leq \bar{x}_N, \\ c_N(x), & x \geq \bar{x}_N, \end{cases} \tag{7}$$

where $c_N(x) = 0$ at $x = \bar{x}_N$, $c_N'(x) > 0$, and $c_N(x) < x$. The function $c_N(x)$ represents the interior portion of the solution where consumption is not constrained by the nonnegativity requirement.

It can be further shown that the marginal utility of wealth declines with age and capital and that the "consumption function" in equation 7 shifts leftward and upward as age increases:

$$w_1'(x) < w_2'(x) < \cdots < w_N'(x) < \ldots,$$
$$c_2(x) > \cdots > c_N(x) > \ldots, \tag{8}$$
$$0 < \bar{x}_2 < \cdots < \bar{x}_N < \cdots.$$

Of course, when $N = 1$, $c = x$.

In the other case, where $\alpha \bar{\beta} \leq u'(0)/u'(y)$, the constraint that consumption cannot exceed capital becomes binding for $N = 2$ and possibly for larger N—when capital is sufficiently small. If there is a value of $x \geq 0$ for which $c_N(x) = x$ then, denoting this value by $\hat{x}_N$, we obtain

$$c = \begin{cases} x, & 0 \leq x \leq \hat{x}_N, \\ c_N(x), & x \geq \hat{x}_N. \end{cases}$$

Again, as age increases, N decreases, the marginal utility of wealth function decreases and the consumption function shifts upward. Consequently the intersection where $c = x$ shifts rightward:

$$\hat{x}_2 > \cdots > \hat{x}_N \geq 0.$$

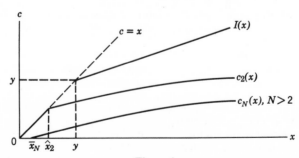

Figure 1

A typical possibility is graphed in Figure 1. This consumption function is of the second type. As N becomes small, the consumption schedule shifts upward. When $N = 2$, the function intersects the $c = x$ line. When $N = 1$, $c = x$ at all x.

The $I(x)$ function is defined in the next section.

CONDITIONS FOR EXPECTED ACCUMULATION

The preceding theorems confirm our expectations about the qualitative behavior of optimal consumption. They do not go far enough to permit inferences about the behavior of capital as a function of age and initial capital. One might ask if the model generates "hump saving" [8, 12], so important in the theory of aggregate capital formation. The "hump saver" saves when he is young and dissaves as he grows older. Therefore we ask: Can one find a value of N sufficiently large to induce the individual to save—more precisely, to cause the expected value of his subsequent capital to exceed the value of his present capital?[8]

Let us define "expected income," $I(x)$, to be the amount of consumption such that the expected value of capital in the next period equals present capital. Now $\exp x_{n+1} = y + \bar{\beta}(x_n - c_n)$. Expected stationarity, $\exp x_{n+1} = x_n$, implies $c_n = (y/\bar{\beta}) + [(\bar{\beta} - 1)/\bar{\beta}]x_n = I(x)$. Expected income is displayed as a function of capital in Figure 1. Our question is then whether, in the limit, as N approaches infinity, $c_N(x) < I(x)$ for all $x \geq y$.

The answer is clear cut when capital is riskless. Then $\beta_i = \beta$ for all i and we obtain the following recurrence relation in the limiting utility of wealth function:

$$w(x) = \max_c \{u(c) + \alpha w[\beta(x - c) + y]\}. \tag{9}$$

The maximum is an interior one for $x \geq y$ so that $c(x)$ defined by

$$u'(c) - \alpha\beta w'[\beta(x - c) + y] = 0 \tag{10}$$

determines c as a function of x.

Differentiating totally with respect to x gives

$$w'(x) = \alpha\beta w'[\beta(x - c) + y] + c'(x)\{u'(c) - \alpha\beta w'[\beta(x - c) + y]\} \tag{11}$$

$$= \alpha\beta w'[\beta(x - c) + y] \qquad \text{(by equation 10)}.$$

Since $w'(x)$ is monotone decreasing, equation 11 implies that $x_{n+1} > x_n$ if and only if $\alpha\beta > 1$. Therefore, denoting the limiting consumption function by $c(x)$, $c(x) < I(x)$ for all $x \geq y$.

---

[8] Of course, an affirmative answer would not be very interesting if the necessary value of N exceeds human life expectancy!

This simple result fails to extend to risky capital. When $\beta_i \neq \bar{\beta}$ for some i, equation 11 becomes

$$w'(x) = \alpha \sum p_i \beta_i w'[\beta_i(x - c) + y]. \tag{12}$$

From equation 12 no general conclusions concerning the conditions for expected capital growth can be drawn. Of course capital cannot be expected to grow very long unless $\bar{\beta} > 1$. But $\alpha\bar{\beta} > 1$ is insufficient to guarantee "expected" capital growth.[9]

It is clear that the critical value which $\alpha\bar{\beta}$ must exceed if capital growth is to be expected will depend upon the distribution of β_i and the shape of the marginal utility function $w'(x)$. The only practical procedure here is to investigate the implications for capital growth of particular classes of utility functions.

IMPLICATIONS OF SELECTED MONOMIAL UTILITY FUNCTIONS

In this section we investigate the implications of certain types of monomial utility functions for the consumption function and for the expected path of capital.

We consider first the utility function[10]

$$u(c_n) = \bar{u} - \lambda c_n^{-\gamma}, \qquad \bar{u}, \gamma, \lambda > 0. \tag{13}$$

Solving successively for the sequence of unknown functions $\{w_n(x)\}$, $N = 1, 2, \ldots$, yields

$$w_N(x) = \bar{u}(1 + \alpha + \cdots + \alpha^{N-1}) - \lambda(\alpha b^{-\gamma})^{N-1}[1 + (\alpha b^{-\gamma})^{\frac{-1}{\gamma+1}} +$$
$$\cdots + (\alpha b^{-\gamma})^{\frac{-(N-1)}{\gamma+1}}]^{\gamma+1}[x + (b^{-1} + \cdots + b^{-(N-1)}y)]^{-\gamma} \tag{14}$$

and

$$c_N(x) = \frac{(\alpha b^{-\gamma})^{\frac{-(N-1)}{\gamma-1}}}{1 + (\alpha b^{-\gamma})^{\frac{-1}{\gamma+1}} + \cdots + (\alpha b^{-\gamma})^{\frac{-(N-1)}{\gamma+1}}} [x + (1 + b + \cdots + b^{N-2})y] \tag{15}$$

---

[9] Several plausible cases are the following. First, there may be no capital level at which the expected returns to saving repay the risks. Or it may be that the individual can "afford" the risks of net expected saving only when capital exceeds a critical value at which $c(x)$ intersects $I(x)$ from above. In the opposite case, additional wealth is worth the risks only as long as capital falls short of the level where $c(x)$ intersects $I(x)$ from below.

[10] The function (equation 13) fails to have the boundedness property assumed up to this point and thus it contradicts the "continuity axiom" mentioned before. Whatever the merits of that axiom, the function has received sufficient study in the context of deterministic models [4, 12, 13] to deserve our attention here.

where

$$b = (\sum p_i \beta_i^{-\gamma})^{\frac{-1}{\gamma}}.$$

If the reader applies equation 15 to $c_{N+1}(x)$ and uses equation 14 he will obtain an expression for $w_{N+1}(x)$ having the same form as equation 14. Note also that if $\alpha = \beta_i = 1$ for all i, formula 15 calls for consuming a fraction $1/N$ of the individual's net worth, $x + (N-1)y$.

Provided that $\alpha b^{-\gamma} < 1$ (for which $\alpha < 1$, $\beta > 1$, $\gamma > 0$ is sufficient in the certainty case), the expressions in equations 14 and 15 converge as N approaches infinity, giving the solutions to the "infinite stage" process:

$$w(x) = \frac{\bar{u}}{1 - \alpha} - \lambda \left[\frac{(\alpha b^{-\gamma})^{\frac{-1}{\gamma+1}}}{(\alpha b^{-\gamma})^{\frac{-1}{\gamma+1}} - 1} \right]^{\gamma+1} \left(x + \frac{y}{b-1} \right)^{-\gamma} \tag{16}$$

and

$$c(x) = [1 - (\alpha b^{-\gamma})^{\frac{1}{\gamma+1}}]\left(x + \frac{y}{b-1} \right). \tag{17}$$

This limiting consumption function is useful as an approximation to $c_N(x)$ for large N.

Properties of the Consumption Function

A number of properties of the consumption functions (equations 15 and 17) can be observed immediately. First, the consumption function is linear homogeneous in capital and nonwealth income. Of two households, both having identical utility functions like equation 13, if one household enjoys twice the capital and nonwealth income of the other, it will also consume twice as much.

Second, consumption is linear in capital and nonwealth income. The coefficient of wealth, $\partial c / \partial x$, may be called the marginal propensity to consume (MPC) out of wealth.

The convergence condition $\alpha b^{-\gamma} < 1$ insures that $\partial c / \partial x > 0$. And $\partial c / \partial x < 1$ for all finite α, $b > 0$.

The coefficient $\partial c / \partial y$ may be called the MPC out of "permanent," sure, (nonwealth) income. Clearly $\partial c / \partial y > 0$ if and only if $b > 1$ (given the convergence condition). What can be said concerning this condition? When capital is risky (that is, when $\beta_i \neq \bar{\beta}$ for some i), then $b < \bar{\beta}$.[11] Therefore the postulate $\bar{\beta} > 1$ does not imply $b > 1$. We see thus that

---

[11] To see this, draw a diagram showing $\beta_i^{-\gamma}$ as a function of β_i. Since $\beta^{-\gamma}$ is a convex function of β, $\sum p_i \beta_i^{-\gamma} > \bar{\beta}^{-\gamma}$ whence $b = (\sum p_i \beta_i^{-\gamma})^{-1/\gamma} < \bar{\beta}$.

Keynes' "psychological law" stating that MPC > 0 applies only if capital has a positive net expected productivity and only if capital is sufficiently productive at that. However, we do observe positive MPC and if we were to fit this model to data we should presumably find that $b > 1$. At any rate, we shall assume $b > 1$ unless we indicate the contrary.

Is the MPC also less than one, as Keynes had it? Of course, with $b > 1$, the MPC out of an income stream beginning sufficiently far in the future is bound to be less than one. Usually one considers the effect on (immediate) consumption of immediate income. To do that in the present model—where the paycheck is received at the end of the period—suppose capital increases by the same amount as y, as if last period's paycheck were increased too. Is this MPC out of "immediate," nonwealth income smaller than one?

This MPC is

$$\left[1 - (\alpha b^{-\gamma})^{\frac{1}{\gamma+1}}\right]\frac{b}{b-1}$$

and is smaller than one if and only if $\alpha b > 1$.

This is an interesting condition. This same condition, we show now, is necessary and sufficient for positive capital accumulation at all possible values of income and capital.

Note first that $c(x) < I(x)$ for all $x \geq y$—causing the expected growth of capital—if and only if $c(y) < y$ and $c'(x) \leq I'(x)$. Now $c(y)/y$ equals the MPC just analyzed so that $\alpha b > 1$ means $c(y) < y$. The condition that $c'(x) < I'(x)$ is

$$1 - (\alpha b^{-\gamma})^{\frac{1}{\gamma+1}} < \frac{\bar{\beta} - 1}{\bar{\beta}}$$

for which $\alpha b > 1$ is sufficient (although unnecessary).[12]

The significance of this exercise lies in the possibility that $1 < b \leq 1/\alpha$, in which case capital will be expected to grow only if it exceeds a certain threshold. Suppose $\alpha b = 1$. Then all nonwealth income is consumed and there is "net expected saving"—that is, $c(x) < I(x)$—only if $x > y$, i.e., only if the individual starts the period with some capital over and above his just-received wage of the previous period. Otherwise there will be no "hump saving" (in this case), even though $\bar{\beta} > 1/\alpha$.

A comparison of the MPC's leads to an interesting finding: The greater nonwealth income, y, as a proportion of total expected income, $I(x)$, the larger is the ratio of consumption to expected income. This is because the MPC out of (sure, immediate) nonwealth income, $c'(x)b/(b - 1)$, is greater

---

[12] Note that all these conditions reduce to $b > 1$ if $\alpha = 1$.

than the consumption effect of that increase in current capital which is required to raise expected income by one dollar. Writing

$$x = \frac{\bar{\beta}}{\bar{\beta} - 1}\left[I(x) - \frac{y}{\bar{\beta}}\right],$$

we see that the latter consumption effect is $c'(x)\bar{\beta}/(\bar{\beta} - 1)$. Recalling that $b < \bar{\beta}$, we find that "sure" income has the stronger effect. This implies that, among households who have like utility functions and who face the same capital growth process, those whose expected income depends relatively heavily on risky capital will be observed to be relatively thrifty. This may help to explain why wealthy heirs, farmers, and certain other groups save a comparatively large proportion of their incomes. Further, the result suggests that capital income and labor income ought not to be aggregated in econometric analyses of consumption.

Variations of Risk and Return

The last question taken up here relates to the effect upon consumption of variations in the riskiness and expected return from capital. Since the consumption function is linear homogeneous we can write

$$c = \frac{\partial c}{\partial x} x + \frac{\partial c}{\partial y} y,$$

whence these variations influence consumption through the marginal propensities, which are a function of b (and independent of x and y).

Let us consider first the effect of variations in risk and return on the value of b.

An increase in the expected return on capital is defined here as a uniform shift in the probability distribution of β_i which leaves all its moments the same except the mean, $\bar{\beta}$. Such a shift *increases* $\bar{\beta}$ and b.

What effect has risk on the value of b? When capital is risky, $b < \bar{\beta}$. Thus the presence of risk (as distinct from marginal increases therein) *decreases* b.

Hence, capital's (net) productivity and its riskiness affect consumption in the opposite direction.

A second kind of risk effect results from a change in the degree of risk, somehow measured.

A probability distribution which offers a simple measure of risk is the uniform or rectangular distribution. This is a two-parameter distribution with mean $\bar{\beta}$ and range $2h$. The variance is $h^2/3$ so that h is the measure of risk.

We show now that increases in h reduce b so that the "structural" and "marginal" effect of risk on b are in the same direction. Noting that $db/dh < 0$ means $db^{-\gamma}/dh > 0$, we examine $b^{-\gamma}$.

By definition of b,

$$b^{-\gamma} = \int_{\bar{\beta}-h}^{\bar{\beta}+h} \beta^{-\gamma} \left(\frac{1}{2h}\right) d\beta.$$

Evaluating the integral we find

$$b^{-\gamma} = \frac{1}{(1-\gamma)2h} [(\bar{\beta} + h)^{1-\gamma} - (\bar{\beta} - h)^{1-\gamma}].$$

Differentiating with respect to h yields

$$\frac{db^{-\gamma}}{dh} = \frac{1}{2(1-\gamma)h^2} [(\bar{\beta} - h)^{-\gamma}(\bar{\beta} - \gamma h) - (\bar{\beta} + h)^{-\gamma}(\bar{\beta} + \gamma h)].$$

Assuming $\gamma > 1$, $db^{-\gamma}/dh > 0$ if and only if

$$\frac{\bar{\beta} - \gamma h}{\bar{\beta} + \gamma h} < \left(\frac{\bar{\beta} - h}{\bar{\beta} + h}\right)^{\gamma}.$$

β equal to zero is excluded, for otherwise b is not defined. Consequently $h < \bar{\beta}$ and the right hand side of the inequality must be positive. But so may be the left hand side (if $\gamma < \bar{\beta}/h$). The following shows the inequality is satisfied for all $\gamma > 1$.

Dividing both sides of the inequality by $\bar{\beta}$, and defining $z = h/\bar{\beta}$, we obtain

$$\frac{1 - \gamma z}{1 + \gamma z} < \left(\frac{1 - z}{1 + z}\right)^{\gamma}$$

which, taking the logarithm of both sides, we find to be satisfied if and only if

$$\log(1 - \gamma z) - \log(1 + \gamma z) < \gamma[\log(1 - z) - \log(1 + z)].$$

Expansion of the logarithmic functions into Taylor's series yields

$$\left(-\gamma z - \frac{(\gamma z)^2}{2} - \frac{(\gamma z)^3}{3} - \cdots\right) - \left(\gamma z - \frac{(\gamma z)^2}{2} + \frac{(\gamma z)^3}{3} - \cdots\right)$$

$$< \gamma\left[\left(-z - \frac{z^2}{2} - \frac{z^3}{3} - \cdots\right) - \left(z - \frac{z^2}{2} + \frac{z^3}{3} - \cdots\right)\right]$$

whence

$$\left(\gamma z + \frac{(\gamma z)^3}{3} + \frac{(\gamma z)^5}{5} + \cdots\right) > \left(\gamma z + \frac{\gamma z^3}{3} + \frac{\gamma z^5}{5} + \cdots\right).$$

This inequality can be seen to hold for all $\gamma > 1$. Therefore a marginal increase in risk reduces the value of b. Recalling that an increase in the expected return increases b, we note that changes in risk and return have opposite effects on consumption.

We consider now the effect of a change in b upon consumption. Does the substitution effect dominate here—so that a rise in b encourages saving and reduces consumption? Or does the income effect dominate?

Turning first to $\partial c/\partial x$, we see from equation 17 that an increase in b raises $\partial c/\partial x$.

Turning next to $\partial c/\partial y$, we note from equation 17 that $\partial c/\partial y = 1/(b-1) \cdot \partial c/\partial x$. It would appear that a rise in b might reduce $\partial c/\partial y$, because of the downward recapitalization (using $1/(b-1)$) of the y stream, if b were sufficiently small ($b > 1$). It can be shown that $d(\partial c/\partial y)/db \geq 0$ if and only if $(\alpha b^{-\gamma})^{-1/(\gamma+1)} \leq (1 + b\gamma)/(1 + \gamma)$. If $\alpha = 1$ this is satisfied for all $b > 1$; otherwise it is satisfied only for values of b above some value $\hat{b} > 1$.

Thus, if there is no utility discount, the income effect dominates here; then a rise in the expected return on capital weakens the incentive to save and an increase in risk compels more saving in order to reduce the insecurity of the future. But if the future is discounted, the individual feels "poorer"; then a rise in the expected return may encourage saving up to a point, after which the income effect dominates; this point comes sooner the smaller is y. In either case, risk and return variations have opposing qualitative effects upon consumption.

Other Utility Function

To see that the implications of the utility function (equation 13) for the effects of variations in risk and return are not general, one has only to modify the utility function thus:

$$u(c_N) = \lambda c^\gamma, \qquad \lambda > 0, 0 < \gamma < 1. \qquad (18)$$

All of equations 14 through 17 continue to hold with the difference that λ and γ are then replaced by $-\lambda$ and $-\gamma$, respectively. Hence the limiting consumption function is

$$c(x) = \left[1 - (\alpha b^\gamma)^{\frac{1}{1-\gamma}}\right]\left(x + \frac{y}{b-1}\right) \qquad (19)$$

where $b^\gamma = \Sigma\, p_i \beta_i^\gamma$.

An increase in $\bar{\beta}$, other moments of the distribution unchanged, will increase b.

Once again the effect of risk is easy to ascertain. Since β^γ is a concave function of β, $\Sigma\, p_i \beta_i^\gamma < \bar{\beta}^\gamma$ whence $b = (\Sigma\, p_i \beta_i^\gamma) < \bar{\beta}$.

Turning finally to the effect of a marginal increase in risk upon b, we find that the "natural" result $db^\gamma/dh < 0$ (meaning that global and marginal risk effects have like signs) depends upon the condition $(\bar{\beta} - \gamma h)/(\bar{\beta} + \gamma h) > [(\bar{\beta} - h)/(\bar{\beta} + h)]^\gamma$, which is satisfied for all $\gamma < 1$.

Once again, risk and return work in opposite directions.

Consider now the effect of an increase in b upon consumption. Unlike the previous example, $\partial c/\partial x$ decreases with increasing b, as can be seen from equation 19; the substitution effect dominates the income effect. And, as equation 19 clearly shows, $\partial c/\partial y$ is also a decreasing function of b for all values of $b > 1$; the downward recapitalization of future income merely reinforces the substitution effect against the weaker income effect.

Thus an increase in expected return encourages saving while an increase of the riskiness of capital discourages saving. The implications of the utility function (equation 18) are essentially opposite to those of the utility function (equation 13).

To what can this contrast of results be attributed? The utility function is determined only up to a linear transformation, meaning that we can set $\bar{u} = 0$ in equation 13 without effect. Doing this reveals that both equations 13 and 18 are constant-elasticity utility functions with elasticity parameter γ. The income effect dominates (unless b is small and y large) in the elastic case and the substitution effect dominates in the inelastic case.

Finally we examine a utility function that can produce some odd results, the logarithmic function in equation 20:

$$u(c_N) = \log c_N. \tag{20}$$

It appears to be impossible to solve for $c_N(x)$ explicitly in terms of x and y except in the case $y = 0$. Then we easily find

$$w_N(x) = (1 + \alpha + \cdots + \alpha^{N-1}) \log x + v(\theta, \alpha, N) \tag{21}$$

where $v(\theta, \alpha, N)$ depends only upon the parameters, denoted by θ, of the probability distribution of β_i, α and N, and not upon x.

Also

$$c_N(x) = \frac{x}{1 + \alpha + \cdots + \alpha^{N-1}}. \tag{22}$$

When the utility function is logarithmic, the optimum consumption rate is independent both of the expected return and riskiness of capital. Consumption is linear homogeneous in capital. As N is increased, the consumption function flattens asymptotically until, in the limit,

$$c(x) = (1 - \alpha)x. \tag{23}$$

A limiting function exists only if $\alpha < 1$.[13]

---

[13] For certain utility functions the existence of a limiting solution does not require $\alpha < 1$. Ramsey [12] argued that boundedness was sufficient but a condition on the elasticity or rate of approach to the upper bound is also necessary, at least in models not containing risk. Samuelson and Solow [14] assume that the upper utility bound is attained at a finite consumption rate, which is not a necessary condition.

REFERENCES

1. Arrow, K. J.: *Bernoulli Utility Indicators for Distributions Over Arbitrary Spaces*, Technical Report No. 57 of the Department of Economics, Stanford University, July, 1958.
2. Beckmann, M. J.: "A Dynamic Programming Model of the Consumption Function," Cowles Foundation Discussion Paper No. 69, March 1959.
3. Bellman, R.: *Dynamic Programming*, Princeton: Princeton University Press, 1957.
4. Champernowne, D. G.: Review of "A Theory of the Consumption Function" by Milton Friedman, *Journal of the Royal Statistical Society*, Series A, Vol. 121, Part I, 1958.
5. Chernoff, H., and L. Moses: *Elementary Decision Theory*, New York: John Wiley and Sons, 1959.
6. Debreu, G.: "Topological Methods in Cardinal Utility Theory," *Mathematical Methods in the Social Sciences*, Stanford: Stanford University Press, 1960.
7. Friedman, M.: *A Theory of the Consumption Function*, Princeton: Princeton University Press, 1957.
8. Graaff, J. de V.: "Mr. Harrod on Hump Saving," *Economica*, February, 1950, pp. 81–90.
9. Koopmans, T. C.: "Stationary Ordinal Utility and Impatience," *Econometrica*, April, 1960, pp. 287–309.
10. Markowitz, H. M.: *Portfolio Selection*, New York: John Wiley and Sons, 1959.
11. Modigliani, F., and R. Brumberg: "Utility Analysis and the Consumption Function: An Interpretation of Cross-Section Data," in K. Kurihara, ed., *Post-Keynesian Economics*, New Brunswick, New Jersey: Rutgers University Press, 1954.
12. Ramsey, F. P.: "A Mathematical Theory of Saving," *Economic Journal*, December, 1928, pp. 543–559.
13. Robertson, D. H.: *Lectures on Economic Principles*, Vol. II, Ch. 5, pp. 69–87.
14. Samuelson, P. A., and R. M. Solow: "A Complete Capital Model Involving Heterogeneous Capital Goods," *Quarterly Journal of Economics*, November, 1956, pp. 537–562.

7

*Estimating the Utility of Wealth from Call Options Data**

RICHARD N. ROSETT

THE MOSTELLER-NOGEE EXPERIMENTAL MEASUREMENT OF UTILITY

Following the model of Friedman and Savage,[1] Mosteller and Nogee[2] in their classic experiment presented subjects with choices of the following sort:

Alternative I: risk neither loss nor gain,

Alternative II: risk the loss of 5 cents with probability $(1 - p)$ or the gain of X cents with probability p.

A subject who was offered this choice repeatedly was assumed to prefer alternative I if he chose it more often, and to prefer II if he chose it more often. If he chose the two equally often, he was assumed to be indifferent

* The research for this paper was begun with the support of a Ford Foundation grant to the Department of Economics, University of Rochester. The major part of the work was carried out under a grant from the National Science Foundation. The final revision was done at the Econometric Institute, Netherlands School of Economics, where the author was a guest during his tenure as a National Science Foundation Senior Post-Doctoral Fellow. Among those who were kind enough to read and comment on this paper, the heaviest debt of gratitude is due to Harry Grubert, whose critical analysis was responsible for the removal of several troublesome errors, and to Fritz Holte.

[1] Milton Friedman and L. J. Savage, "The Utility Analysis of Choices Involving Risk," *Journal of Political Economy*, Vol. LVI (August 1948), pp. 279–304.
[2] Frederick Mosteller and Philip Nogee, "An Experimental Measurement of Utility," *Journal of Political Economy*, LIX (October 1951), pp. 371–404.

between them. Holding p fixed at some value, p^*, the subject was offered various values of X so as to determine the particular value, X^*, for which the subject was indifferent between I and II. This determined one point on the utility function.

Let

$$U(-5) = -1,$$

and

$$U(0) = 0.$$

This is equivalent to selecting the constant term and scale of the utility function. Having determined X^* such that the subject is indifferent between I and II for the given value of p^*, solve the equation

$$(1 - p^*)U(-5) + p^*U(X^*) = U(0)$$

for $U(X^*)$. This gives

$$U(X^*) = \frac{1 - p^*}{p^*}.$$

Additional points on the utility function are found by varying p and repeating the procedure.

Except for reasons of simplicity, nothing prevented the experimenters from using a gamble for alternative I instead of a sure thing. They could have selected two sums of money, Y and Z, and defined $U(Y) = -1$ and $U(Z) = 0$ (where $Y < Z$). Fixing p_1, p_2, p_{11}, and p_{21}, they could have determined, experimentally, sums of money X_1 and X_2 such that

$$p_1 U(Y) + (1 - p_1)U(Z) = p_{11}U(X_1) + (1 - p_{11})U(X_2)$$
$$p_2 U(Y) + (1 - p_2)U(Z) = p_{12}U(X_1) + (1 - p_{12})U(X_2).$$

These equations could be solved for $U(X_1)$ and $U(X_2)$.

If the general form of the utility function is specified to be a polynomial of degree n, its parameters can be determined provided it is possible to find, for each parameter to be determined, a pair of probability distributions, f_t and g_t (where t ranges over the number of parameters to be determined), such that the subject is indifferent between them.

Write

$$\int f_t(X)U(X)\, dx = \int g_t(X)U(X)\, dx \quad (t = 1, \ldots, n - 1).$$

Select zero as the constant term of U and select the scale so that the coefficient of the linear term is equal to one. Then

$$\mu_{f_t}{}^1 + \sum_{i=1}^{n-1} \mu_{f_t}{}^{i+1} a_i = \mu_{g_t}{}^1 + \sum_{i=1}^{n-1} \mu_{g_t}{}^{i+1} a_i \quad (t = 1, \ldots, n - 1)$$

where $\mu_{f_t}{}^i$ is the ith moment around the origin of the distribution, f_t. These $n - 1$ equations can be solved for the parameters a_i.

Of course it is unlikely that observations obtained in such an experiment will exactly fit the postulated function, and if more than $n - 1$ comparisons are made it is necessary to use some statistical technique for determining the function. Mosteller and Nogee, in determining seven points on the utility function, offered each subject 686 choices—168 for each point. For each value of p (seven were used to obtain seven points) seven different values of X (judiciously selected) were offered. Each value of X was offered 14 times. It was found that for some value of X, X_L, the gamble was selected less than 50% of the time, and that for the next larger value of X, X_H, the gamble was selected more than 50% of the time. Linear interpolation was used to find X^*, the value of X for which the gamble would be selected exactly 50% of the time. Thus, of the 168 offers made in determining a single point on the utility function, only 28 (X_L and X_H were each offered 14 times) actually entered into the estimate of X and hence into the estimate of the point on the utility function. It will be shown later how it is possible to use all available information in the determination of the utility function.

THE MARKOWITZ MODIFICATION OF FRIEDMAN-SAVAGE

In discussing possible criticisms of their work, Mosteller and Nogee deal with the question of the triviality of the sums involved in their experiment. The question of triviality of sums should really be regarded as two questions:

1. Are the sums involved so small that, over the range of possible gains and losses, changes in the level of utility cannot be detected?

2. Are the sums involved so small that during the period of the experiment uncontrolled variation in the wealth of the subjects is of an order of magnitude equal to or greater than that of the sums offered in the experiment?

Regarding the first question, Mosteller and Nogee have provided experimental evidence to the contrary. The curves show considerable variation in utility over ranges as small as 50 cents. This fact unfortunately raises serious problems of the following sort: Subject B-IV was found to associate 10 utiles with the sum of 50 cents. Suppose we define his utility at the beginning of some session to be zero utiles. The first gamble offered is attractive and he accepts, winning 50 cents as a consequence. If he is now at 10 utiles, Mosteller and Nogee should account for that in interpreting the results of the next offer. But they don't. They assume that he is still at zero utiles.

The question of whether Mosteller and Nogee were measuring the utility of income or of wealth might be raised here, but it would only confuse the issue. They were measuring the utility of whatever they were offering; the thing they were offering was a chance to win X cents. Starting from zero and having won X cents is the subject still at zero utiles, or is he at some higher utility level?

The 1952 paper by Harry Markowitz[3] offers an interpretation of the Mosteller-Nogee results. Put most simply, Markowitz suggested that the utility function is just a device for explaining and predicting responses to choices involving risk. As wealth increases, Markowitz required that the utility function satisfy certain criteria based on casually observed gambling behavior. These criteria led him to a specification of the slope of the utility function. It is possible to raise equally plausible casual arguments against the slope specified by Markowitz, but to do so here would be to digress. Most significant is the fact that Markowitz proposed a departure from the traditional idea of a utility function. One would ordinarily mean, when speaking of a utility of wealth, a function which enables us to predict the choice between gambles *at any level of wealth*. The Markowitz utility function enables us to predict choices only at the present level of wealth since changes in wealth will change the utility function. For a small change in wealth the change in the function is small and gambling behavior remains almost unchanged.

If Mosteller and Nogee were to argue that, over the experimental period, changes in wealth (both those due to the experiment and those which were uncontrolled) were so small that changes in the Markowitz utility function were trivial, they could interpret their function as one which will predict choices in situations involving risk, but which cannot be interpreted as giving the effect of changes in income or wealth. This interpretation also disposes of the second problem connected with triviality of sums. Except in the light of the Markowitz modification of Friedman-Savage, the Mosteller-Nogee experiment is extremely difficult to interpret. Given the modification, however, the experiment and its results make very good sense.

THE CALL OPTIONS MARKET AS A SOURCE OF DATA FOR ESTIMATING THE UTILITY OF WEALTH

According to the latest edition of the *Financial Handbook*

A "call is a contract whereby the holder gets the privilege of purchasing a given number of shares of a given stock from the maker within a certain time and at a certain price. It is purchased by those who hope to profit from a rise in the shares.[4]

---

[3] Harry Markowitz, "The Utility of Wealth," *Journal of Political Economy*, LX (April 1952), pp. 151–58.

[4] J. I. Boyer, editor, *Financial Handbook*, Roland Press, 1952, p. 93.

The following illustration of a call option transaction comes from a typical dealer's guide.

A call on 100 shares of *XYZ* at 52 for 90 days is purchased for $475. After 85 days, *XYZ* is selling at 68. The call is exercised and 100 *XYZ* is purchased for $5,200. On the same day 100 *XYZ* is sold in the open market for $6,800. Profit is $1,600 less the cost of the call. Profit on the investment of $475 is $1,125 (commissions and taxes not considered).

Dealer's guides list several uses to which call options might be put, but it is likely that almost all options are purchased for the purpose suggested in the last sentence of the definition above, speculation. This view is supported by a recent S.E.C. study of the options market.

> The brokers interviewed were unanimous in the opinion that the reason most persons bought options was the opportunity it afforded them for speculation on a small amount of capital. This was borne out by the fact that when an option holder exercises a call he usually resells the stock he has acquired immediately.[5]

This same study also revealed that, while the above quotation from the dealer's guide may be typical of dealers' guides, it is not typical of call buyers' experiences. Of 380.9 thousand shares covered by calls written in June 1959, only 42.7% were exercised. Of those exercised, the cost of the call was recovered in only 42.5%. The remaining 57.5% of calls exercised were unprofitable. Thus only 18.1% of all calls earned a profit for the purchaser. The expected return to a dollar invested in calls during the month covered by the study was −42¢.[6]

---

[5] Security and Exchange Commission, *Report on Put and Call Options*, August 1961, p. 77.

[6] The data used in my study were drawn from among all options sold through a single large brokerage firm during the years 1957–60. For the purpose of calculating average profitability of call options, all options written on the ten most frequently optioned stocks were used. These accounted for about 20% of all options sold by this firm during the period covered. The results were as follows: Of 118.2 thousand shares worth of options (about 1 thousand options) purchased during the years 1957–60, only 50.4 thousand were exercised. Generously assuming that stock called under an option was resold at the high on the day the call was exercised, the average loss was 37 cents per dollar invested. If stock, on the average, was sold at 25 cents below the day's high, the average loss was 40 cents. Among the next fifteen most popularly optioned stocks (about one thousand options), the proportion exercised was 0.41 or about the same as in the top ten. To have calculated the average profit on all twenty-five top stocks would have involved the key-punching of about 25 thousand stock prices. In view of the close agreement of the results already obtained and those of the S.E.C. the expenditure seemed unwarranted.

For the purposes of this paper it will be assumed that daily changes in the prices of stock listed on the New York Exchange are generated by a random process as follows:

$$P_t = P_{t-1}e^{X_t},$$

where P_t is the price of a stock on day t and where X_t is a normally distributed random variable with mean μ_t and standard deviation σ_t. It is also assumed that

$$E[(X_s - \mu_s)(X_t - \mu_t)] = 0. \qquad (s \neq t)$$

In other words the ratio P_t/P_{t-1} is a lognormal random process.[7]

If it were possible to obtain data regarding the decisions of stock purchasers confronted with choices between securities, a utility function could be estimated similar to that estimated by Mosteller and Nogee. The call option market is one possible source for such data.

The assumptions regarding the purchaser of call options are as follows:

1. Call options represent a small proportion of the investor's wealth. Wealth includes discounted future income as well as all other assets.

2. Other assets in the investor's portfolio are riskless. While this is certainly never the case, since even if all other assets are riskless the mortality table makes future income a risky asset, call options are so very risky that most other assets are comparatively riskless.

3. The investor behaves as if he knows the distribution of returns associated with the call option he buys. His knowledge is based on an estimate of μ_t and σ_t obtained from the recent performance of the market. Whether the investor actually knows μ_t and σ_t is beside the point. He is assumed to respond to changes in them as though he knew how they had changed. Evidence against this assumption could, for example, consist of data showing that the relation between μ_t and σ_t on one hand and the choice between holding or exercising an option on the other hand is either non-existent or unstable.

4. If a call option owner exercises his option at a profit, his level of customary wealth is increased, and in the neighborhood of the new level of wealth the shape of his utility function, as suggested by Markowitz, is very close to the shape of his utility function in the neighborhood of his former level of wealth. He will therefore purchase a new option very similar, from the point of view of the distribution of return, to the option he bought originally. On the date of purchase, an option is associated

---

[7] For evidence that this is not an unreasonable assumption, see Case M. Sprenkle, *Warrant Prices as Indicators of Expectations and Preferences*, Ph.D. dissertation, Yale, 1960, pp. 55–58.

with some distribution F_{t_0}. From day to day the distribution changes in a manner described below. The current distribution F_t is compared daily with F_{t_0} and, if F_t is preferred, the option is not exercised. If F_{t_0} is preferred, the option is exercised and replaced with one having a distribution as close as possible to F_{t_0}. This may require buying an option on a different stock from the one owned originally.

5. All investors' utility functions are of approximately the same shape, the scale on the horizontal axis varying directly with the level of wealth. Thus if the value of options purchased varies directly with wealth, the utility function can be determined by considering choices between a dollar's worth of old option and a dollar's worth of new option. The function is assumed to be approximately cubic.

For the purpose of estimating the coefficients of the utility function, the origin in each individual's wealth-utility plane is shifted so that the wealth, exclusive of options, is zero. Together with assumption 2, this simplifies what follows.
Define:

Π = the profit from a call option.

P_s = striking price (the price at which stock may be purchased with the option).

P_t = market price of the stock at time t.

$R_t = P_s/P_t$.

$D = \begin{cases} 0 \\ 1 \end{cases}$ indicates that a currently held dollar's worth of option $\begin{cases} \text{is not to be exercised.} \\ \text{is to be exercised.} \end{cases}$

Δw = the addition to other (nonoption) wealth if the currently held option is exercised.

$$Q\left(\frac{x-\mu}{\sigma}\right) = \int_{\frac{x-\mu}{\sigma}}^{+\infty} \tfrac{1}{2}e^{-t^2}\lambda t. \tag{1}$$

If the utility of wealth, w, is

$$U = \alpha_1 w + \alpha_2 w^2 + \alpha_3 w^3, \tag{2}$$

then the expected utility of an option involves $E(\Pi)$, $E(\Pi^2)$, and $E(\Pi^3)$.

$$E(\Pi) = P_t e^{\left(\mu_n + \frac{\sigma_n^2}{2}\right)} Q\left[\frac{\log_e R_t - (\mu_n + \sigma_n^2)}{\sigma_n}\right] - P_s Q\left(\frac{\log_e R_t - \mu_n}{\sigma_n}\right) \tag{3}$$

$$E(\Pi^2) = P_t^2 e^{2(\mu_n + \sigma_n^2)} Q\left[\frac{R - (\mu_n + 2\sigma_n^2)}{\sigma_n}\right]$$

$$-2P_s P_t e^{\left(\mu_n + \frac{\sigma_n^2}{2}\right)} Q\left[\frac{R - (\mu_n + \sigma_n^2)}{\sigma_n}\right] + P_s^2 Q\left(\frac{R - \mu_n}{\sigma_n}\right), \tag{4}$$

and

$$E(\Pi^3) = P_t^3 e^{\frac{3}{2}(2\mu_n + 3\sigma_n^2)} Q\left[\frac{R - (\mu_n + 3\sigma_n^2)}{\sigma_n}\right]$$

$$- 3P_t^2 P_s e^{2(\mu_n + \sigma_n^2)} Q\left[\frac{R - (\mu_n + 2\sigma_n^2)}{\sigma_n}\right]$$

$$+ 3P_t P_s^2 e^{\left(\mu_n + \frac{\sigma_n^2}{2}\right)} Q\left[\frac{R - (\mu_n + \sigma_n^2)}{\sigma_n}\right]$$

$$- P_s^3 Q\left(\frac{R - \mu_n}{\sigma_n}\right). \tag{5}$$

Holding n, the number of days remaining under the option, constant, all three moments increase as P_t increases, although if the second and third moments were taken around the mean instead of the origin, the second would increase and the third would decrease as P_t increased. This is because the distribution of Π looks exactly like the distribution of P_{t+n} except that it is truncated on the left at P_s. P_s in the distribution of P_{t+n} corresponds to zero in the distribution of Π. As P_t increases, the mean of P_{t+n} increases, the variance of P_{t+n} increases, and the distribution of P_{t+n} becomes less skewed. This all follows from the assumption of lognormality. Correspondingly, since the distribution of Π is simply a left truncated version of the distribution of P_{t+n}, its variance increases faster than that of P_{t+n} and its skewness decreases faster. Also, its mean increases slower than the mean of P_{t+n} as P_t increases. Holding P_t constant and decreasing n, all three moments of the distribution of both P_{t+n} and Π decrease.

Let us now examine the history of an option. An investor has purchased a call at time $t = 0$. The profit to be earned from the call, Π_0, has a distribution determined by μ, σ, n, P_t, and P_s. At some later date n is smaller and suppose P_t is higher than P_s. He could exercise the option and allocate the profit, buying another option having the same distribution as Π_0. Designate the profit to be earned by continuing to hold the present option as Π_1. His choice is determined by a comparison of $E[U(\Pi_0 + \Delta w)]$ and $E[U(\Pi_1)]$. If $E[U(\Pi_0 + \Delta w)]$ is greater, he will exercise the option he is holding, buy a new option, and add to his wealth. Otherwise he will continue to hold the present option.

Thus the decision model is

$$D = 0 \qquad E[U(\Pi_0 + \Delta w)] - E[U(\Pi_1)] - \epsilon < 0 \tag{6}$$

$$D = 1 \qquad E[U(\Pi_0 + \Delta w)] - E[U(\Pi_1)] - \epsilon > 0. \tag{7}$$

Where ϵ is a normally distributed variable with zero mean and unit variance, accounting for differences between individuals. The expression

$$E[U(\Pi_0 + \Delta w)] - E[U(\Pi_1)]$$

can be written

$$\alpha_1 E[(\Pi_0 + \Delta w) - \Pi_1] + \alpha_2 E[(\Pi_0 + \Delta w)^2 - \Pi_1^2]$$
$$+ \alpha_3 E[\Pi_0 + \Delta w)^3 - \Pi_1^3].$$

If μ, σ, n, P_t, P_s, and D are known, α_1, α_2, and α_3 can be estimated using multivariate probit analysis.[8] If the model described above is correct, it should turn out that

$$\frac{\partial E(U)}{\partial E(\Pi)} > 0. \tag{8}$$

It has commonly been supposed that call buyers, being gamblers, like variance, so that one might hypothesize

$$\frac{\partial E(U)}{\partial E[(\Pi')^2]} > 0; \tag{9}$$

where

$$\Pi' = \Pi - E(\Pi). \tag{10}$$

However, the most notable feature of an option is the skewness of its distribution. This suggests that

$$\frac{\partial E(U)}{\partial E[(\Pi')^3]} > 0, \tag{11}$$

or that option buyers like options because they are right skewed. If this is so, it becomes possible that

$$\frac{\partial E(U)}{\partial E[(\Pi')^2]} < 0. \tag{12}$$

In other words, since option buyers almost certainly do not like options for their negative first moments, they must like them because of some higher moment. It is usually assumed that it is the large second moment that option buyers like. But if option buyers like large third moments, the attitude toward second moments becomes open to question.

Data for this study were supplied by a brokerage firm which chose to remain anonymous. The data consist of:

1. The date on which each option was written.
2. The date on which it expired.
3. The striking price.
4. The cost of the option.
5. The stock against which the option was written.
6. The number of shares optioned.
7. The disposition of the option. If the option was exercised, the date was recorded.

---

[8] James Tobin, "An Application of Multivariate Probit Analysis to Economic Survey Data," Cowles Foundation Discussion Paper Number 1 (revised), July 1955.

From these it is possible to calculate n, P_s, and D for every day on which the option presented its owner with a choice.

By assuming that the option owner could sell stock at the market high on the day called, it is possible to obtain P_t.

Estimates of μ and σ were obtained simply by regarding the thirty days prior to any time t as a sample from which μ and σ could be estimated. A computer program was written which read each option and, for every profitable day until it was exercised or expired, computed

$$E[(\Pi_0 + \Delta w) - \Pi_1],$$
$$E[(\Pi_0 + \Delta w)^2 - \Pi_1^2],$$

and

$$E[(\Pi_0 + \Delta w)^3 - \Pi_1^3].$$

Values of Π_0, Π_1, and Δw were divided by C, the cost of an option, to give profit and addition to wealth per dollar's worth of option.

Options written in the four most popularly optioned stocks in the years 1957–1960 were used. The stocks were American Motors, Boeing, Chrysler, and General Dynamics. There were 398 options written in these four stocks. These generated 9836 observations of days on which P_t was greater than P_s. Of these, only 52 were days on which options were exercised, not counting options exercised on the last day. All observations of expiration dates were eliminated because they do not represent choices for the option holder, assuming he regards wealth as a desirable good. An option for which $P_t > P_s$ on the last day can be exercised at a profit or allowed to expire.

THE ESTIMATES

Table 1 gives the results of the estimation of α_1, α_2, and α_3 of equation 2. From the estimates of α_i it is possible to evaluate the partial derivatives

$$\frac{\partial E[U(x)]}{\partial \mu_1},$$

$$\frac{\partial E[U(x)]}{\partial \mu_2'},$$

and

$$\frac{E[U(x)]}{\partial \mu_3'},$$

where μ_1 is the first moment around the origin, and μ_2' and μ_3' are the second and third moments around the mean.

$$E[U(x)] = \alpha_1 \mu_1 + \alpha_2 \mu_2 + \alpha_3 \mu_3 \tag{13}$$

Table 1 Estimates of α_1, α_2, and α_3

	α_1	α_2	α_3	Log Likelihood
Trial Values	0.1696	−0.01880	0.0004455	−5811
Iteration number:				
1	0.8065	−0.0188	0.0002349	−5811.
2	1.1689	−0.1549	0.004472	−3550.
3	1.4078	−0.2044	0.006463	−3244.
4	1.6177	−0.2540	0.008755	−3062.
5	1.7359	−0.2865	0.01050	−3000.
6	1.7745	−0.2976	0.01112	−2995.
7	1.7764	−0.2981	0.01115	not computed
$S_{\hat{\alpha}_i}$	0.0294	0.00567	0.000252	

where μ_2 and μ_3 are second and third moments around the origin. But

$$\mu_2' = \mu_2 - \mu_1^2. \tag{14}$$

$$\mu_3' = \mu_3 - 3\mu_2\mu_1 + 2\mu_1^3. \tag{15}$$

Solving for μ_2 and μ_3,

$$\mu_2 = \mu_1^2 + \mu_2', \tag{16}$$

$$\mu_3 = \mu_3' + 3(\mu_2' + \mu_1^2)\mu_1 - 2\mu_1^3. \tag{17}$$

$$\frac{\partial E}{\partial \mu_1} = \alpha_1 + 2\alpha_2\mu_1 + 3\alpha_3(\mu_2' + 3\mu_1^2)$$

$$= 1.7764 - .3962\mu_1 + .03345(\mu_2' + 3\mu_1^2). \tag{18}$$

$$\frac{\partial E}{\partial \mu_2'} = \alpha_2 + 3\alpha_3\mu_1 = -.2981 + .03345\mu_1. \tag{19}$$

$$\frac{\partial E}{\partial \mu_3'} = \alpha_3 = .01115. \tag{20}$$

From equation 20 the preference for right skewness is unambiguous.
Since α_1, α_2, and α_3 were estimated using transformed data, the transformation must be accounted for in evaluating equations 18 and 19.

For instance, μ_1 is the expected return per dollar invested in options only. For all values of μ_1 up to 8.91, small values of σ^2 are preferred to large. Similarly, μ_2' is the variance of return per dollar invested in options. Within reasonable ranges of these values it can be seen that equation 18 is positive and equation 19 is negative. Thus large values of expected return are preferred to small, small values of variance are preferred to large, and right skewness is desirable.

It should be pointed out that the estimated relationship can be used to calculate, given the relevant moments, the probability that an individual will exercise a currently held option. If we calculate

$$Y = \alpha_1[E(\Pi_0 + \Delta w) - E(\Pi_1)] + \alpha_2[E(\Pi_0 + \Delta w)^2]$$
$$- E(\Pi_1^2) + \alpha_3[E(\Pi_0 + \Delta w)^3] - E(\Pi_1^3), \quad (21)$$

Y is a unit normal deviate such that

$$\int_{-\infty}^{Y} \frac{1}{\sqrt{2\Pi}} e^{-\frac{1}{2}x^2 \, dx}$$

gives the probability that the currently held option will be exercised.

It can be seen that equation 21 implies that if the currently held option is identical to its potential replacement, the probability that the call will be exercised is 0.5. This of course is a requirement imposed by the original statement of the model. For the purpose of testing the significance of this relationship, it is proper to test it against the null hypothesis:

$$\alpha_1 = \alpha_2 = \alpha_3 = 0.$$

The null hypothesis implies that the probability that an option is exercised on a profitable day is 0.5. Based on this assumption, the value of the natural log of the likelihood function, L_0, would be $9836 \times \log_e (0.5) = -6818$. But from Table 1, $L_1 = -2995$. The statistic

$$-2 \log_e \lambda = 2 \log_e \left(\frac{L_0}{L_1}\right) - 2(-6818. + 2995.) = 7646$$

is chi-square distributed with 3 degrees of freedom. It is obvious that the relationship is significant.

The requirement, implied by the model, that an option be exercised with probability 0.5 if it is identical to its potential replacement was relaxed, and equation 2 was replaced by

$$U = \alpha_0 + \alpha_1 w + \alpha_2 w^2 + \alpha_3 w^3. \quad (22)$$

Estimates of α_0, α_1, α_2, and α_3 are given in Table 2. Here the appropriate test of $\hat{\alpha}_1$, $\hat{\alpha}_2$, and $\hat{\alpha}_3$ is as follows: The null hypothesis is that $\alpha_1 = \alpha_2 = \alpha_3 = 0$. In this case, the maximum likelihood estimate of α_0 is given by

$$\int_{-\infty}^{\hat{\alpha}_0'} e^{-\frac{1}{2}x^2} \, dx = Pr \text{ (option is exercised)} \quad (23)$$

$$= \frac{52}{9836} = .00528,$$

Table 2 Estimates of α_0, α_1, α_2, and α_3

	α_0	α_1	α_2	α_3	Log Likelihood
Trial Values	-0.2883	0.2260×10^{-2}	-0.2031×10^{-3}	0.3320×10^{-5}	-293.8
Iteration number:					
1	-1.3617	0.1117×10^{-1}	-0.9993×10^{-3}	0.1643×10^{-4}	-976.1
2	-1.9491	0.3466×10^{-1}	-0.3063×10^{-2}	0.5105×10^{-4}	-412.0
3	-2.2034	0.8562×10^{-1}	-0.7516×10^{-2}	0.1320×10^{-3}	-309.0
4	-2.4439	0.1511	-0.1300×10^{-1}	0.2367×10^{-3}	-294.6
5	-2.4810	0.1810	-0.1530×10^{-1}	0.2804×10^{-3}	-293.8
6	-2.4842	0.1836	-0.1549×10^{-1}	0.2838×10^{-3}	not computed
S_2	0.5457×10^{-1}	0.1485×10^{-1}	0.5893×10^{-2}	0.1512×10^{-3}	

Thus $\hat{\alpha}_0' = -2.55$. L_0, the value of the likelihood function under the null hypothesis is

$$L_0 = (0.00528)^{52}(0.99472)^{9784}. \tag{24}$$

$$\text{Log}_e\, L_0 = 52 \log_e 0.00528 + 9784 \log_e 0.99472 = -325. \tag{25}$$

$$-2 \log_e \left(\frac{L_0}{L_1}\right) = -2(294 - 325) = 62.$$

This is chi-square distributed with 3 degrees of freedom and is significant.

Since α_0 is significantly different from zero, equation 22 cannot be regarded as a utility function in the sense of Mosteller and Nogee. It can, however, be regarded as a decision function which determines the probability that an option will be exercised given the distribution of possible outcomes. The inferences which can be drawn with respect to attitudes toward first, second, and third moments are not affected either by the new interpretation, or by the estimates obtained for equation 22.

EVALUATION OF THE ESTIMATES

Regarding the validity of the assumptions on which the estimates are based, there is little evidence. The most important assumption is the implicit one that there is a stable relationship between the performance of the market and the response of the investor. For the purposes of this paper it is not necessary that the investor understand what is going on in the market, merely that he always respond in the same way to the same events. It would be very damaging to the estimates presented here if it could be shown that an investor buys his first option under the impression that he is certain to make money and that he continues to buy options only as long as the market is kind enough to provide him with no contrary evidence. Such an investor would be changing his response to the market, and no estimate of his utility function could be obtained until the relationship between the market's behavior and his became stable. Discussion with about a dozen brokers strongly suggests that option buyers are as perennial as horse players. The only other evidence which is available is less promising. It was possible to obtain a list of the customer's account numbers from a ledger in which option purchases were recorded. These account numbers are not dated, but are listed in chronological order of posting (not purchase). A casual look at the pages of the ledger suggests that there are considerable delays between purchases and posting, and that some sort of systematic sorting occurs between purchase and the posting of the purchase. This fact reduces the usefulness of these account numbers, but they represent the only evidence available and are therefore presented.

If call buyers are really as perennial as the brokers believe they are, an individual account number, whatever the frequency with which it occurs, should be distributed more or less uniformly over the total list of account numbers. There are 5219 transactions represented in the list of account numbers, and these involve 2586 separate accounts. Among all accounts which occur twice, the average number of transactions separating the pair should be about 2600. Table 3 gives the distribution of account

Table 3 Frequency of Account Numbers and Transactions

Frequency with Which Account Number Appeared on List	Number of Account Numbers	Number of Transactions
1	1756	1756
2	400	800
3	166	498
4	74	296
5	63	315
6	31	186
7	22	154
8	13	104
9	17	153
10	5	50
11	7	77
12	7	84
13	9	52
14 or more	21	694
Total	2586	5219

numbers according to the frequency with which they occurred.

The distribution shown in Table 3 is consistent either with the hypothesis that investors continue to buy options only as long as they win, or with the hypothesis that they buy options perennially and that rate of purchase is correlated with wealth. Table 4 gives estimates of the transactions rates for each frequency group. The hypothesized rates are based on the assumption that if X purchases are made the transaction rate must be $X/5219$. The estimated rates are significantly higher in every case. This means that, although the data cover a year, the average investor made all of his purchases over a period significantly shorter than one year. The assumptions on which this evidence is based are as open to question as the assumption on which it is brought to bear. My own judgment is that in spite of the results shown in Table 4 the following valid general statements

Table 4   Estimated and Hypothesized Transaction Rates

Transaction Frequency	Hypothesized Transaction Rate	Estimated Transaction Rate and (Standard Error)
2	0.0004	0.0006 (0.00003)
3	0.0006	0.0008 (0.00004)
4	0.0008	0.0010 (0.00007)
5	0.0010	0.0016 (0.00009)
6	0.0011	0.0014 (0.00013)
7	0.0013	0.0016 (0.00017)
8	0.0015	0.0019 (0.00019)
9	0.0017	0.0025 (0.00013)
10	0.0019	0.0096 (0.00072)
11	0.0021	0.0039 (0.00035)
12	0.0023	0.0042 (0.00037)
13	0.0025	0.0038 (0.00049)
14	0.0027	0.0174 (0.00085)

can be made on the basis of the utility functions estimated using the call options data.

1. The average purchaser of calls is risk averse in the sense that he would prefer less variance if he could get it, all other characteristics of the distribution being equal.

2. Without taking account of higher moments of the distribution associated with call options, incorrect inferences concerning the utility function would be drawn. It is possible that moments higher than the third enter into decisions involving risk.

3. While the data employed here are such that they must be used in conjunction with very strong assumptions if a utility function is to be estimated, the world does generate data that can be used for this purpose. If data having to do with investors' wealth had been available, some of the stronger assumptions could have been relaxed.

Cumulative Author Index

This index includes names appearing in Monographs 19, 20, and 21 of the Cowles Foundation Monograph series. The boldface roman numerals indicate monograph numbers.

Adams, E. S., **XX,** 157, 159
Aitchison, J., **XX,** 174
Alhadeff, Charlotte, **XXI,** 5
Alhadeff, David, **XXI,** 5
Anderson, T. W., **XIX,** 112
Anderson, W. M., **XX,** 194
Archibald, G., **XIX,** 64
Arrow, K. J., **XIX,** 61, 142, 153; **XXI,** 13
Aschheim, Joseph, **XXI,** 45, 94

Baumol, William, **XX,** 70, 102, 104
Bear, D. V., **XXI,** 139
Beckhart, B. H., **XX,** 123, 126, 155
Beckmann, Martin J., **XIX,** 139, 153; **XXI,** 92
Bellman, R., **XIX,** 153
Benishay, Haskel, **XIX,** 73
Berki, Sylvester, **XX,** 1
Bloch, Ernest, **XIX,** 58
Bollinger, L. L., **XIX,** 57, 107
Borch, K., **XIX,** 123
Bossons, J., **XIX,** 114
Boyer, J. I., **XIX,** 157
Brainard, William C., **XX,** 66, 171; **XXI,** 3, 48, 55–93, 94–141
Brechling, F. P. R., **XIX,** 40
Brill, Daniel, **XX,** 66
Broida, Arthur, **XXI,** 168

Bronfenbrenner, M., **XXI,** 144
Brown, A. J., **XXI,** 144
Brown, E. C., **XIX,** 54
Brown, J. A. C., **XX,** 174
Brownlee, O. H., **XIX,** 28, 40
Brumberg, R., **XIX,** 153
Brunner, K., **XXI,** 99
Budd, Edward, **XX,** 66
Butters, J. K., **XIX,** 57, 107–108

Cagan, Phillip, **XX,** 72
Cagle, Caroline H., **XX,** 122
Cannan, Edwin, **XXI,** 38
Carson, Deane, **XXI,** 1, 96
Chambers, David, **XX,** 118, 173
Champernowne, D. G., **XIX,** 153
Charnes, Abraham, **XX,** 118, 173
Chernoff, H., **XIX,** 153
Chudson, Walter, **XX,** 74
Clarkson, G. P. E., **XIX,** 62
Conard, Joseph W., **XXI,** 149, 192, 210, 229
Cowles, Alfred, **XIX,** 111
Culbertson, John M., **XX,** 242; **XXI,** 178, 191

Davidson, D., **XIX,** 60–61
Debreu, G., **XIX,** 142, 153
Dernburg, Thomas F., **XX,** 24

Dodd, David L., **XIX,** 70–71, 73
Domar, E., **XIX,** 54–56
Doob, J. L., **XXI,** 40
Duncan, Acheson J., **XX,** 72, 102
Durand, D., **XXI,** 193, 197, 200
Dvoretzky, Aryeh, **XXI,** 41

Eckert, James, **XX,** 118, 150
Edgeworth, F. Y., **XXI,** 13–14
Elsom, Harold B., **XIX,** 72

Farrar, D. E., **XIX,** 124–125
Feeney, George J., **XIX,** 48, 110–138
Fellner, W., **XIX,** 8, 76
Fisher, Irving, **XXI,** 190
Fisher, L., **XXI,** 193
Foulke, Roy A., **XX,** 123
Friedman, James, **XX,** 171
Friedman, M., **XIX,** 12, 64, 153–154,
    157; **XX,** 70; **XXI,** 94–95, 99, 124

Gantmacher, F., **XXI,** 139
Garvy, George, **XX,** 124
Gerstenberg, C. W., **XX,** 74
Goldenweiser, E. A., **XXI,** 95
Gordon, M. J., **XIX,** 73
Graaff, J. de V., **XIX,** 153
Graham, Benjamin, **XIX,** 70–71, 73
Granville, J. E., **XXI,** 218
Grubert, Harry, **XIX,** 154
Gurley, John G., **XXI,** 3, 5, 95–96, 154
Guthmann, Harry G., **XX,** 123
Guttentag, J. M., **XX,** 119, 176–177

Hahn, F. H., **XIX,** 40
Hall, Challis, **XIX,** 1, 57
Hamada, Koichi, **XIX,** 27–40
Harris, S., **XIX,** 8
Harris, T., **XXI,** 13
Hart, A. G., **XXI,** 95
Hayes, A., **XX,** 134
Haynes, A. T., **XX,** 192
Henderson, James, **XXI,** 94–95
Herstein, I. N., **XIX,** 12, 60
Hester, Donald D., **XIX,** 41–50, 110–
    138; **XX,** 1, 40, 66, 81, 118–170, 171,
    175–178; **XXI,** 189
Hester, Karen, **XXI,** 142
Heston, Alan W., **XX,** 66–117; **XXI,** 94
Heston, Wilma, **XXI,** 142

Hickman, W., **XXI,** 193, 200
Hicks, J. R., **XIX,** 33–34, 37, 40, 52;
    XX, 242; **XXI,** 16, 149, 178, 190–191,
    195, 222
Hodgman, Donald, **XX,** 120–121, 176
Holte, Fritz, **XIX,** 154
Hotelling, H., **XIX,** 112; **XX,** 81, 133

Johnson, Harry, **XXI,** 3, 96, 99
Jorgenson, Dale, **XX,** 171

Kaldor, N., **XIX,** 8
Kalecki, M., **XXI,** 144
Kareken, J., **XX,** 127, 129
Katona, George, **XX,** 40, 119, 125
Keaton, James, **XIX,** 110
Kendall, M. G., **XIX,** 112, 125; **XX,** 100
Keynes, J. M., **XIX,** 3, 7–8, 148; **XXI,**
    39, 98, 143
Khusro, A. M., **XXI,** 144
Kirton, R. J., **XX,** 192
Kisselgoff, Avram, **XX,** 70–72, 79, 101–
    102
Koch, Albert, **XX,** 74
Komiya, Ryutaro, **XIX,** 27
Koopmans, T. C., **XIX,** 142, 153
Kreps, C., **XXI,** 95
Kurihara, K., **XIX,** 153

Lange, O., **XIX,** 53
Lapkin, D., **XXI,** 95
Latane, H., **XIX,** 62; **XX,** 72; **XXI,** 144
Leontief, W., **XIX,** 8
Lepper, Susan J., **XIX,** 51–109
Lerner, A. P., **XIX,** 109
Lindbeck, A., **XXI,** 37
Lintner, J. H., **XIX,** 28, 30, 40
Liviatan, N., **XIX,** 27
Lovell, Michael, **XXI,** 94
Luce, R., **XIX,** 61
Lutz, F. A., **XIX,** 52; **XX,** 72, 79, 130;
    XXI, 149, 190–191

Mack, Ruth, **XX,** 40
Madden, Carl H., **XX,** 71
Makower, H., **XIX,** 53
Markowitz, H. M., **XIX,** 24, 28, 40–41,
    48, 50, 54, 61, 62, 64, 69, 84, 124–
    125, 153, 156–157, 159; **XX,** 121, 126,
    191; **XXI,** 22, 102

Marschak, J., **XIX,** 12, 53; **XXI,** 13
Mayer, Thomas, **XXI,** 144
Meltzer, Allan H., **XX,** 106
Menger, K., **XIX,** 142
Milnor, J., **XIX,** 12, 60
Minsky, Hyman, **XX,** 71
Modigliani, F., **XIX,** 153
Moore, George S., **XX,** 126
Morgenstern, O., **XIX,** 12, 53, 60, 141–142
Moses, L., **XIX,** 153
Mosteller, F., **XIX,** 154, 156, 157, 159, 167
Murad, A., **XXI,** 20
Murray, A. C., **XX,** 195
Musgrave, R., **XIX,** 54–56; **XX,** 127, 130–131, 148

Nagle, John, **XX,** 1
Negishi, Takashi, **XIX,** 27
Neumann, J. von, **XIX,** 12, 53, 60, 141–142
Nogee, Philip, **XIX,** 154, 156–157, 159, 167

Okun, Arthur, **XIX,** 1, 19; **XX,** 1, 66, 118, 191; **XXI,** 94, 142–188, 189
Orcutt, Guy, **XX,** 40, 51–52

Patinkin, D., **XXI,** 41
Penman, W., **XX,** 193
Phelps, C. D., **XIX,** 71; **XXI,** 142
Phelps, Edmund S., **XIX,** 139–153
Pierce, James L., **XX,** 171–190
Porter, Richard C., **XX,** 66, 118, 173; **XXI,** 12–54, 102
Powell, Raymond, **XX,** 118
Pratt, Eleanor, **XX,** 66
Puryear, Alvin, **XX,** 1
Pye, Gordon, **XIX,** 27

Ramsey, F. P., **XIX,** 139, 152–153
Richter, M. K., **XIX,** 56, 69
Ritter, L. S., **XX,** 72, 119
Robertson, D. H., **XIX,** 153
Robinson, Joan, **XXI,** 151
Robinson, Roland I., **XX,** 118, 121, 123–124
Roosa, R. V., **XX,** 127

Rosett, Richard N., **XIX,** 154–169
Roy, A. D., **XIX,** 53
Royama, Shoichi, **XIX,** 27–40

Salant, Walter, **XIX,** 1
Samuelson, Paul A., **XIX,** 2, 31, 40, 152–153; **XX,** 127
Sauvain, H. C., **XIX,** 71
Savage, L. J., **XIX,** 12, 59–60, 64, 154, 157
Scott, I. O., **XIX,** 28, 40; **XX,** 127, 129; **XXI,** 22, 35
Seldon, Richard T., **XX,** 70
Shaw, F. S., **XXI,** 3, 5, 95–96
Shelby, Donald, **XXI,** 96
Silberman, C. E., **XX,** 74, 79, 97, 101
Simons, Henry C., **XIX,** 109
Sloane, Peter E., **XXI,** 189–245
Smith, W. L., **XXI,** 51, 96, 207
Snodgrass, Donald, **XXI,** 189
Snyder, Edward P., **XX,** 149
Solow, R. M., **XIX,** 152–153
Sprenkle, Case M., **XIX,** 159
Srinivasan, T. N., **XIX,** 139; **XX,** 66; **XXI,** 189
Stedry, Andrew C., **XX,** 72; **XXI,** 144
Streeten, Paul, **XIX,** 54
Summers, Robert, **XX,** 1
Suppes, P., **XIX,** 61
Suviranta, B., **XXI,** 13

Tachi, Ryuichiro, **XIX,** 27
Telser, T. G., **XIX,** 53
Theil, H., **XIX,** 112
Thompson, L. E., **XIX,** 57, 107
Tobin, James, **XIX,** 1–26, 37–38, 40–41, 50, 54, 56, 124, 162; **XX,** 1–39, 40–66, 70, 72, 102, 104, 118, 132, 152, 166, 171, 191; **XXI,** 1–11, 22, 43–44, 48, 55–93, 94–96, 98, 99, 102, 110, 126, 129–130, 143–144, 153, 189, 237
Tolley, George, **XXI,** 95

Uzawa, Hirofumi, **XIX,** 27

Wall, Alexander, **XX,** 123
Wallich, Henry, **XX,** 118, 122, 127, 129, 148, 159; **XXI,** 161

Warburton, Clark, **XX,** 72
Watts, Harold W., **XX,** 1–40, 81; **XXI,**
    189
Wehrle, Leroy S., **XIX,** 1; **XX,** 191–248;
    XXI, 191
Winn, W., **XXI,** 193, 197, 200
Winter, S. G., **XIX,** 139

Working, E. J., **XX,** 132

Yaari, Menahem, **XXI,** 94
Yule, G. Udny, **XX,** 100

Zoellner, J., **XX,** 175, 178
Zorn, Eugene, **XX,** 118

Cumulative Subject Index

This index includes subjects covered in Monographs 19, 20, and 21 of the Cowles Foundation Monograph series. The boldface roman numerals indicate monograph numbers.

Accelerator model, **XIX,** 120–121
Account, capital, *see* Capital account
  income, *see* Income account
Assets, **XX,** 172; **XXI,** 3, 14, 15, 57, 100
  complements, *see* Complements
  demand for, **XIX,** 27–36; **XXI,** 3, 4,
    102–104, 148
  exchange costs, *see* Transactions costs
  gross liquid, **XX,** 55–56
  inferior, **XIX,** 33
  liquid, **XX,** 55, 59, 64–65; **XXI,** 147,
    154
  net position, **XX,** 56–57
  normal, **XIX,** 33
  portfolio composition, *see* Portfolio
  properties of, **XIX,** 70–73; **XX,** 172,
    175–177, 192–193
  return, *see* Rates of return
  substitutes, *see* Substitutes
Availability of credit, *see* Credit

Balance sheet, corporate, **XX,** 73
  financial intermediaries, **XX,** 57; **XXI,**
    3–4
  households, **XX,** 1, 39
  see also Assets; Net worth
Balances, *see* Cash

Bank deposits, *see* Demand; Savings;
  Time deposits
Bank loans, availability, **XX,** 106, 127–
  128, 148; **XXI,** 3, 234
  short term, **XX,** 67, 73, 77, 83, 105–
    106, 124
  supply of, **XX,** 128–129, 178
  see also Loan offer function
  term, **XX,** 126, 134–149, 163, 166
  terms of, **XX,** 120–122, 132, 162,
    164–165, 177
  see also Credit
Bills, *see* Treasury bills
Bills only doctrine, **XX,** 246; **XXI,** 179,
  234
Bonds, **XXI,** 3, 114–115, 132–135, 189–
  245
  price pegged, **XIX,** 39; **XXI,** 198
  see also Consols; Interest rate; Trea-
    sury bills
Budget constraint, **XIX,** 50

Call, margin, **XIX,** 42
  option, defined, **XIX,** 157
  option market, **XIX,** 158, 169
  provision, **XIX,** 71–72; **XX,** 195;
    XXI, 152

Canonical correlation applied to, bank lending, **XX,** 133, 160–165
corporate balance sheets, **XX,** 80–83, 105
Capital account, **XX,** 1–39, 171–172; **XXI,** 98–99, 138
see also Household worth; Net worth
Capital gains, **XIX,** 4, 42; **XXI,** 150, 192, 196, 216, 225–228, 237
tax treatment, *see* Tax
uncertainty about, **XIX,** 9–11
Capital losses, *see* Capital gains
Carry back, *see* Tax
Carry forward, *see* Tax
Cash, **XXI,** 15, 21, 184–185
corporate holdings, **XX,** 66–117
demand for, **XIX,** 18, 25–26; **XX,** 89–92; **XXI,** 118, 131
in banks, **XX,** 9; **XXI,** 65–73, 156
multiple alternatives, **XIX,** 21–25
precautionary, **XX,** 55
speculative, **XIX,** 3–4, 7–9, 20–21, 25–26
transactions, **XIX,** 2–3; **XX,** 4, 55, 70, 102, 105; **XXI,** 170, 235
see also Transactions costs
Certificates of deposit, **XX,** 188
Complements, **XIX,** 27, 33, 35–38; **XXI,** 66–67, 69–70, 72, 78, 126, 131, 133
Consols, **XIX,** 4, 9
demand for, **XIX,** 18–19, 20–21
interest rate of, **XIX,** 4–21
see also Bonds; Treasury bills
Consumer, expenditures, **XX,** 1–39, 40–65
price index, **XIX,** 73–74
survey of finances, **XX,** 41
Consumption, function, **XIX,** 139–141, 144–145, 147–149
optimal lifetime, **XIX,** 139–153
Corporation, assets, **XX,** 66–67, 105
current accounts, **XX,** 66, 73, 77
nonfinancial, **XX,** 66–117
Cost of financial transactions, *see* Transactions costs
Credit, availability, **XX,** 127–128, 148, 167, 179; **XXI,** 3, 37, 96, 172, 234
doctrine, **XX,** 128, 167–168

Credit, control, **XX,** 126, 147, 165–167
new theory of, **XXI,** 37
constraint, **XIX,** 50
installment, **XX,** 9, 23–24, 73
rationing, **XX,** 129, 141, 157, 159, 167

Debt, **XXI,** 64
household, **XX,** 4, 40–65
see also Balance sheet; Bonds; Mortgage debt; Treasury bills
Debt policy, **XX,** 245–247; **XXI,** 142–189
Default risk, *see* Risk
Demand deposits, **XX,** 172, 175, 184; **XXI,** 2, 4–7, 57–58, 65, 70, 94, 113, 126, 156, 185
Deposit rate, **XXI,** 66–73, 77–84, 87–92, 122–125, 127–129, 129–132, 133
see also Interest rate
Depreciation, **XX,** 8
Diffusion index, **XIX,** 79
Discount window, **XXI,** 9, 20
Diversification, *see* Portfolio
Diversifier, **XIX,** 11, 14, 16–17, 19; **XXI,** 45
Dominant set of assets, **XIX,** 23–24
Dow Jones average, **XIX,** 110–138
Durable goods, **XX,** 3–4, 7–12, 24, 45, 64
depreciation, *see* Depreciation
second hand market, **XX,** 2
valuation, **XX,** 8
see also Inventory cycle
Dynamic programming, **XIX,** 142–143

Efficiency frontier, *see* Opportunity locus
Efficiency locus, *see* Opportunity locus
Equilibrium, **XIX,** 8, 25; **XXI,** 59, 63, 71, 74, 104–107, 120–122, 130, 195–196, 235–236
general, **XXI,** 55, 95, 97, 99–139, 148
partial, **XXI,** 96, 97
stability, *see* Stability of equilibrium
Equity, **XXI,** 210, 216, 235, 241
classification, **XIX,** 72
see also Net worth
Expectations, **XIX,** 58, 82, 103, 105; **XXI,** 146, 177, 191, 192, 195,

Expectations, 196, 208, 214, 219–223, 229, 231, 237–242
  adaptive, **XIX,** 61
  Hicks elasticity of, **XXI,** 16, 191, 225
  horizon, **XIX,** 62, 68; **XXI,** 149–150
  inelastic, **XIX,** 4–5, 8, 25; **XXI,** 143, 177–178, 190–191, 222–223, 224, 228
  price, **XIX,** 35, 39
  rate of return, **XIX,** 59
  static, **XXI,** 41
  sticky, **XIX,** 5, 9, 26
Expected income, *see* Income
Expected return, *see* Rates of return
Expected utility, *see* Utility

Federal funds, **XX,** 184; **XXI,** 9, 17
  market, **XX,** 126
Federal Reserve, **XIX,** 42; **XX,** 126; **XXI,** 144–147, 155, 161, 172, 176, 179, 210
  Business Loans Survey, **XX,** 149–150, 156

Household, capital account, **XX,** 1–39, 64–65
  current account, **XX,** 1

Income, expected, **XIX,** 145
  household, **XX,** 1
  permanent, **XX,** 4, 11, 26, 37
  transitory, **XX,** 26
Income account, **XXI,** 138
Income-averaging scheme, *see* Tax
Income effect, **XIX,** 18, 27, 67, 95, 106, 140, 151–152; **XX,** 59–61; **XXI,** 45, 170
  see also Wealth
Interest rate, **XXI,** 59–60, 63, 66, 142–169, 172–175, 222–223, 234
  bond, **XIX,** 71, 103; **XX,** 147, 150, 156–160; **XXI,** 99, 108–109, 115, 118, 125, 127, 133, 148, 189–245
  consol, **XIX,** 4–6, 9, 20, 25
  critical, **XIX,** 5–7
  Keynesian theory of, **XIX,** 8, 52; **XXI,** 99, 154
  legal ceiling, **XXI,** 7–8, 10–11, 55, 66–73, 95, 107, 113, 122–130
  loan, **XX,** 120, 129–131, 140, 143,

Interest rate, loan, 145, 150–151, 155; **XXI,** 59, 63, 101, 118, 125, 128–129, 177
  prime, **XX,** 132, 140, 146–147, 156, 165–166; **XXI,** 30–31, 193–194, 214, 225
  tax exemption, **XIX,** 103
  treasury bill, **XX,** 73, 83–88, 95, 105, 147, 156; **XXI,** 157–158, 164, 169, 175–177, 179
  see also Rates of return; Yield curve
Inventory cycle, **XX,** 23–24, 76–77

Life cycle, *see* Consumption
Life insurance, **XX,** 3–4
  companies, **XX,** 191, 247; **XXI,** 4, 7, 58, 151
  contract, **XX,** 192–196; **XXI,** 5
  investment principles, **XX,** 192–196
  premiums, **XX,** 9, 24
Line of credit, **XX,** 52
Liquidity preference, **XIX,** 1–25, 53–54; **XXI,** 62, 148, 153–154
  Keynesian, **XIX,** 3–9, 25; **XXI,** 143–144
  schedule, defined, **XIX,** 1
Loan demand function, **XX,** 178; **XXI,** 30, 68, 75, 115–117
Loan offer function, **XX,** 118–170, 178
  defined, **XX,** 119
  partial, **XX,** 132–133, 143, 153
Loss carry back provision, *see* Tax
Loss carry forward provision, *see* Tax
Loss offset, *see* Tax

Margin call, **XIX,** 42
Margin loan, **XIX,** 41–42, 45, 50
  interest rate, **XIX,** 42, 44, 48
Margin requirement, brokers, **XIX,** 42
  Federal Reserve, **XIX,** 42, 44
Markets, capital, **XX,** 245, 247–248; **XXI,** 55, 192, 210
  financial, **XXI,** 55, 67, 94–141, 148, 172, 177, 195–196, 210, 234
  imperfect, **XX,** 2–3, 119; **XXI,** 30–32, 160–161, 176, 195–196, 226
  money, **XX,** 126, 184; **XXI,** 9, 67, 70, 80, 195, 214, 225, 235
Maturity yield function, *see* Yield curve

Money, **XXI,** 2, 96, 145, 147, 152, 154, 156, 158, 175–176, 235
    bank, **XXI,** 1, 5, 8
    creation, **XXI,** 1–11, 38, 97, 147
    government, **XXI,** 2, 8, 148
    quantity theory of, **XIX,** 2; **XXI,** 38
    reserve base, **XXI,** 9, 97, 147
    velocity, **XIX,** 2; **XXI,** 2–3, 38–39
    see also Cash
Mortgage debt, **XX,** 1, 9; **XXI,** 58
    and inventory cycle, **XX,** 23–24
Mutual fund portfolio, **XIX,** 124–125

Net worth, **XX,** 2, 10, 65, 124; **XXI,** 3, 15, 24, 27, 105
    constraint, **XIX,** 42, 50

Open-market operation, **XIX,** 7; **XXI,** 10–11, 37, 107–112, 127–129, 130, 145–146, 160–161, 166, 168, 176–177, 233
Opportunity locus, **XIX,** 11, 20, 43–47, 54–55, 69, 80; **XX,** 120, 125, 132, 165; **XXI,** 22, 44, 239
Optimal lifetime consumption, *see* Consumption
Optimum assets curve, *see* Opportunity locus

Pin-in effect, **XX,** 247; **XXI,** 16, 18
Plunger, **XIX,** 11, 14, 16, 19
Portfolio, balance, **XIX,** 9, 12; **XX,** 152–153; **XXI,** 21–22, 59, 63–64
    choice, **XIX,** 9; **XX,** 171–190, 191; **XXI,** 3, 12–54, 57, 62, 66, 97, 102, 117–118, 194
    determinants of, **XX,** 4, 39
    diversification, **XIX,** 16, 25, 52, 54; **XX,** 126; **XXI,** 12, 14
    efficient, defined, **XIX,** 41
Precautionary demand, *see* Cash
Private wealth, *see* Wealth
Purchasing power variation, **XIX,** 73

Quadratic programming, **XIX,** 29, 125
Quadratic utility function, *see* Utility

Rates of return, **XIX,** 110–138, 140;

Rates of return, **XXI,** 59–60, 61–62, 68, 71–72, 97, 99, 101–107, 109, 119–120, 239
    correlation matrix, **XIX,** 110, 124–125, 130
    covariance matrix, **XIX,** 28, 110, 114, 124, 125–126, 130–131
    defined, **XIX,** 9, 110
    expected, **XIX,** 9, 13, 28, 45, 49, 53, 75–79; **XX,** 180–184; **XXI,** 149–151
    principal components, **XIX,** 110–138
    relation to taxes, **XIX,** 20–21, 32, 35, 52, 79–109
    variance of, **XIX,** 53
Real bills doctrine, **XXI,** 38
Receivables, **XX,** 66–67, 74–76, 83–97, 105–107
Reserve requirement, **XXI,** 2, 5–11, 21, 37, 55, 64–65, 66–73, 82–84, 90, 94, 103–104, 118–122, 126, 130, 145, 155, 166, 168, 176, 177, 179, 185
Reserves, **XXI,** 17, 18, 56, 97, 132, 135–136, 184–185
    net free, **XXI,** 9–10, 95, 215
    required, **XXI,** 9–10, 95
    unborrowed, **XXI,** 9–10
Return, *see* Rates of return
Risk, **XXI,** 42–45, 140, 149–151, 192, 193, 208, 239–240
    alternative measures, **XIX,** 10–11, 53, 56–57
    and policy, **XIX,** 20–21, 51–52, 57, 109
    aversion, **XIX,** 1–26; **XX,** 179; **XXI,** 45, 143, 151
    averter, **XIX,** 11, 13, 15–17, 50; **XXI,** 43, 151, 239
    capital value, **XIX,** 9; **XX,** 195; **XXI,** 143, 151, 225–226
    default, **XIX,** 71; **XX,** 121, 123, 126, 152–153, 176, 192–195, 243–244; **XXI,** 3, 14, 19–20, 30, 57, 63, 75, 148, 189–190, 193, 194, 215, 216–217, 239, 241
    income, **XX,** 192–195, 219; **XXI,** 151, 194
    lover, **XIX,** 11, 13, 15–16, 50
    of deposit change, **XX,** 125–126, 152,

Risk, of deposit change, 175; **XXI,** 13, 17–19, 23–25, 26, 39–42, 51–52
portfolio, **XIX,** 10–11
Robert Morris Associates, **XX,** 242

Sales finance paper, **XX,** 71
Saturation, effect, **XX,** 51
of wants, **XX,** 5
Saving, *see* Consumption
Savings and loan association, **XIX,** 49; **XXI,** 5–7, 58, 113
Savings deposits, **XX,** 172, 175, 184; **XXI,** 2, 4–5, 10, 58, 70, 95, 124–125
Securities, attributes, **XX,** 192–193; **XXI,** 15, 19
demand for, **XX,** 66–78, 89, 92, 105, 191–248; **XXI,** 28–29, 145
Short sale, **XIX,** 30, 39, 41–50, 126
and risk averters, **XIX,** 48–50
and risk lovers, **XIX,** 48, 50
defined, **XIX,** 41
Short term credit, *see* Bank loans; Receivables
Slutsky equation, **XIX,** 33
Speculative demand, *see* Cash
Stability of equilibrium, **XXI,** 67, 78
Stationary state, and interest rate, **XIX,** 9, 25
Substitutes, **XIX,** 27, 33, 36–38; **XXI,** 4–5, 58–59, 62, 64, 66, 68, 69–70, 72–73, 78, 102–103, 108, 126, 131, 149, 151, 196, 217, 236–237
Substitution effect, **XIX,** 18, 27, 32–39, 106, 140, 151–152

Tap issue, **XX,** 247
Tax, and expected returns, **XIX,** 20, 103, 105, 107
and risk, **XIX,** 20–21, 97–103
anticipation certificate, **XX,** 71, 73, 79
capital gains treatment, **XIX,** 20, 93–96, 101, 106
income-averaging scheme, **XIX,** 57
loss offset, **XIX,** 35, 56–57, 82–89, 97–99, 109
as countercyclical tool, **XIX,** 99, 109
as investment stimulus, **XIX,** 101

Tax, loss offset, complete, **XIX,** 20, 82–87
partial, **XIX,** 87–89
loss carry back, **XIX,** 57, 87, 92
loss carry forward, **XIX,** 57, 88, 89, 91, 92, 93, 97
lump sum, **XIX,** 32, 35
on expected earnings, **XIX,** 20–21
on interest income, **XIX,** 20–21, 103
on investment returns, **XIX,** 51
progressive income, **XIX,** 89, 99–101, 103, 106
with loss offset, **XIX,** 89–93, 95–97, 99–101
proportional income, **XIX,** 82
with complete loss offset, **XIX,** 82–85
without loss offset, **XIX,** 85–87, 106
with partial loss offset, **XIX,** 87–89
Time deposits, **XX,** 172, 175, 184; **XXI,** 2, 4, 10, 48–51, 70, 94, 122–125
Transactions costs, **XIX,** 2–4, 42, 50; **XX,** 70; **XXI,** 151, 161, 191, 193–194
Transactions demand, *see* Cash
Treasury bills, **XX,** 71, 73, 79, 193; **XXI,** 148, 151
see also Bonds; Consols; Open market operation

Utility, cardinal, **XIX,** 16, 53
expected, **XIX,** 13–16, 60, 141–143
function, **XIX,** 12, 55–56, 141–142, 151, 152
linear, **XIX,** 60, 63
logarithmic, **XIX,** 152
monomial, **XIX,** 140, 146–147, 151, 152
quadratic, **XIX,** 14–16, 19, 28, 38–39, 41, 64, 68–69, 95, 110, 124–125, 140, 145–152; **XX,** 152; **XXI,** 102
von Neuman-Morgenstern, **XIX,** 12, 28, 53, 140
marginal, **XIX,** 64, 144, 146
of income, **XIX,** 64; **XX,** 120
of rate of return, **XIX,** 9, 12–13, 16, 56, 63–64, 124, 157
of wealth, **XIX,** 28–29, 63–64, 143, 144–146, 154–169

Variance, as measure of risk, **XIX,** 10–11, 53, 67, 79, 105–107

Wealth, **XXI,** 6, 60–62, 65, 103, 130, 148, 152–153, 157, 176, 187–188
   effect, **XIX,** 33, 38–39
   real, **XIX,** 28

Yield, Moody rating of new issue, **XX,** 211–214; **XXI,** 148–149, 197–198, 200
   see also Rates of return
Yield curve, **XX,** 193, 196, 228, 242–243; **XXI,** 193, 194, 195, 196, 197, 200, 210, 226, 231, 240